Mondays at Gaj's

Mondays at Gaj's

The Story of the Irish Women's Liberation Movement

Anne Stopper

The Liffey Press

Published by
The Liffey Press
Ashbrook House
10 Main Street
Raheny, Dublin 5, Ireland
www.theliffeypress.com

A catalogue record of this book is
available from the British Library.

ISBN 1-904148-94-8

Printed in Spain by Graficas Cems Ltd.

Contents

About the Author .... *vii*

Acknowledgements .... *ix*

Introduction 1

1   Not Just a Restaurant... 9

2   The Universal Activist 21

3   A Journalist Crosses the Pond..................................... 33

4   Daughter of the Liberties... 47

5   Two Different Doctors 57

6   Chains or Change 69

7   Paying the Price... 79

8   Hats and Hotpants 91

9   Showtime... 105

10   Finding Her Place... 117

11   Standing Room Only... 133

12   Odd One Out 147

13   Learning Feminism Backwards.................................. 159

14   All Aboard... 167

15   The Derrywoman 191

16   Where They Are (and What They Think) Now 211

Notes... 233

Index 241

About the Author

Anne Stopper is a journalist and former Fulbright scholar to Ireland who lives, works and studies between the United States and Ireland. Her articles have been published in newspapers and magazines from Washington, DC, to Northeastern Pennsylvania. She has also worked in the broadcast media as an intern for National Public Radio's flagship news programme *Morning Edition*. This is her first book.

Acknowledgements

Thanks to David Givens, Brian Langan and Heidi Murphy of The Liffey Press for publishing this book, and to Sinéad McKenna for her excellent design work. Thanks to Carmel Coyle and the staff at the Irish Fulbright Commission for thinking this was a worthwhile project. Ailbhe Smyth, Katherine O'Donnell, Ursula Barry and all of the staff of the Women's Education, Research and Resource Centre (WERRC) at University College Dublin provided constant warmth, support, and guidance. Professors Wendell Cochran, Rick Rockwell, Lenny Steinhorn and Rodger Streitmatter at American University's School of Communication were the best of mentors, and Mrs Angela Schoebel was the first teacher who told me I could write. The staff of National Public Radio's *Morning Edition*, especially executive producer Ellen McDonnell, taught me that creativity, collaboration and meticulous research are the staples of out-standing journalism.

Thanks also to John Furlong for opening the door into the most welcoming house in Dublin for me, and to Matteo Beghetti and Letty Stegeman for keeping it that way. Thanks to Síne Quinn for her help and guidance. Thanks to Karen Campos McCormack, Katie Mazzari, Cristina O'Connor, Jenny Flament, Adam Good, Lauren Squires, Marisha Goldhammer, Brett Zongker, Margaret McElligot, Andy Peternith, Edel Kenny, Anne-Marie Keane and Claire Foskin for the laughs. My sincerest thanks to all the people who consented to interviews for this book, especially to the founders of the Irish Women's Liberation Movement, who delved back through their memories and photographs and were so generous with their stories and their time. Without them it would not have been possible to write this book; nor would there have been a book to write. Mary Maher in particular provided great assistance and direction. A very large thank you to Derek Speirs for generously allowing the use of his photographs. Thanks also to Frank Crummey for his stories, sense of humour, and eagerness to feed starving artists. Thanks to my parents, with whom it is always so much fun to kick around new ideas, for their unfailing love, enthusiasm, and encouragement, and to my brother Matt and sister-in-law Susan for the same. Finally, thanks to Phil Hourihane for more than I have the space or the words to convey.

For my family

Introduction

"And the trouble is, if you don't risk anything, you risk even more." — Erica Jong, American writer, b. 1942

IN the late summer of 1970, five women from dramatically different backgrounds met in a popular Dublin café in the late summer and decided that it was time for some drastic changes in Irish women's lives. The five knew each other well from gathering at one of the women's restaurants in Baggot Street where artists, journalists, politicians, and a wonderfully eclectic assortment of others congregated for good home-cooked meals and marathon conversations. That day over coffee and tea in Bewley's, the women talked less about what they wanted to do and more about who they wanted to ask to join them. It wasn't difficult for them to think of other women who would be interested in helping lead the fight for women's equal rights. The group that the women started that day in the café, the Irish Women's Liberation Movement (IWLM), was the country's first radical women's liberation group. Now, more than three decades after the IWLM's short but profoundly significant life, Irish women are living the very changes that the group fought for. As evidence of the impact of the IWLM's work, two of the most outrageous injustices against women that the group worked hardest to change – the illegality of contraception and the presence of the marriage bar in the workplace – are simply unfathomable today.

Of the dozen or so women who founded the IWLM in Dublin, there was a majority of journalists among them, including the women's page editors at two of the national newspapers, the *Irish Press* and the *Irish Independent,* and the former women's page editor of the third, *The Irish Times*. My first interest in the IWLM was linked to my fascination with journalism and the reporter's role in society, and one of the questions bouncing around newsrooms through the ages: should journalists objectively reflect society or actively, and subjectively, become leaders in changing it? For the IWLM journalists, there was never any doubt between them that they should combine their journalism and their activism in their fight for women's equal rights. They would use every influence they could at their publications and through their colleagues in the broadcast media to get their message out to Irish women. The time had come for them to take a long, hard look at how their country was treating them in terms of the laws, education system and workforce. They wrote stories that depicted society as it was, holding a mirror up to the public face that reflected hypocrisy and cruelty where women were concerned. Many disliked what they saw. This was one of the IWLM's first real steps in provoking change: helping enough people to recognise the flaws in the status quo, and forcing them to think more deeply about the reasons behind society's oppressive laws and attitudes as many never had before.

These women's influence in the media is what made all the difference in terms of the IWLM's impact on society during the short period of time the group was together. If the founders had not been able to use the media as effectively as they did, it is unlikely that Irish women outside of Dublin would have known much of their existence and their aims. But as it was, they went about the business of creating a nationwide dialogue on issues that literally had never been addressed in the public arena before. One of the most difficult tasks for Irish women on their path to liberation in the sixties and early seventies was the development of a new language to put words to their oppression. The IWLM journalists were introducing into Irish society and debate a whole new vocabulary to describe the origins and foundations of discrimination against women.

The IWLM was neither the beginning nor the end of the women's movement in Ireland. There were important groups that came before it, and certainly many that followed. Although it is very difficult to define exactly what its effects on society were, few would deny the IWLM's significance in helping Ireland break its silences in so many areas of women's suffering. The poet who was present at some of the IWLM's early meetings herself, Eavan Boland, expertly expressed the conundrum of measuring social change in her introduction to a 1984 collection of journalist and IWLM founder Nell McCafferty's articles, *The Best of Nell*:

> What is much harder to measure, to quantify, are shifts of perception. They are the slow, unseen rock-slides that begin in every generation without anyone being aware of the first slip, the first boulder loosening and scattering small pebbles. I have no doubt, and equally no proof, that there have been such shifts and changes in the climate of thought in this country in the last ten or fifteen years.[1]

I likewise have neither doubt nor proof that the IWLM contributed to these shifts of perception, but it is my intention that this book might begin to compensate for that lack of proof by providing some insights and explanations into who some of the revolutionaries were, how they connected with each other, how they worked together, and how they eventually separated. It is really only when one begins to understand the motivations of the people behind the movement that one can understand the movement, and its significance, itself.

The IWLM founders weren't only journalists, and the diversity of the core group is one of its most intriguing characteristics. Among the first five women who met in Bewley's café was a medical doctor, an American-born *Irish Times* journalist, a Sinn Féin official, a left-wing political activist and trade unionist, and the owner of one of the city's most popular restaurants. The differences among them stretched across class, age and nationality. The group was, from its very conception, as University College Cork sociologist Linda Connolly has said, "simultaneously about solidarity and difference". The solidarity emerged very early on in the meetings at Gaj's restaurant in Baggot Street, the IWLM's eventual meeting place, when the women began to realise that discrimination knew none of the boundaries that they imagined separated them – especially class. It didn't matter how much money a woman had or if she was a professional; she still needed her husband's signature, for example, to open a bank account, and it was still likely she'd be fired from her job upon marriage due to the marriage bar.

The differences between the women, though, were also strong, and although the IWLM members reconciled those differences better than history has sometimes given them credit for, there were arguments that were difficult to resolve so the group could function to the best of its ability. Still, when assessing the IWLM's impact and the incredible strides it made in the space of less than one year, it is becoming increasingly clear that the founders accomplished all they did not *despite* their diversity, but *because* of it.

Nuala Fennell was one of the most conservative IWLM members, and the one who publicly expressed her dissatisfaction with the group upon her resignation in 1971. But even Fennell realises today that the IWLM provided exactly the jolt that Irish society needed at the time by shocking the public, which was a task that a more structured, formal, homogenous group probably would not have been able to carry off. The spontaneity that the gathering of such a diverse group of women allowed was exactly what the time called for.

And yet for all the spontaneity, excitement, and allure that surrounded the IWLM, and for all of the group's efforts to be an unstructured organisation with no designated leaders, the founders were often able to organise themselves extremely well. When scratching beneath the surface of what went on at meetings and how the women reached a consensus about when and how to take action, a structure, however loose, and a system, however vague, emerges. Even if it simply meant that there were unspoken rules about discussion topics at meetings (the North being one that the group carefully and deliberately excluded) there was still a sufficient level of organisation that allowed the IWLM to get on with its work and, for the most part, avoid arguments on many of the most potentially divisive subjects. The emotions that often accompanied the most heated disagreements were tempered with an underlying, if obscured, mutual respect of others' viewpoints. This respect was one of the most positive results of the group's use of consciousness-raising, a tactic borrowed directly from the American women's liberation groups that involved small numbers of women talking about their own experiences in every context from the workplace to the bedroom. Such frank and personal discussions created a bond of sympathy even between women who had come from drastically different backgrounds, which was a major factor in the IWLM's ability to stay together and function cohesively for the months that it did.

What the IWLM accomplished was formidable. Sociologists have noted that a successful movement is the point of intersection between personal and social change.[2] Even as the IWLM founders were discovering their individual feelings and developing their own language through the consciousness-raising sessions, they were spreading their ideas and messages on the women's pages of the nation's three largest newspapers. They were responsible for many "firsts" for Irish women. They designed and developed their mantra in the form of a booklet titled *Chains or Change,* which they published in March 1971, about six months after their first meeting. The booklet was the first single document that detailed the inequalities Irish women suffered in the workplace, in the education system and under the law. They orchestrated demonstrations, pickets, and protests, some of them at the Dáil, at churches, and at the Archbishop's residence. They planned an appearance on the most popular television show of the time, *The Late Late Show* with Gay Byrne. The group's 1971 appearance on the show marked the first time that an entire television programme was devoted to women's issues in Ireland. They organised their first mass meeting at the Mansion House the following month, which more than 1,000 women attended, and they accomplished all this in less than one year, the length of time the group existed from its formation to disintegration.

I realised during my earliest interviews with the founders how heavily I would be relying on other people's memories, which is a major difficulty when attempting to study a time and a place of which one has no personal recollection. Within the first few weeks of interviews, I had already encountered significant differences between several individuals' accounts of the same meeting. One woman had no memory whatsoever of several American feminists' influence on the group's synthesis, but many others claimed it was the Americans' conversation with one of the group's founding members that acted as the catalyst for the beginning of the whole movement. It was circumstances such as these in which I had some difficult decisions to make – whom to believe? In the end, I tried to piece the different accounts together as best I could to create the most accurate possible picture of events while taking everyone's versions into consideration. I agree with historian Mary Cullen's assertion that "history, in the sense that it is the closest approximation of what really happened that can be achieved, will always need the convergence of as many different stories from as many different points of view as possible".[3]

The advantage of coming to a history project involving events and people of which I had no preconceived notions was that I was able to collect vivid descriptions from the minds of women who, even if they couldn't remember an exact date or detail, had particularly clear recollections of some of the most exciting and important events of their lives. Put another way, I had to "take their word for it" because I had few other means besides their words for tracing the history of their movement. Although there's no question that memories become distorted over the years, the passage of time also allows for further insight and reflection that can be equally, if not more, valuable than a perfectly accurate description of any one event. For example, we know from the Dáil records that Mary Robinson attempted to get a reading of her Contraception Bill in 1971; but how did the protestors outside react to IWLM founder Mary Kenny's rendition of "We Shall Not Conceive" sung impromptu to the tune of "We Shall Overcome"? How is it that so many women in the group can remember the exact colour of a pair of satin hotpants, all the rage in 1970, that Kenny wore to one of the meetings, even as she smoked one of her famous long-stemmed velvet pipes? The great American oral historian Studs Turkel once said that his work was not *history*, but *memory*; he was searching not for the facts, but for the truth behind the facts, which is often more telling.

Like the women's liberation movement itself, or any social movement for that matter, memory is not static. It changes with experience. It is unlike the printed words on the pages of minutes from meetings and memos, letters and newspaper articles, recorded television images, or any of the other materials that comprise part of the historical record. The difficulty with the IWLM is that few of these solid records exist to help with the documentation of the details of the group's existence. The meetings were supposed to be informal and relatively unstructured; no minutes were taken. RTÉ has no existing recording of one of the group's most famous activities, its appearance on *The Late Late Show*. There are many newspaper articles that provide a general outline of the group's goals, but not much detailed information about the group members themselves or how the IWLM operated. For these kinds of insights, then, the only sources are the women themselves and those who knew them best.

Even for a group that was together for as short a time as the IWLM was, with its entire life span of seven or eight months at most, it is difficult to trace its origins and endings completely. There were so many groups, individuals and social factors that precipitated the group's formation that I know I've only been able to provide a glimpse into what I see as some of the most important influences. But above all, what I hope I've been able to capture is the personality and spirit both of the IWLM as a group, and of its individual members. By charting their personal backgrounds and delving into the individual motivations behind their activism, I believe I have been able to explain how these particular women came together as a group and boldly challenged nearly every notion that society and tradition had taught them about what it meant to be a woman in Ireland. The enormity of their task and the seriousness of its purpose has been somewhat lost, if not forgotten, over the years. But what's even more extraordinary to discover about the women themselves is the amount of grace, good humour, and wit they possessed in the face of their fight for equal rights. Many of the founders believe they wouldn't have been able to accomplish what they did unless they each, as individuals, had a good dose of these particular qualities – especially good humour – along with all of their determination, intelligence and courage.

Why was it that these particular women were some of the first to take the risks involved with stepping outside of the boundaries of polite society toward what they saw as a better deal and a better future for Ireland's women? It is my hope that this work will provide a little more insight into that question. Social movements are often started by a surprisingly small number of people, but even for as small a country as Ireland is, the IWLM was unique – and wonderful – in this respect. The IWLM founders proved that even a very small number of true believers who have the courage to fight discrimination wholeheartedly, at great personal risk and sacrifice, can change the course of history. For women, for journalists, and for people who are not and have never been content to encounter injustice without fighting it, the IWLM is an example of the power of a small group of people with a large vision – a few pebbles that started a landslide.

1

Not Just a Restaurant

"Of all the lunchtime places, Gaj's still holds first position for straightforwardly good food and incredible value. None of the main courses are more than 5/- and they include pork cutlets, mutton cutlets, casserole or stews. All main courses are served with fresh vegetables – Mrs Gaj believes this to be an absolute necessity for all her customers. The restaurant is always bubbling over with people so don't go expecting a quiet candlelight lunch – they haven't got time for those kind of trimmings." — Rosita Sweetman, from the *Irish Press* Women's Page, 9 April 1970[1]

"I suppose there's always somebody and some place in every city who looks after the poets and the artists and maybe the druggies and the politicos, and Mrs Gaj was that person." — Rosita Sweetman

"People were drawn in there. It was like a magnet. It was an amazing, amazing place." — Marie McMahon

Frank Crummey remembers exactly how the conversation usually started at his regular lunchtime table at Gaj's restaurant, 132 Baggot Street, Dublin, through the better part of the late sixties and early seventies. Lady Christine Longford would look around the table and say, "And who will start the stories today?" The collection of people she addressed included a doctor, two bank robbers, a prostitute, the restaurant owner herself, and Frank, then a social worker. One of the bank robbers, as Frank recalls, was never caught or convicted in court of a robbery, and upon his retirement he wrote a letter to the local Gardaí telling them they might as well give up now, as his working days were finished.

Twenty-six years after closing her Baggot Street restaurant, eighty-seven-year-old Margaret Gaj often dreams about the place and her staff. As important a forum for discussion and exchanging ideas as any Dublin pub of its time, Gaj's was the place to meet for people who were interested in changing the world. Politicians, artists, journalists, travellers, activists, prostitutes, students and business people alike all gathered at Gaj's. Patrons would drop in assured of hearty home-cooked food at fabulously low prices and conversation with people from all walks of life about anything from politics and court cases to art and music. Someone had to feed the revolutionaries, and Mrs Gaj knew just what to put on her menu – tasty, no-frills food that, aside from the wonderful burgers and chips, was relatively healthy. Frank remembers one of Mrs Gaj's sons making those burgers upstairs in the restaurant from a secret recipe that he never revealed. Stews, casseroles, bacon and cabbage, Scotch eggs – solving the world's problems tended to work up an appetite that required a lot of high-energy protein-laden dinners. Gaj's was a place where the usual boundaries that kept people from being able to relate to one another more freely – class, age, political affiliations – seemed to soften to allow for new ideas and even alliances to emerge. Both the atmosphere of the restaurant, which was small, naturally wood-furnished and always had fresh flowers on tables, and the menu reflected Mrs Gaj's preference for simplicity and straightforwardness.

If every city has its renegade social workers disguised as teachers, shopkeepers or restaurant owners, Margaret Gaj was the greatest of these in the Dublin of the sixties and seventies. Those who know her well speak of Mrs Gaj as an imposing, straightforward, wise and extremely generous woman, large in body, vision and spirit. Born in Scotland to Irish parents in 1919, she was a pacifist and conscientious objector, refusing to join the army when war broke out in 1939 as her two brothers and sisters had done. Instead she joined the Red Cross as a nurse because she saw nursing as the one thing she could do that would cause the least harm during the war. While nursing she met her husband, a badly injured Polish prisoner of war. Later, Mr Gaj was an artist who made copper jewellery in Celtic designs, which were displayed and sold at the restaurant. Her husband has now been dead for more than three decades, but Mrs Gaj says he lived a lot longer than she had expected him to.

Although she has never stated publicly why she and her husband chose to move to Ireland towards the end of the war, her Irish roots and the fact that it was one of the few countries that remained neutral made it appealing to her. Ironically, she was attracted to the country on the basis of its neutrality, but became so deeply involved with such a range of political issues that she was anything but neutral herself. She seems to have been born with an interest in politics; there was no single incident that she can trace it back to. Politics, she says, was simply something that was part of everything back then – part of being.

"I started with more money than sense, and ended with more sense than money," Mrs Gaj says of her life in the restaurant business. When she opened the restaurant she had no background in business at all, but thought that if she had good food and served it cheaply, that's all she needed to be successful. And yet, Mrs Gaj's definition of success is probably markedly different from most others' in the business, both then and now. She was lucky enough to be able to start her restaurant with a little bit of her own money, so financial gain was never her primary concern in opening Gaj's. She had a saying with some customers, "double or quits", so sometimes people would pay her double and sometimes nothing for a meal, depending on their circumstances. The waitresses knew the names and faces of the certain customers that were never to be handed a bill – those who didn't have the price of the meal and whom Mrs Gaj was happy to take care of without embarrassing. There were four or five seats at the counter, and often a small group of travellers would come in early to whom Mrs Gaj would also give a meal free of charge. For all the meals that Mrs Gaj gave out, some of her patrons might have wondered how she ever made any money at all if it weren't for the fact that the place was crowded day and night, during opening hours and after. In any case, she figured that once you had enough money to survive, what was the use in trying to make more?

The staff remembers that people weren't hired at Gaj's, but taken on for a week on a probationary basis to see if they fit in. Then the staff would decide collectively and democratically whether to ask the person to stay. This made perfect sense to Mrs Gaj because she wasn't the one who had to work directly with new people, and so the current employees should have the final say. A young waitress who joined the staff in the early seventies, Deirdre Shannon-Shiel, says she would have worked there for nothing save the stimulation of the conversation and the energetic buzz about the place. She remembers Mrs Gaj "holding court" over the restaurant at about four o'clock, after the frenetic lunchtime rush had died down, sitting in her designated chair in the corner and falling into conversation until about six o'clock when the dinner crowd would start streaming through the place. Shannon-Shiel remembers music that Mr Gaj selected playing in the background – gypsy music from Hungary, Poland and Russia, and Soviet military marches – but you could seldom hear the music over the constant din of the talking. In another life, Shannon-Shiel says, Mrs Gaj could have been a brilliant barrister or Minister for Human Rights because she sponsored everybody and argued her points masterfully, often bailing people out of jail or standing up for them in court as a character witness. It would have been difficult to find a more committed champion of the underdog.

Indeed, one of Mrs Gaj's most defining characteristics is her sense of equality and social justice that was obvious in the universal generosity she demonstrated toward her patrons and more overtly with her political affiliations. She was instrumental in the creation of the Prisoners' Rights Organisation in 1973 along with Joe Costello, now a Labour TD, and had a keen sense of the deprivation of rights and privileges that the poor endured. She would have her journalist friends in *The Irish Times* announce "bring-and-buy" days that she'd sponsor at the restaurant around Christmastime, charity days to benefit Dublin's poor and homeless. Costello remembers Mrs Gaj as an extraordinarily determined woman who was sincere but blunt. "She was tough-minded and probably ruthless," Costello says. "I think she'd go a long way to carrying out what she believed in." She was also clearly no woman to trifle with. Mrs Gaj's bad side was not a pleasant place to find oneself. One night just after she had gotten home from the restaurant, she received a call from a waitress that a man was causing trouble by exposing himself. The staff may have had permission from Mrs Gaj to put customers in their place without fear of consequence, but this was a problem they hadn't encountered before and they were unsure how to handle it. Mrs Gaj returned to the restaurant, went straight over to the man and told him to "just cover that thing up and get out". "And he did, just meek as a lamb," she says.

Frank Crummey remembers just how far Mrs Gaj would go for her cause sometimes, with his own full support and assistance. Crummey was a Gaj's regular and a good friend of Mrs Gaj's when he lost his job as a social worker with the Irish Society for the Prevention of Cruelty to Children (ISPCC) around 1970 because he was involved in setting up the first family planning clinics in Dublin. The society felt that it was "inconsistent" for a good social worker to be involved in family planning. He bounced from job to job, trying to look at his situation as an opportunity to try out new and different lines of work. One summer, while he was doing maintenance work at a sizeable Dublin law firm, two of the partners unwittingly scheduled holidays for the same two weeks. Frank heard them discussing their troubles; either they had to find someone to run the office, or one of them would have to change his booking. The quick-thinking Frank offered to look after the business for them and found himself taking care of the office single-handedly for the two weeks – he was, after all, familiar with most of the cases and clients. Mrs Gaj always said that Frank could "talk the hind legs off a donkey", but he was also curious about everything, and a fast learner – he could listen as well as he talked. The solicitors returned to offer Frank an empty back office, and he set about learning the ins and outs of the law. Although he never received his law degree, he spends most of his days now arguing cases in court and is recognised there as a solicitor. Soon after he began studying the law and learning the job, it became a favorite pastime of his and Mrs Gaj's to personally track down people whom they felt needed to be brought to justice. Frank had grown up with no father, in an entirely female household with his mother and sisters, and has great respect for the strength of women.

Frank remembers one man whom he and Mrs Gaj knew was planning to desert his wife by fleeing the country. They wanted to catch up with him before he could escape because the wife was a friend of theirs and there were no laws at the time that allowed deserted wives any kind of recourse once their husbands left the country. The man knew they were after him, and he would look up and down the street as he came out of his house. But Frank knew that he and Mrs Gaj would get him. The pair drove to the man's house one night and let the air out of his back tyres. The next morning they parked at the end of the street, Mrs Gaj at the wheel and Frank crouched in the back seat, waiting. Mrs Gaj narrated the scene from the front seat to Frank, who couldn't see any of the action from his covert position. The man was getting into his car, pulling away, stopping, getting out, examining the trouble, and opening the boot. Mrs Gaj floored the accelerator and Frank jumped out of the back seat, yelling "Gotcha!" while shoving solicitor's papers at the man. "They were building a supermarket and the muck was everywhere and he would have killed me if he got me, but I was a good runner," Frank says. Mrs Gaj met Frank at the end of the street in the getaway car and the sneak attack was successfully completed without much bodily harm having been done to either of them. Frank remembers another "mission" with Mrs Gaj, though, when a man pulled a gun on them. But Mrs Gaj was afraid of no one. "I wasn't afraid of many people either," Frank says, "and yet I was ridiculously small and she was ridiculously large." It conjures an image of a dynamic, if somewhat unlikely, duo; rogue crusaders whose home base of operations and planning was the Baggot Street restaurant. All that was missing were the capes, masks, and theme music.

They'd always laugh about their escapades at the restaurant over lunch with the same gang. Mrs Gaj liked ordinary people who were interesting, no matter what their backgrounds, as was reflected by the diversity of her lunchtime table. Lady Longford was never disappointed when she asked who would start the stories for the day – whoever it was and whatever they talked about, they were bound to be good. Dr Noel Browne, the Minister for Health in the late 1940s and early 1950s, was a great friend of Mrs Gaj's, and he would tell the table about the politicians who were annoying him in the Dáil. Lyn Madden was a prostitute and another great friend of Gaj's, and she would regale the table with stories about her clients – which politicians were paying for sex and who the kinky guys were. The bank robbers would tell about their last jobs, and one lunchtime could never have been enough to fit everything, everyone's stories, in.

Frank reckons that any political group worth anything in the sixties and seventies held its first meeting in Gaj's. And if you wanted to make sure that every penny would be accounted for and save yourself the hassle of financial problems, you'd make Mrs Gaj the treasurer. For a woman who was genuinely never particularly concerned with making money for herself, she was awfully good at keeping track of it for other people. Posters announcing meetings, protests, teach-ins and demonstrations constantly appeared on the walls as the politically aware went about their business in the city and then brought their debates about their business into the restaurant. Free speech and a diversity of opinions reigned in Gaj's, as Mrs Gaj wished. The tables were thrown over more than once in heated discussions between those at opposite ends of the political spectrum, and the cooks knew to leave the kitchen windows open if patrons like Frank needed to exit the building in a hurry – jumping onto the roof of the neighbouring building – while being chased. Some would always sit with their backs to the wall to avoid being punched or otherwise caught unawares because you never knew who might walk through the door. Everyone went there. Those whom Mrs Gaj barred would come back in a few days, begging to be let back in. She had one strict rule with her staff, and it was that the customer was always wrong. If patrons were rude or simply annoying, the staff had every freedom to deal with them as they saw fit. Mrs Gaj, running a restaurant seemingly against every written or unwritten rule of the business, would never want for customers.

The groups that met at Gaj's and the discussions that went on within its walls had everything to do with the changes that Dubliners – especially youth – wanted to see in their city, in Ireland, and in the world. The main issues of the day were the housing crisis, the Vietnam War, apartheid in South Africa and, as the seventies began, women's liberation. "Debates, pickets, public meetings, occupations and sit-ins were the order of the day, whether against American imperialism or the jailing of the Irish telephonists or the Griffith Barracks campaign to civilise the lives of Dublin's homeless," trade unionist Des Geraghty wrote in his 1994 biography of Dubliners folk singer Luke Kelly.[2] The Dublin Housing Action Committee was one of the largest organisations of those years, and it encompassed a large alliance of the homeless, workers, students and members of nearly every left-wing political party – the Labour Party, Sinn Féin, the Communist Party of Ireland (then called the Irish Workers' Party), and others. Geraghty detailed the tremendous feelings of hope and possibility among the young that they really were going to change their world, spurred on by developments in the media like the new RTÉ programmes on social issues and current events and the radicalisation of *The Irish Times* under the stewardship of news editor Donal Foley. There was a general feeling that Ireland was, as Geraghty put it, "finding its soul" as it broke free from the restrictions enforced by the orthodoxy of the church, state and Irish business class. The area around Merrion Row was made up of a string of pubs and restaurants, from O'Donoghue's down to Gaj's, and Geraghty remembered that those with the stamina could make it in one night to all of the establishments where the lefties and revolutionaries thrashed out their ideas.[3]

One of the causes that Margaret Gaj herself believed most passionately in was the fight for Irish women's liberation. She put her social and political connections from the restaurant into action in late 1970 to help orchestrate the gathering of a group of young, passionate women in the fight for women's equal rights. Her circle of friends and associates was wide enough to include women like Sinn Féin official Máirín de Burca, who in the summer of 1970 received a visit in the organisation's Dublin office from two American feminists who happened to be looking for information on Irish Republicanism. The two feminists ended up staying to talk with de Burca about the American women's liberation movement. The Americans were curious about Irish women's current situation.

Mrs Gaj had also asked to see, or had "sent for", American-born *Irish Times* journalist Mary Maher after seeing Maher's byline over stories about the Dublin Housing Action Committee, the Irish Voice on Vietnam, and other left-wing and socialist groups. Maher already knew de Burca from reporting on such groups, many of which de Burca was involved with; but if she hadn't, Mrs Gaj would have ensured that the two like-minded women met in her restaurant. She had always been like that, a person who found it rewarding to connect people whom she thought would get on well and be able to accomplish something together. Both Maher and de Burca were friendly with Dr Moira Woods, another regular Gaj's customer, from their mutual membership in the Irish Voice on Vietnam. And Maher knew another Dublin woman and a member of the Communist Party, Máirín Johnston, through mutual friends in the Labour Party, with which Johnston was also an activist. Johnston was heavily involved in the trade unions and other workers' rights groups, and naturally would have frequented Gaj's. Mrs Gaj had known de Burca, Maher, Woods and Johnston individually before they all had been formally introduced to each other.

It was these five women – Gaj, de Burca, Maher, Woods, and Johnston – who gathered in the late summer of 1970 at Bewley's Café on Westmoreland Street at what was the first meeting of the collection of women who were to form the Irish Women's Liberation Movement (IWLM), the country's first radical women's group. Mrs Gaj was a Bewley's regular, stopping there for a bit of breakfast almost every morning before opening her own restaurant. The Bewley's staff knew her well, and, as in her own restaurant, she had her designated spot in the café.

The IWLM women often referred to Mrs Gaj as "mother". She was about twenty years older than the average age of the other founder members, and something of a nurturing, protective influence on the younger women. Máirín de Burca recalls with great gratitude the fact that she could always depend on Mrs Gaj, no matter what the hour, to bail her out of jail. Few other women could have helped in the same way because Mrs Gaj had her own car and was very respectable. (Most of the IWLM women never dropped the "Mrs" when addressing her, as a matter of tacit respect.) She was phenomenally good at organisation, both with money and human resources. As with so many other upstart organisations, she was the unofficial treasurer of the group, collecting two shillings per person each week as a contribution toward the "rent" of the place. Once the IWLM had been together several months and the group was planning more activities and protests, she would also occasionally suggest that the women break up into smaller groups to work on a specific task. Mary Sheerin, another IWLM founder member, remembers her as a kind of Buddha figure.

The IWLM might not have technically been born in Gaj's, but it certainly grew and did the bulk of its work in the upstairs room over the restaurant. The founders met every Monday night, including bank holidays, and they lived for the meetings. They couldn't wait to get there. Although Mrs Gaj was one of the original five members of the IWLM and was tremendously influential in the synthesis of the group, she has never been fond of interviews and is highly protective of her privacy. It is perhaps for this reason that her role in the beginning of the women's liberation movement of the seventies has been largely overlooked, but then it is sometimes the great thinkers and visionaries who are the most modest of all.

Mrs Gaj worries that nowadays there's no place in the city like Gaj's where the same kinds of people mix and meet. Bewley's cafés in Grafton and Westmoreland Streets, which paralleled her own restaurant in its eclectic collection of patrons, closed in the winter of 2004. The chairman of the Campbell Bewley Group, Patrick Campbell, cited high rents and competition as two of the chief reasons for Bewley's closure. The day prior to the announcement, Grafton Street was named as the fifth most expensive street in the world in which to run a shop, after New York, Paris, Hong Kong and London.[4]

The absence of a restaurant like Gaj's is due, Mrs Gaj says disdainfully, to the fact that the Dublin restaurant business is so much more competitive now and the overwhelming emphasis is on making money and getting as large a volume of people in and out each day as possible. That means rushing people through their meals and simply not allowing them the time it takes for thoughtful debate and deep conversation. "That was the end of a restaurant where people mattered," she says. Dubliners have changed a great deal since the days when her restaurant was overflowing with people, and even if some of her memories are fading, she's sure she's not at all pleased with what she sees as the every-man-for-himself attitude that prevails today. She also thinks people were generally more interested in politics three decades ago. Having an interest in politics and discussing important issues was just innately more of a part of people's existence back then. Indeed, the restaurant and its patrons came to symbolise the vitality and idealism of the first generation of young people in Dublin who believed any kinds of changes were possible, and for many of them, Gaj's closing represented the passing of that mentality:

> The 1970s had been a decade of growth and expansion. The hope for the 1980s was that this would continue. A prophetic note was struck, however, in April 1980, when Margaret Gaj closed her restaurant. It was situated on the first floor in Baggot Street and for twenty-one years Margaret had presided over a meeting-place which became as much club as café. You would see all kinds of people there – journalists, tourists, travellers, unemployed people, prostitutes, politicians, business people, actors, civil-rights activ-

ists. The colourful mix seemed to encompass the spirit of a time when barriers between differing groups were being broken down. When it closed, many of us felt we had lost something special.[5]

Frank Crummey often visits Mrs Gaj at her house these days and they talk about the restaurant, the conversations, the craic, and the faces at the table that have long since disappeared. But neither is one to live life in the past, and, like the old days, they're both still acutely interested in politics, even if their personal involvement as active members of protest groups isn't what it used to be. The ever-changing titles of the books on Mrs Gaj's table are some of the latest, yet they seem to reflect old interests. One of the most recent ones was *Reading Lolita in Tehran,* Azar Nafisi's story of her time as a professor in Tehran teaching banned Western literature to a study group of young Iranian women. For his part, Frank will get just as riled over America's 2003 invasion of Iraq as one could imagine him getting over the laws banning contraception in Ireland at the start of the women's liberation movement. Irish neutrality, both politically and individually, has always frustrated him. "Neutrality, to me, is the refuge of the scoundrel," he says. Right or wrong, you've got to nail your colours to the mast, and why should it be impossible for Ireland to agree with America on some issues while disagreeing on others, he asks? True friends, he argues, will speak their minds honestly with each other, especially if they think the other is in the wrong. That's how it always was at Gaj's; you could disagree on every issue but still be engaged and interested in someone else's views, and in fact be great friends, without ever really falling out. The way Frank sees it, if he's walking down the street and he sees something going wrong, he's got a moral obligation to interfere. There is simply no question of *not* doing something to try to correct injustice.

That's one characteristic that Mrs Gaj shared with the other women who began the IWLM – none of them was neutral. None of them remained neutral on any issue, and all of them were willing to go down for their principles. They simply didn't care about going to jail. In any case, the prevailing belief seemed to be that if you were fighting for basic civil rights, and fighting for the justice that every citizen deserved, no matter the particulars of the cause, you couldn't really go wrong. Risk-takers though they were, however, it didn't hurt to know that if you landed yourself in a jam, there was always someone to depend on to help you.

A practical and even-handed decision-maker, Mrs Gaj had always sworn the day she was no longer able to take over the cooking duties in the kitchen herself if need be was the day she would close her restaurant, and so it was in the spring of 1980. As the place was put up for sale, her patrons agreed that the worst thing would be if someone took it over and tried to run a restaurant under new management. That's exactly what happened, and it lasted a few months before failing and closing for good.

Neither Frank Crummey nor Mrs Gaj would trade the advancements of the past thirty years in Ireland for the old days, but that doesn't mean they don't miss the spirit of involvement, possibility, and excitement of the sixties and seventies. "We went to meetings and protests and demonstrations like the young ones today go to the cinema," Frank says. "That was our entertainment. It was a fantastically exciting time." He throws a mischievous glance at Mrs Gaj and proclaims that a good part of the fun of those days was that they were all slightly nuts to do the things they had done, take the risks they had taken. She seems to agree, and there's no indication of regret on either of their parts for anything they'd done for any of their causes. When the restaurant closed, her patrons booked a dinner at a hotel and took Mrs Gaj out for a celebration of all that she had meant to them. Frank remembers TD Garret FitzGerald, who would be elected Taoiseach the following year, commenting that no Dubliner's education was complete unless they had spent some time in Gaj's. But when asked about her impact on the city and her customers over the years, Mrs Gaj says simply, "I was better off for knowing them."

"We had some good laughs, didn't we, Margaret?" Frank says at the end of one of his visits. You can tell he's pleased with himself.

Mrs Gaj just looks at a black-and-white photograph of herself behind the counter in her restaurant, circa early 1970s, and smiles.

The Universal Activist

"I wouldn't have given up every other cause and only did the women's issue. It wouldn't have been in me to do it." — Máirín de Burca

"De Burca, Máirín. Secretary of Sinn Féin (Gardiner St.). Dedicated left-wing republican with strong feelings for the underdog; quick-tempered but actually full of common sense, efficiency and good humour. Began life as a shop-girl but today is in the mainstream of policy-making and leadership in radical groups here. Not to be underestimated." — From the *Irish Press*'s list of the 25 most influential Irish women, 9 March 1971[1]

The IWLM's permanent home was the room above Gaj's restaurant, and Mrs Gaj became a Godmother-type figure who watched over the group as it grew. But it was Máirín de Burca who actually made the very first phone call with the idea of organising an activist group for women's rights, setting the chain of events in motion that resulted in the formation of the IWLM. Other group members name de Burca as a pillar of logic and common sense. Just as important, or even more so in the context of the IWLM, de Burca's years of involvement with political groups had taught her how to organise people and resources to their best possible potential.

De Burca was born in Dublin in 1938 but spent her early childhood in America, where her father was the head carpenter at the Marshall Field Building in Chicago. Her parents would have returned to Ireland earlier than they did, when Máirín was about nine years old, if the Second World War had not prevented their passage. As it was the de Burcas were on one of the first ships back, and they settled in Newbridge, County Kildare, where Máirín left school at an early age. De Burca encountered the problem of not being able to sit the leaving certificate exams because she'd never had the opportunity to learn Irish during her early education in America. The nuns in Newbridge were willing to teach her, and had asked her mother if she wanted to learn, but her mother said no. The fact that she never learned Irish is one of Máirín's great regrets. She saw no real point in staying in school any longer than was absolutely necessary, so she left and went to work on her fourteenth birthday at a shop in Newbridge.

De Burca eventually moved to Bray and then to Dublin, still working in shops. She claims she was the worst shop assistant in the world because she hates dealing with the public. Regardless of whether that's true, de Burca is extremely well-respected among her former colleagues in the IWLM. Máirín Johnston speaks of the impossibility of walking down any main street in Dublin with de Burca, then and now, without getting stopped every few minutes by someone wanting to say hello and have a chat with her. True, Dublin remains a friendly city, and de Burca has been living in it practically her whole life. But the high regard that her fellow revolutionaries maintain for de Burca more than three decades after the height of her activism is indicative of her deep and enduring commitment to the causes she saw reason to fight for. For someone who doesn't see herself as a people person, de Burca has done far more than most in her efforts over the years to help people who didn't have the power or means to help themselves. Margaret Gaj insists that although de Burca lacks a formal education, she was one of the cleverest and most committed of all the women in the IWLM. There is a certain kind of intelligence that Mrs Gaj sees as separate from that which is enhanced by a university degree, the sort that allows you to be far outside of society's conventions in your thinking without being afraid of the gulf between you and the majority. The ability to be such a free thinker is often at odds with formal education, so in that sense de Burca was fortunate to have left school at such an early age.

De Burca joined Sinn Féin on the very first day that was possible, her sixteenth birthday. She had a great deal of freedom from an early age.

Her parents had lost a young son before she was born, and she had only one other brother, on whom she says all of her mother's love and attention was focused, leaving Máirín to do mostly as she pleased. So at the age of sixteen, Máirín would cycle out to political meetings that would go on until two or three in the morning without being asked where she was or whom she was with. She learned to look after herself. Even as she found her mother's lack of concern unusual, and no doubt a bit hurtful, she looks on it now as an asset to her life. She reasons that she might not have become so involved in politics at such an early age if it hadn't been for the freedom she enjoyed.

After moving to Dublin, she broke off her activities with Sinn Féin for a year or two because, in retrospect, she thought the group was becoming too right-wing for her. What eventually attracted her back to the group was Sinn Féin's support for the telephonist strikers – they were paid a pittance – as they demonstrated for higher wages in the late sixties. De Burca realised that the group had moved substantially to the left while she had been away from it, and she now felt it was a better fit for her. When the Troubles broke out in the North in 1969, she quit her shop job and went to work full-time in the party's head office in Dublin. Máirín recalls that 1970 was the year of the Sinn Féin split that resulted in the formation of the Provisionals, the branch of the IRA that was in favour of acquiring arms and taking violent action against the British Army in the North. She remembers it as an awkward time for her with the party because she was a pacifist. She says that the other branch of Sinn Féin, the Officials, was not completely against the arming of the Provisionals, but she was.

Besides Sinn Féin, de Burca was involved in several other political groups, the main ones being the Dublin Housing Action Committee, the Irish Voice on Vietnam, and the Irish Anti-Apartheid Movement. But it is the Vietnam War that de Burca speaks the most fervently about. To de Burca, Vietnam defined her generation. "I remember being so, so passionate about it. I would have done anything to try to stop it. I would have done anything," she says.

What she did do was spend three months in jail in 1971 for her conduct during an anti-war demonstration at the American Embassy. At the height of the IWLM's public activities, de Burca's involvement in the Irish

anti-war movement was unfaltering. April 24, 1971, marked a day of co-
ordinated international mass protests against the war, with thousands turning out all across America and a large protest at the American Embassy in
Dublin. As usual, de Burca was one of the most forceful protestors at the
Embassy, and she joined others in smashing large bottles of cow's blood
over the Embassy steps, and taking the American flag down from its pole
and setting fire to it. The Gardaí arrested de Burca and fellow IWLM
founder Marie McMahon for their part in the demonstration, and they
were sentenced to three months each in Mountjoy prison on charges related to the damage they had done to the Embassy's property. De Burca
recalls that their sentences did not begin until the following autumn because of the slow pace of the courts.

De Burca had had her fair share of arrests previously, but she'd yet to
be in jail for months at a time. Fellow IWLM founder and then-*Irish
Times* columnist Nell McCafferty wrote about de Burca's court record in
the final instalment of a three-part series titled "Women in Court" in
May 1971. At the date of publication, McCafferty reported that de Burca
had appeared in the courts no less than seventeen times in the previous
three years on various charges related to her actions during demonstrations on a range of social and political issues.[2] McCafferty's article detailed how de Burca appealed to the Supreme Court, disputing a sentence
of two months' imprisonment for painting slogans on an American bank
after American troops had invaded Cambodia. She was fined five pounds
for breaking a window in the German Cultural Institute during a Sinn
Féin protest, although, she told the judge, she had mistaken the building
for the British Embassy, which she had been aiming for. Burning the
Union Jack and participating in a sit-in protesting the jailing of squatters
were some of the additional reasons for her court appearances. She was
charged with obscene behaviour in a place of worship, riotous behaviour
and breaching the peace when she called for the release of prisoner Dennis Denehy at the Dáil's nineteenth commemoration mass, which Eamon
de Valera was attending. She had been fined for cutting down the British
flag at the RDS and throwing eggs at President Richard Nixon's car during his October 1970 visit to Dublin. On that particular occasion, de
Burca and two other activists were each fined two pounds for throwing
eggs at Nixon's car, but de Burca's aim had been particularly sharp and

she had managed to land one squarely on the presidential windscreen. A guard told the *Irish Press* that he had taken de Burca over to the footpath near the Winetavern Street Bridge because the crowd was hostile to her. There were shouts of "throw her in the river", and one woman attempted to strike de Burca, calling, "lynch her".[3]

"I am using the law against itself," de Burca told McCafferty of her protest history in McCafferty's *Irish Times* piece. "I want it to be seen, and proved, that people do have the right to protest against what they consider to be injustice; that they need not fear the remote anonymous control of their lives which they see embodied in the magisterial trappings of the law and the system." Leaving school at fourteen had not hindered de Burca's ability to communicate her ideas and convictions articulately.

De Burca's experience in jail was so unsettling that she found it difficult to talk about it for a long time afterwards. She and Marie McMahon had had their differences over the North (de Burca was a staunch pacifist and completely against the arming of the Provisional IRA, while McMahon was not) but the two decided that if they were going to be in jail together they ought to try to stick together. They also agreed that a cause like Vietnam was worth burying some of their other differences over. De Burca remembers their first morning at Mountjoy together. At that time, the cells were left open in the women's unit and McMahon had come racing into de Burca's cell, upset that one of the prison guards had ordered her to call her "Miss".

"Marie was all fed up that this was unfair and we shouldn't do it and I said *sit down* for a minute. We're going to be here for three months, and if we're going to have a row we're not going to have a row about this," de Burca says. She was about nine years older than McMahon, and although McMahon was also very active in political protests and demonstrations herself, she didn't have as much experience as de Burca yet in dealing with law enforcement officials.

De Burca had already served a week in jail for a previous charge, and she had a marginally better idea of how to handle the inevitable struggles with the prison guards. If peaceful resistance worked outside jail, there was a chance it might be effective inside as well. That same first morning that McMahon had been so upset about the prison guard's demand, all the women were ordered after breakfast to go down to the workroom. De Burca knew that all prisoners were entitled to one hour of exercise outdoors, and she, McMahon, and another inmate sat down and refused to move until they had had it. The prison guards were annoyed because they conceded that de Burca, McMahon, and the other inmate did have the right to exercise, and they knew from de Burca's history and commanding demeanour that she wouldn't budge. But they had to work out between themselves who would go outside with the three prisoners, and it was an inconvenience for them. When the three returned inside, some of the other inmates asked where they'd been. De Burca told them, adding that everyone was entitled to a daily hour of outside exercise. The next day the rest of the women insisted on exercise, and the guards made them go out without their coats. It being November, they never asked to go out again. "At least they knew they were entitled and if you wanted to, you could," de Burca says. She, McMahon, and the third inmate who had gone out on the first day continued to insist on exercise every day, standing their ground. "We just wouldn't move unless we got our exercise. So we kind of stuck together in that kind of way, and if one wanted something we'd make sure she got it."

The other inmates had trouble understanding why de Burca and McMahon had risked jail for a political demonstration. Most of them were extremely poor and were serving time for petty theft, begging, drunk and disorderly conduct, and a range of other crimes based on desperate social conditions. They all thought de Burca, McMahon, and the one other female inmate serving time for political reasons were mad. "Try explaining that to some poor sod who is in there because she hasn't a ha'penny, who has never had any money, who is living in the flats, and who probably had parents who were alcoholics," de Burca says. "It got to the point where I would do a lot *not* to explain what I was in there for."

De Burca read Germaine Greer's *The Female Eunuch* while serving her time in Mountjoy. That text, along with Betty Friedan's *The Feminine Mystique,* were the two bibles that de Burca remembers from the women's liberation movement. A friend and fellow feminist had sent her Greer's book, the cover of which depicted a nude female torso made to look like a shirt on a clothes hanger. All the books had to pass through the prison matron's office, and the matron called de Burca in to talk to her about this one. She thought it was pornography, and she did her best to make de Burca feel ashamed and a "little bit grubby" about reading it before finally handing it over to her. "I always remembered that; I can actually see her looking at it in that sort of way — like she didn't even want to touch it," de Burca says.

It was de Burca's encounter with the Gardaí and the courts in August 1971 that put her into the history books. She was protesting outside the Dáil against the passage of the Forcible Entry and Occupation Bill, still waiting to hear about her sentencing for the Vietnam protest four months previously, when she was arrested again along with fellow IWLM founder and *Irish Independent* journalist Mary Anderson. Socialist and leftist groups deplored the bill because it would grant extra powers of arrest without warrant to the Gardaí, place the onus of proving innocence on the accused, legalise notions of guilt by association and, some journalists felt, threaten press freedom. The bill was specifically designed to give the Gardaí more leverage in dealing with and arresting squatters who were driven to their situations by a combination of poverty and the severe housing crisis in Dublin at the time. Sinn Féin was one of the groups that had been helping families with nowhere else to go move into empty properties.

The August night in 1971 that the bill was passed, many of the activists in the Dublin Housing Action Committee, as well as the women involved in the IWLM, were out in full force protesting at the Dáil. De Burca, Anderson and the rest of the crowd were waiting outside for the politicians so they could shout at them as they drove away in their cars. Today, de Burca looks back on their plan as a plain measure of their innocence in contrast to the terrible violence some protestors are willing to carry out now. Although the protest remained peaceful, de Burca and Anderson were arrested for being particularly vocal and aggressive, and the two opted to have a trial by jury instead of a summary trial, which would have involved only the solicitors and a judge. De Burca's solicitor thought this might be best for her since she had been through the courts so often, reasoning that if she was brought before a sympathetic jury it was possible she would be let off altogether. At some stage in the course of discussing their case, however, de Burca and Anderson realised that the only possible jury they were to appear before would be an all-male panel. A woman, as long as she was a property owner, could apply to serve on a jury, but women were not actively called to serve. Men who were not property owners were also excluded from jury service.

The *Irish Independent* had published a well-researched article titled "Why don't Irish women make good jurors?" just three months before de Burca's and Anderson's arrest, explaining the specifics of the existing Juries Act and the reasons women weren't called to serve under it. In April 1962 the Committee on Court Practice and Procedure had recommended that women should be liable for jury service, but three had dissented, saying the "domestic inconvenience" that jury duty would impose on most women was so serious a consideration as to render invalid the argument for changing the law. Employing a rationale which was difficult to comprehend even in the context of the Ireland of the sixties and seventies, the dissenters stated: "If a married woman returns to her home at seven o'clock in the evening and finds an irate husband and three hungry children waiting for her, we think it unlikely that they will accept the importance of jury service as a convincing excuse".[4] Not only did the existing law keep women out of the jury system, but it was also in deliberate breach of the United Nations' 1954 International Convention on the Political Rights of Women. Ireland had ratified the Convention in 1968, but stood firm on its belief that its failure to call women for obligatory jury service was not a discriminatory practice.

De Burca and Anderson decided to challenge the law with a court case of their own. Through the poet Eavan Boland, a mutual friend of de Burca and then-Senator Mary Robinson, Robinson volunteered her assistance as part of the legal team that took de Burca's and Anderson's case, knowing that they may or may not end up getting fees for their work. After being turned down by a High Court judge, and after Robinson and the rest of the legal team had been working on the case intermittently since 1971, the Supreme Court finally changed the law in December 1975 so that jury service would be open to anyone over the age of eighteen who was on the register of electors. In the ten years prior to the ruling, only nine Irish women had sat on juries at all. An *Irish Times* editorial the day after the ruling noted that women had been liable for jury service before independence and were only excluded by an Act of the Free State in 1927, marvelling that it had taken 44 years for someone to challenge the law. The editorial went on to state that the decision ". . . may well indicate to women that some of the more fundamental discriminations may well be more effectively pursued through the courts than by political lobbying".[5] It is somewhat ironic that the paper upheld an action brought to court by a woman like de Burca as an example of the effectiveness of the slow, arduous process of legislative reform in changing society. De Burca had been the strongest advocate of provoking change through radical strategies, outside the established system, during her years "on the barricades" and out in the streets. But with her successful challenge to the discriminatory Juries Act, she showed a willingness to change her preferred tactics of activism. After all her court appearances, she must have had some sense of pride at using the system against itself to benefit women.

De Burca remembers the day of the decision as a terrific day. Not many people were at the court, she says, because of the gap between when she and Anderson had first brought the case and when the decision was handed down. "I kept writing to them saying, I could be dead by the time this comes through. I still don't know why it took so long," de Burca says. The day after the decision, de Burca received a phone call at work at the Sinn Féin office from an irate woman who asked her how dare she make women sit on juries. It just drove the point home to de Burca that there were still many women in 1975, four years after the IWLM's disintegration, who were staunchly opposed to women's liberation. "You have that sort of woman, scared, scared of what she saw coming, which was that if they got all these equal rights they were going to have to think for themselves," de Burca says.

Another oppressed group with which de Burca sympathised was the freedom fighters in the black civil rights movement in America, which had peaked a few years earlier, in the mid-sixties. Her parents had been fiercely bigoted, and blacks were never referred to as anything other than "niggers" in her house. A childhood memory, when she first began to realise that there was a discrepancy between her own experience with blacks and the way her parents spoke about them, is imprinted on her mind. At the end of the street in de Burca's working-class white Chicago neighbourhood was a laundry staffed entirely by black people. One day as a very young de Burca was riding her tricycle, a black woman waiting at the bus stop called her over and pointed out a penny on the ground. She kindly told de Burca to pick it up and take it home, calling her "honey". De Burca may have been raised to be a bigot, but she was raised to be a polite bigot, and she asked the woman if she was sure she didn't want it for herself. De Burca remembers the woman insisting that she take the penny for herself.

"And I remember, in a childish sort of way, feeling rather than even making an idea of it, that this did not accord with my mother and father's way of speaking about black people," she says. Years later, back in Ireland, de Burca's father came home from the pub and told the family that a black man had come in for a drink and the barman had refused to serve him, asking him to leave. "And I remember saying to him without thinking, without even planning to say anything, 'If I had been there I'd have walked out with him,' totally astonishing both my father and myself because I didn't know where it had come from," she says. "But I think, it's really weird how something gets into you as a child and it sits there and festers."

Considering de Burca's political background and the extent of her involvement with so many left-wing organisations, the only thing that's surprising about her pivotal role in the IWLM was that she didn't start it sooner. The Dublin Gardaí knew de Burca very well because she was out on so many protests, but she saw a great link between the injustices that the many and varied groups she was involved in were fighting. The Gardaí would often cite de Burca and her colleagues as agitators, saying they were out on every march, no matter what the cause. But like the true revolutionary, de Burca felt it was impossible to fight for one oppressed group and not another. She saw all the movements as blending into each other, and it only seemed right to her to participate in every fight for equal rights.

"You couldn't discriminate. One of them led into the other and you felt that you couldn't demonstrate for Black America or Native America without demonstrating for women," she says. She describes how she saw the civil rights movement as sparking women's desire in America to begin their own equal rights movement. "I suppose what happened with women was that women were saying, blacks are entitled to equality, but then so are women. The same hit us in Ireland, only slightly later, because we got everything later. We had to read about it in the papers first and digest it and sort of say, 'Oh, yes! This happens here too, only worse!'"

Like fellow IWLM founder Máirín Johnston, de Burca had a strong sense of history and of what the radical Irish women who had gone before her had endured in the struggle for their own rights as well as in the larger national struggle in the War of Independence. "Women did everything during the War of Independence, they were there in the GPO and in the Rising for the whole three or four years of the War, and they took great risks. They risked their lives on a daily basis, and not one woman was appointed to the peace delegation. And that had never occurred to me; I just took it for granted that there were five or six men," she says.

In the best of all possible worlds, de Burca says, there would have been a big group concentrating solely on women, a group devoted to Vietnam, another for housing, and another for anti-Apartheid, but in Dublin in 1970, the people who were heavily involved in politics moved in tight circles. De Burca wasn't by far the only one involved in several different prominent political organisations, but she was one of the most visible and well-connected. And since her days as a shop assistant in the union fighting for better wages for women (never mind equal pay, she says, just better wages) she was acutely aware of all the work there was to be done to ensure Irish women's equal rights.

By the time the two American feminists walked through her door at Sinn Féin headquarters in Dublin in the summer of 1970, de Burca was more than ready to begin dismantling the structures of discrimination against women; she just didn't quite know it yet. She'd been reading scores of newspaper articles about the women's movement in America, and, like the Vietnam war protests and the civil rights movement, she felt that it was only a matter of time before the impetus for collective action drifted across the Atlantic and took hold in Ireland. The two Americans were, in a sense, the physical embodiment of the journey of those ideas. The time was ripe in Ireland for women to begin questioning the reasons for their oppression, and the other IWLM founders were more than ready in their own ways to join de Burca in the cause. Like her, though, they needed a push from someone or something to get them together.

De Burca thought about which women she knew who might be interested in contributing their ideas and talents to this new group. She rang her friend Mary Maher at the *Irish Times*, whom she knew from Maher's journalistic interest and participation in many of the issues and political groups in which Máirín, too, was so active. They also knew each other from their mutual affinity for Gaj's restaurant. This phone call between friends, the first of many, was the beginning of one of the most startling social movements Ireland had ever seen.

A Journalist Crosses the Pond

"The great part about being young is that you can tackle anything if you think, 'oh yes, this needs to be done'. . . .Once the women's movement started it was like wildfire because we were onto something that needed to be done, and then." — Mary Maher

Mary Maher, who was to become the first editor of the *Irish Times* women's page, walked into the *Chicago Tribune* newsroom in 1962 at the age of 21 and decided on the spot that she wanted to be a journalist. Her decision had nothing to do with journalism. Maher, fresh from sixteen years of all-girls' classes at her Chicago Catholic high school and college, was looking over the society editor's shoulder at a sea of men and boys of every shape and size. When the editor asked her if she was accurate with facts and if she wanted to be a journalist Maher answered with an enthusiastic yes, adding that she'd always wanted to be a journalist.

Maher, born and raised in Chicago, lived away from her family home for a short period of time following her college graduation and worked at the *Tribune* for a few years. As she moved through her early twenties, the feeling that she had to leave Chicago in order to grow up grew stronger. She had also broken off her engagement to a fellow Chicago journalist just a few days before her wedding. At the time, she didn't quite know how to explain her feelings, but she felt certain that she saw her life ending with marriage, and she knew she could not go through with the wedding. Aside from not loving her fiancé, she had a gut feeling

that getting married was the wrong decision for her. The whole experience was jolting. She identified with feminist Betty Friedan who wrote
in her breakthrough book *The Feminine Mystique* about the difficulty of
articulating feelings. Maher had belonged to a book club for graduates
from her Catholic Chicago college, where they had read *The Feminine
Mystique* when it was published in the US in 1963. She remembers being
the only one who said she thought Friedan was right about the "problem
with no name", which was how Friedan referred to the restlessness, dissatisfaction and frustration with housework and child-minding felt by
housewives who otherwise appeared to have perfectly content and comfortable lives. Friedan was the first to attempt to pinpoint the reasons that
many American housewives felt deeply unhappy and desperately
trapped, and further, why there was so much difficulty in articulating
those feelings. The rest of the women in the book club thought the book
was nonsense and had no bearing whatsoever on their own lives. Maher
more than sympathised with Friedan's ideas; she *felt* them very strongly,
experiencing them herself in her own reservations about her marriage.

She applied to a few newspapers in Boston and, through someone she
knew at the Irish Counsel in Chicago, *The Irish Times*. She was given an
interview with *The Irish Times* and travelled to Dublin for it, bringing
along a smattering of cuttings from the three years she had spent writing
for the *Chicago Tribune*. She happened to walk into the Dublin newsroom in 1965 the week management had decided they needed more
young women on the paper. Maher was hired on three months' probation,
though no one ever told her in her more than three decades at the paper
whether she had passed whatever test it was she was given.

If she had a rough plan at all, Maher thought she'd stay in Dublin a
while and get some different experience, and come back with something
more interesting to offer in whatever job she got in America. But by the
time she'd been in Dublin and at the *Times* three months, she knew she'd
never return to live in the US. She loved the work and was having far too
good a time. She found that she was treated more equally to the men at
the *Times* than she had been at the *Tribune*. At the *Tribune*, which employed very few women as journalists, Maher had worked solely for the
society desk. The desk's staff was made up of five women at the time, a
Presbyterian, a Methodist, an Episcopalian, a Catholic and a Jew, organ-

ised to cover Chicago's full ladies' social calendar. At the *Times*, though, under the hugely respected and legendary Donal Foley, who became news editor in 1965, Maher got to do things she feels she never would have been given the opportunity to do on any American newspaper at the time. She covered the North, politics, health and the arts, the same topics to which the male journalists were also assigned and all areas in which she was interested.

Maher settled into Dublin life, eventually marrying trade union activist Des Geraghty. As she found her niche at the newspaper, she also rapidly became immersed in left-wing causes, including the Irish Voice on Vietnam. She had written a letter in the paper about how many Americans also felt that America should not have got involved in the conflict, and was immediately recruited by the group. Foley himself was a socialist, and like Maher he was interested in seeing the paper cover the activities of the energetic leftist activist groups. Maher described her first meeting with Foley to her former colleague Elgy Gillespie for Gillespie's collection of *Irish Times* women journalists' pieces:

> Donal Foley looked at me glumly and asked my opinion of John F. Kennedy. With all the pompous assurance of youth, I replied that despite his good points Kennedy had failed to initiate the social change urgently needed in the USA. Had I been less gauche I would have waffled nicely on that one, because the assassinated president was still greatly mourned in Ireland. But since Donal Foley held much the same view, I was rapidly vaulted to the second stage of the interview.[1]

What Maher identified as the "pompous assurance of youth", others, including Foley, might have viewed as a brassy willingness to express her opinions regardless of consequence or fear of unpopularity – a very desirable quality in the kinds of journalists Foley liked, and one that Maher shared with many of her fellow IWLM founders. In 1967, after Maher had been with *The Irish Times* for two years, Foley asked her if she'd be interested in starting a women's page, an idea that Maher was completely against at first. Her vision of women's pages was something akin to what she'd worked on at the *Tribune*: social calendars, wedding announcements and knitting patterns. But Foley eventually won her over to the idea with the promise that she could have exactly the kind of page that she wanted by starting to change people's perceptions of what constituted "women's stories".

With her half page per day, Maher and her staff did things that no other page was doing or could have done at the time. Considering the issues they covered, the page became as much a health page, a sociology page, and a psychology page as it was a "women's page". "We did cover a lot of social issues and we began covering the feminist issues and this was very important because the *Irish Press* came six months later and then the *Irish Independent* followed suit, so you had three women's pages all run by young women, instead of a forty-five-year-old woman in a hat," Maher says. It was, of course, Mary Kenny (who did happen to like hats herself – just not the same kinds that forty-five-year-old women liked) who took the reins at the *Press*, and the late Mary McCutchan who ran the *Independent's* page. All three women were in their twenties, and all three were future members of the IWLM.

Maher sees Foley's cajoling her into the women's page editorial position as one of the most significant driving forces for the beginning of the radical Irish women's movement and the revolution in the way newspapers covered women and women's issues. Often the material in the women's pages would be controversial enough to make readers open to that page first. Men, although loathe to admit it, were reading the women's pages just as voraciously as women were because it was often the most interesting section of the paper. "It was very funny; you'd get men who would say, 'I was locked in the toilet for four hours with nothing else to read so I had to read your page', and they were all reading it, of course," Maher says.

Maher's focus on such controversial issues during her years editing the women's page incited many women – and men – to write in denouncing the journalists' immorality, a phenomenon that Kenny and McCutchan also experienced at their respective papers. Articles on single mothers (in those days referred to only as "unmarried" mothers), deserted wives, equal pay and especially contraception were enough to make the letters of protest pour in to Maher's desk.

Maher's work on the women's page foreshadowed her later involvement with the IWLM. As early as September 1968, articles about equal pay, Dublin's housing crisis, civil rights activists in the North, and contraception appeared under either her byline or her editorial eye. She reviewed books with titles like *The Sexual Wilderness* (by American doctor Vance Packard) and printed short pieces on fashion urging women to take risks like wearing trousers at places other than the beach and garden. She interviewed women who were successful and confident in careers at a time when most Irish women were still expected to work only at low-level, low-paying jobs, and then only until they got married. At the same time, Kenny and McCutchan at the *Press* and the *Independent* were similarly starting to write articles on subjects that no one had ever read about before.

The silence blanketing such issues as sexuality, contraception, broken marriages and domestic violence was so complete that Irish women literally did not know how to begin the conversations that were essential to addressing the sources of their discrimination. They lacked the necessary tools of the language that would help them put words to their oppression. Some IWLM founders even argue that women, themselves included, were unaware of the reality of their own oppression because of the simple fact that it was never discussed or addressed. In this sense, the women's pages were crucial in striking the initial spark of the women's liberation movement because they were taking the very first steps in presenting the articulation of these previously *verboten* subjects to the public.

Anything having to do with sexuality was risky, Maher remembers, but one article in particular which she worked on in 1970 was completely uncharted, untouchable territory. Maher, who had recently handed the editorship of the women's page over to Maeve Binchy, had received a letter from a homosexual woman asking if a women's page reporter would be interested in meeting her and telling her story. The subject of lesbianism was so taboo and poorly understood at the time, Maher says, that the assumption, even among most *Irish Times* reporters, was that if you knew a lesbian you must be one yourself – guilt by association. Maher was already married and didn't want people to feel sorry for her husband, thinking the poor man had not known he was marrying a lesbian! Maeve Binchy was not yet married and wasn't keen on the idea of ruining her dating options. So although the two reporters had interviewed the woman and had written the two-part story together, the article appeared in the paper under the byline "Irish Times Reporter". In those days, it was not uncommon for articles on which several staff members had collaborated to be presented that way, but Maher does recall the anxiety that she and Binchy both felt in reporting the story. The joke in the newsroom as the two set off to do the interview had been that if they hadn't returned within a reasonable amount of time, the paper should send guns, money and lawyers. The article itself was a sympathetic portrait of a woman who had been taught from very early in her life that she was intrinsically abnormal and flawed:

> But what about the female homosexual? Much less is known about her, and there is some reason to believe she is subject to even more suspicion and hostility than her male equivalent. Ironically, the reason why lesbianism is not illegal in England (or, in fact, in Ireland) is given as the reluctance of civil servants to inform Queen Victoria of the existence of such a horrible vice when the first anti-homosexual laws were drafted in the 19th century . . . in the 1970s in Ireland there are lesbians living in isolation, loneliness and extreme fear of being discovered . . .[2]

Of course, years later, Ireland was to discover, along with the rest of the world, that homosexuality among both males and females was much more common than anyone in the sixties and seventies could have imagined. Nell McCafferty, journalist and fellow IWLM founder member, had joined the *Irish Times* six months before Maher and Binchy wrote their article on the female homosexual. In her 2004 memoir, at age sixty, McCafferty wrote for the first time about her own experiences as a lesbian woman. But she remembers hoping that if the 1970 article was causing as much of a stir in the newsroom as it was, none of her colleagues must have suspected that she was gay. At the time she was grateful for that, but she was also thinking, how could they *not* know? She couldn't wait to read the article, but when she did, she wasn't impressed. "I remember thinking, she sounds really boring. They haven't met a proper lesbian woman," McCafferty says.

Maeve Binchy, later to achieve great success as a novelist, was an enthusiastic supporter of the women's movement without joining the IWLM or any other political protest group herself. She felt that to join a radical group like the IWLM that was in the business of breaking the law would shame and embarrass her father, a barrister, although she would have loved to participate in some of the IWLM's protests. "I'm not proud or ashamed of it, but that's just the truth of how it was. Things were different then," Binchy says.

Although she was not out on the barricades herself, Binchy always tried to write what she believed in, and many of her articles from the time period are just as forceful as those written by the journalist IWLM founder members. Binchy could not entirely escape from the fear of what other people were thinking about her behaviour and support of women's liberation, but she tried to empower women with some of the confidence that she had gained from both her own mother and her work as a journalist. "I think why so many journalists ended up being strong feminists is because there is always this open door; if you wanted to meet someone, you could meet them, and that gave you great confidence," she says. Binchy was also delighted by the women in the Irish Women's Liberation Movement, most of them newspaper colleagues and friends of hers. "I think they were very important, and courageous. Ireland could have stayed a small backwater country where women continued to be restricted in so many ways, but it didn't because of them and their work in the media," she says. "They were very successful in getting attention and changing people's opinions."

As the women's page writers were introducing new topics to society, creating a new language for women by arming them with the courage to begin talking about formerly unspeakable issues, they were also changing the existing language in the newspapers that was degrading to women. Binchy remembers an obituary about an unmarried woman who had died at home of natural causes, whom a journalist referred to in the obituary as a "spinster". First of all, there was no comparable word for a man who had never been married that carried with it the same kind of negative connotation. Second, Binchy says, you got the feeling from the article that somehow the woman would have been all right had she been married. Binchy and the other women's page writers would bring such offences to the attention of the editors, and gradually, *slowly*, the language began to change and such words have been all but phased out of the public vocabulary. It would be a shock to see "spinster" used in a newspaper to describe an unmarried woman today.

There was a great deal of fun for the women's page journalists in the fact that they could behave just as badly, or as "unladylike" as they wished. It was expected that they would go to the same pubs as their male colleagues, most often either the Pearl Bar or Bowes, and talk and drink with journalists from the other papers, even though the barmen would never serve women full pints, only half pints. Being in the news-paper business, especially if you were a woman, was a bit risqué at the time. If you didn't know that beforehand, you got the idea pretty quickly when you found yourself being interviewed in the pub, as was Donal Foley's preference.

By late 1970 when the IWLM was forming, the women who staffed all three newspapers' women's pages knew each other particularly well. There was a friendly rivalry, and an equally good deal of co-operation and concerted effort among them. If there was any event like a cooking demonstration by the Irish Fisheries Board, they were certain to run into each other because they were all fairly badly paid and they went to any-thing that had food! "You'd go at six o'clock and you'd eat absolutely everything in sight and you'd pick what you go to depending on the grub," Maher says.

There was a lot of overlap on the issues that the papers covered on their women's pages and, significantly, very similar articles sometimes appeared in all three papers at crucial points in the IWLM's chronology of activities, a sure sign that the editors were working very closely with each other. During the late summer and autumn of 1970, right around the time the IWLM members were beginning their first meetings at Gaj's, all three newspapers printed articles about women's liberation and what it might mean to Irish women. Mary Kenny was relentless in the *Press* dur-ing August 1970, running articles either directly or indirectly related to women's liberation nearly every week. An article published on 24 Au-gust titled "What is Women's Lib About?" was scornful in its accusation that a women's liberation movement would never materialise in Ireland because radical Irish women were too involved with other revolutionary causes to devote the necessary attention to a women's movement.[3] Ex-actly a week later, Kenny published another article, "Just One More

Time", vowing that she just meant to clarify some of the misconceptions about women's liberation and would then leave the topic alone for a while (a promise which was predictably false). "Some will think Women's Lib is absurd in its seeming extremism; how can throwing off the bras and discarding cosmetics add to the sum of human wisdom in any way? Yet they will be just a tiny bit bolstered by it too. They will think just a bit more of themselves for it. They will think, heck, I am a woman and I like being a woman, but I'm a person, too," Kenny wrote.[4]

It was in the summer of 1970 that Máirín de Burca received her visit from the Americans in the Sinn Féin office. The five original IWLM members held their first meeting in Bewley's shortly afterwards, and after that, things moved quickly. The other journalists from the women's pages were instantly recruited, as well as young women involved in left-wing politics from Margaret Gaj's clientele, until about a dozen women were set to meet in Mary Maher's house in north Dublin. They held another meeting soon after in Mary Kenny's flat, when they decided the upstairs room in Mrs Gaj's restaurant was the best meeting place from then on. One rule they had agreed upon for the meetings said that no one was to bring or serve food at all, in an effort to begin the break with the traditional stereotypes of women's roles at gatherings. At Gaj's they could get a dinner if they hadn't had time to eat before rushing from work to the meeting. Most of the original members would have eaten in Gaj's several times a week anyway, and this arrangement would be very convenient.

October of 1970 was a watershed for both the women's pages of the three newspapers and the IWLM's development. The first week of October saw the *Irish Times* devoting the entire week to women's liberation – how the movement had taken off in America, some of the misconceptions about the movement's aims, the particular problems and complexities that Irish women faced if such a movement were ever to develop in Ireland, and, finally, the opinion columns of four "Women First" writers – Mary Maher, Nell McCafferty, Maeve Binchy, and Mary Cummins – on what women's liberation meant to them. Today, Maher classifies her piece as "positively finger-wagging", but it exhibits the conviction of her writing and the resonance it held:

The critics still squirm. Fair enough, right the wrongs, they say;
but why resort to this flamboyant, faintly embarrassing word,
"liberation"? The answer is that until we free ourselves from
thinking in sexual stereotypes no piecemeal reform will be
enough. The people who stand most to gain by women's liberation are, or course, men – men who have been burdened with
such dreadful stereotypes for so long. There are countless boys
afraid to study poetry or music because it isn't manly; numerous
fathers who feel lonely in their own homes because they have left
the child-rearing to their wives; plenty of sad old men and young
men who can't look after themselves because they learned to
think of cooking, sewing, washing as women's work. If we can
liberate ourselves from vague, unfounded ideas of what "femininity" and "masculinity" are, we might, both sexes, learn to be a
great deal more human.[5]

The *Independent* likewise ran a slew of stories that October to do with
women's liberation, and, like the other two newspapers, it called women
to action and emphasised that it was they themselves who had to work
for the changes they wanted. Janet Martin, who like Maeve Binchy wrote
strong pieces about women's rights while choosing not to join the
IWLM, was particularly forceful on the *Independent*'s women's page:

Nobody has the right any longer to sit back and say, "I'm all
right, Jack", or, "What do you want to go kicking up all that fuss
for?" There are a lot of people in Ireland who have got something
to fight about and the tragedy is, very few will. Some people honestly do not know where to begin and the rest just don't bother.[6]

One of the reasons that the staffs of the competing newspapers seemed to
be so comfortable sharing ideas and socialising so closely at times was
that there simply wasn't that much competition among them. Today, this
sounds ludicrous, but there seemed to be an unwavering faithfulness on
the part of readers to their particular preferred newspaper. Each of the
newspapers had a very clear demographic to which it appealed, and an
Irish Times reader was very unlikely to stray to the *Irish Press*, an *Irish
Press* subscriber wouldn't suddenly switch to the *Irish Independent*, and
so on. Of course, the journalists admit that they enjoyed getting a story

first and thereby scooping the competition, but much of the fun in that must be diminished if it's not going to entice more people to read their paper. Founder IWLM member Mary Sheerin, who was then a publicist for the Gaiety Theatre and a freelance journalist, thinks that the kind of co-operation between competing newspapers, television and radio programmes that existed in the seventies simply wouldn't be possible today because of the growth of the Irish media. "Nowadays there's a host of radio stations all over Ireland, all over Dublin and all over the rest of Ireland. And of course there are more newspapers and there's great competition and there's great tensions and all of that. That didn't exist then," Sheerin says. So the women's pages in those days really were able to become important forums during the women's liberation movement – in a sense, they were the culmination of the journalists' meetings, deliberations, and arguments.

Like any wise editors, Donal Foley and his counterparts at the *Press* and the *Independent* knew that women's liberation would sell papers, and having energetic young women editing the women's pages was a great asset. Whether or not the majority of the public agreed with the IWLM, people were undeniably fascinated with the women and their activities. Foley wrote in his 1977 autobiography *Three Villages* about the importance of women in the newsroom in the sixties and seventies as he saw it:

> The importance of women in Irish journalism, long before the Women's Liberation Movement began in Ireland, was recognised in *The Irish Times*. The Women's Page "Women First" became a forum for discussion of social, political and philosophical questions. Women reporters were appointed on an equality basis with men and at one period their numbers were exactly half and half. The paper carried reports from every part of Ireland and as a result was able to lose its image as a purely Dublin paper . . . No cows were sacred and reporters and writers were given their heads to express the more unorthodox views.[7]

Although Mary Maher did her fair share of reporting straight news stories without editorialising during her thirty-five years at *The Irish Times*, she never would have gone into journalism if she could not have practised the kind of advocacy journalism that she was allowed to practise on the women's page. If she had been born ten years later, when it wasn't as widely accepted that girls could be overeducated and thus harder to marry off, Maher says she would have liked to have gone to law school to become a civil rights lawyer. In any case, she makes a very clear distinction between the news pages and the features pages, the latter being the category the women's page would fall into if it had to be categorised. On the news pages, there was the usual standard for any journalist – objectivity. Or, for those journalists who believed objectivity wasn't really possible, fairness and balance. Features, however, were different kinds of stories, and when writing features journalists had more freedom to express strong opinions. "On the feature pages, with a byline, you were allowed to hold forth. Advocacy journalism," Maher says. "And we held forth."

Following the June 2004 death of her hugely respected *Irish Times* colleague Mary Holland, Maher edited a collection of Holland's articles and wrote a foreword in which she expressed some of her views on journalism. "Learning history from journalism," she wrote, "is . . . like learning history as it happens. This is the best of what journalism can do, record the moment so vividly and perceptively – and often with such comic wit – that to read it is to re-live the moment." Maher went on to say that a journalist of Holland's ability "places a handprint on history itself".[8] Reading the women's pages that Maher wrote and edited, and the articles by the other women's page journalists in the late sixties and early seventies, is to get as close to re-living those moments as possible. There is an immediacy, an urgency in their voices that comes through their writing on those pages that more than three decades has done little to dull. Their articles provide a chronological primer of the early days of the women's liberation movement as useful for a historian as any map is for an explorer.

Maher is one of the original IWLM founders to say, laughingly, that if they had all known about the enormous amount of attention the IWLM was to receive – that the group would capture the imaginations of so many Irish women – they never would have begun meeting in the first place. The prospect would have been too intimidating, even for women as strong and energetic as they all were. It is obvious, though, that she and the other founders were pleased, in the end, with how the group they started incited women to action, even if its messages were sometimes misunderstood, its image distorted and its disintegration haphazard.

When Maher talks about the IWLM today and her own role in it, she is somewhat bemused. It is always difficult to look at yourself as you were thirty years ago and be able to objectively judge your actions and their effects. Looking back and realising that the group existed for less than a year, and considering that most of the IWLM founders were working full-time jobs and raising families at the same time as they were attending weekly meetings, planning protests, making media appearances, putting together their charter to be published, and, in a few cases, even getting arrested, it does seem extraordinary that the group accomplished everything it did. But that was largely because every member contributed some different skill. If Margaret Gaj was an excellent organiser and Máirín de Burca knew how to plan protests and demonstrations better than anyone, Maher's skills as a bridger of divides within the group was equally important to its functioning, perhaps even more so considering the diverse backgrounds of the IWLM founders. It was often Maher who would try to make sure everyone got a chance to speak and that everyone was heard. Although her own politics and beliefs fell very much in line with those of Máirín de Burca's and the other women with strong ties to the left, she tried to include the viewpoints of the women with whom she disagreed as well. In the end, the overriding conclusion to which most of the founders have come when reflecting on their roles in the IWLM is as Maher has articulated it: "I'm sure glad I was there."

When Maher received Máirín de Burca's call about the Bewley's meeting in the late summer of 1970, she thought about who else might want to be included in discussions about beginning the long overdue fight for women's rights. The first person who came to mind was Máirín Johnston, a warm woman with strong links to the trade unions and the fight for workers' rights. Johnston, iron-willed and articulate, grew up in Dublin's Liberties. She could also sing the songs of the Irish revolutionaries of old like she meant them. Maher was sure that Máirín Johnston would be thrilled that Ireland could be expecting some big changes very soon, and that she could play a part in the beginning of them.

4

Daughter of the Liberties

"You had to shock. You had to shock in order to make things better." — Máirín Johnston

An oft-overlooked but basic fact about the beginnings of social movements is that they all start with people whose belief in the necessity of major societal changes outweighs whatever discomfort they may feel about seriously challenging the status quo. Sometimes there are only very few people who take the initial steps that eventually incite others to action. Sometimes those initial steps start with something as simple as a few phone calls, and a conversation among friends in a small city coffee shop. This was the case with the IWLM.

Máirín Johnston was the third person in the phone chain that Máirín de Burca had started when she rang Mary Maher, and Johnston thought the idea of getting together to discuss Irish women's rights was fabulous. It was about time. Maher had met Johnston through a mutual friend who was a Labour Party politician, and had already run into her at Gaj's and many of the pubs which served as unofficial meeting spots for left-wing activists in those days.

If anyone had experienced first-hand in her childhood how difficult life could be for an Irish widow with children, it was Máirín Johnston. Born Máirín Moorhouse in the Liberties in 1931, she came from a family of very strong trade unionists. Her mother had been involved in the 1913 strike at the Jacob's Biscuit factory, when the workers had been told that they would be sacked if they remained members of the union. Johnston's mother refused to quit the union and wasn't taken back, at large financial sacrifice to her family.

When Johnston's mother met her father, he was separated from his wife, with whom he had children. He moved in with Johnston's mother, even though this was unheard of at the time. At a very early age, Máirín Johnston was aware that her mother was different in her attitude to authority, in particular the church's authority, than the majority of Irish women, in that she wasn't intimidated or cowed into living her life according to the church's rules. Johnston and her four siblings were all born out of wedlock. "You're not supposed to say 'illegitimate' now, but that's what we were," she says. The result of her family's circumstances was the church not allowing Johnston's mother through its doors. Nonetheless, Johnston recalls that her mother was never anti-religious. "She was anti-church, though, kind of the organisation," she says. Although she never stopped Johnston and her brothers from doing their religious duties while in school, she never encouraged them in that direction either.

Johnston's father, Jack Moorhouse, died when she was very young, leaving her mother with five children to raise on her own. Her younger brother was killed in an accident shortly after her father's death, and her mother fell into a deep depression that never entirely ebbed. If it weren't for Johnston's granny – her mother's mother – she says her family could not have survived. There was no widow's pension when her father died, and Johnston's granny went out to work so the family could eat while her mother looked after the children. Such arrangements were not uncommon in working-class Dublin, and there was a strong matriarchal tradition in Johnston's own family. When she traced her family's history back as far as the famine, she realised that it was mostly the women who were responsible for raising the children and making all the decisions because so many of the men had died quite young.

Johnston's brothers went to England to work during the Second World War. Johnston had been attending school at St Brigid's in the Coombe but, like Máirín de Burca, she left when she was fourteen and went to work in various shirt and glove factories. The first job she took was a non-union job and Johnston remembers her mother telling her that if there wasn't a union where she was working it was up to her to start one. Johnston's mother was always putting the worker's point of view first. Eventually, against her mother's wishes but because the wages were better than other factory jobs at the time, Johnston started working at the same Jacob's biscuit factory from which her mother had been sacked years earlier for refusing to give up her membership in the trade union.

Apart from the sense of social justice and workers' rights that Johnston's mother instilled in her, as well as a healthy questioning of authority, there were many serious debates in the house about politics and the family was always encouraged to read and develop different interests. Her mother was a great reader, and although Johnston and her family members lacked a formal education, she feels that it didn't matter as much because they were all gaining knowledge through books and family discussion.

Although Johnston left school early, she became involved with left-wing political groups at a very young age. She joined the Democratic Youth Movement when she was fifteen or sixteen and started participating in demonstrations on many issues, including the Dublin housing crisis, a cause she shared with Máirín de Burca. Through these movements Johnston met many different kinds of people from whom she was constantly learning more about politics, history, the media and the finer points of organising effective demonstrations. She met one young Trinity physics student with whom she got along particularly well despite their very different socio-economic backgrounds. Roy Johnston came from an intellectual middle-class family, and she remembers that his parents were horrified at the match. Johnston could understand that, because her own mother's reaction was the same. "She kind of said this won't work out, he wouldn't be interested in someone like you," Johnston says. With her involvement in so many leftist causes and the strength of her self-education, though, Johnston had already proven herself to be more engaged in and aware of the world around her than the average factory worker. She and Roy Johnston were married and they moved to France on their wedding day.

Although Máirín and Roy Johnston eventually separated, she looks back on her two years in France in the mid-fifties as an incredible learning experience. Her husband introduced her to new literature, people and ideas. Through these experiences, he instilled a confidence in her that she had lacked. Johnston discovered for herself the truth of the old adage that people only fear what they don't understand, and although her mother had been a great reader and had encouraged Johnston and her siblings to read as much as possible, it was a narrow selection of Irish authors. In France, Johnston discovered a diversity of literature from around the world. She had access to a whole new intellectual world that she would never have had in Ireland. In addition, she worked as an assistant in her husband's laboratory and learned how to use the microscopes to study atoms, and upon their return to Dublin she worked for another two years at the Institute for Advanced Studies, then in Merrion Square, training women in the same laboratory skills.

Now seventy-five, Johnston has her thick hair pushed back from her face with a headband, and with rosy cheeks and quick eyes, she looks at least ten years younger than her age. "I never really tell this to anyone, because it seems too outlandish," she says with slight embarrassment. "I have no education and yet to be working in the Institute for Advanced Studies, you know? Now this was a huge difference from working in the factory."

Johnston's job at the Institute was technically that of a Civil Servant because it was funded by the government, and as such she normally would not have been able to work due to the marriage bar that forced women to retire upon marriage and prohibited the hiring of already married women. But since the kind of skills she was training women in were just coming into Ireland and she had learned them in France, she was something of a rarity, so she was allowed to stay at the Institute until she had her first child. While recognising the injustice inherent in that system, she welcomed the opportunity to stay home with her baby.

After leaving work and having her first child, Johnston attributes her ability to stay quite active in her political groups to her mother, who was very good about looking after the baby and encouraged her daughter's participation in political groups. Johnston found her membership in the Communist Party especially exciting because its members attended so many protests and were very politically active. Childcare was also an issue about which Johnston cared deeply; she realised how lucky she was to have a mother to look after her children and how many women were so much more restricted because they lacked proper childcare resources. She started an organisation for childcare workers and took a few jobs herself looking after children, realising that what prevented many women from taking a more active role in political organisations (specifically women in the trade union movement who were just beginning to fight for equal pay and better working conditions) was the fact that they didn't have anyone to look after their children while they attended meetings.

Johnston did not just look after the children of the trade unionists; when the Women's Political Association (WPA), a group of mostly middle-class women who trained in public speaking and canvassed for women election candidates, formed in IWLM's aftermath, she took what was essentially a travelling crèche to their conferences. She saw her contribution to the childcare problem as a partial solution to one of women's most basic obstacles in becoming more politically involved. Before her experiences in the IWLM, Johnston was less sympathetic to the plight of middle-class women like the majority of those involved in the WPA. But working so closely with women from such diverse backgrounds in the IWLM – in terms of class, political affiliations and age, among other things – taught her that discrimination against women knew no boundaries.

"I really had a narrow vision of discrimination and exploitation before that," Johnston says. "I saw it as a class thing because I had this class attitude to everything and I realised listening to other people who were middle class, and some of them very upper class, that there was more to it than that. Being a woman was very, very difficult no matter what level of society you happened to be at. And I have to say that with all that went on even at that first meeting, my eyes were opened and I thought I knew it all, but I didn't," Johnston says.

Johnston had always felt that working-class women had been kept down and discriminated against to a greater degree than middle- and upper-class women because they had always been deprived of education and employment opportunities. She saw herself as an anomaly – she was extremely lucky to have been brought up by a mother who valued reading and political debate so highly, and to have been presented with the opportunity to further educate herself through her marriage. Almost all of the other girls whom Johnston had grown up with and worked with in the factories had no such opportunities; they were stuck in their jobs for life, making barely enough to survive.

In a sense, Johnston had been able to transcend her place in the class system through her education, even if it was not a formal education and she had not received a university degree. Like Máirín de Burca and several of the other IWLM founder members whose families had not had much money while they were growing up, though, Máirín Johnston realised that education was the only way she could break free from the barriers to which the "working-class" label confined her. It was perhaps this realisation that inspired, at least in part, the IWLM founders to place such importance on the education of other women concerning the particulars of the discrimination through their work in the media. They knew, collectively, how well knowledge had served them as individuals in the past, and they knew it was the key to opening women's minds to new possibilities. As a result, it is difficult to assign any class distinction or label to several of the IWLM founders – not just Johnston, but also Máirín de Burca and Marie McMahon – whose early economic backgrounds and lack of any formal education at the time would otherwise have distinguished them clearly as "working-class".

Despite Johnston's experiences and how well-read she was, she felt inferior because, unlike some of the women, she lacked a formal university degree. There were times when she felt inadequate even though she had been friends with several of the founders before the group began meeting. There were also people in the IWLM, Johnston says, with whom she didn't have much in common, apart from being the same sex and having the same feeling that something had to change in the way women were being treated. But she can pinpoint the exact moment during an early IWLM meeting, possibly the very first one that took place in Bewley's, when her own opinion about the relationship between class and discrimination began to change. The women were sharing examples, personal stories, of how they had been mistreated on the basis of gender. Dr Moira Woods told a story about how she had tried to get a charge card at one of the largest shops in the city and was told she needed her husband's signature. Dr Woods had thought that because she already had her own bank account, a rare feat in itself in the early seventies even for a professional woman, she would not have had any problem getting the card. Johnston was astounded. She had never thought that a woman like Woods – wealthy, highly educated – would have been subject to the same restrictions that the rest of the women lived under. Without even fully realising it herself, Johnston had always assumed that there were special privileges or exceptions in the system for women like Woods to which she and other

working-class women had never been privy. "It just illustrates that no matter where you were in society, being a woman meant you were going to be
discriminated against," Johnston says.

While Johnston didn't feel that class differences should be ignored
completely in the women's liberation movement, she did understand the
need for women to work together regardless of their backgrounds to find a
way of tackling the pervasive problems of women's inequality. A common
criticism of the women's liberation movement, both in Ireland and in the
rest of the western world, is that it was conceived and carried out more or
less exclusively by middle- and upper-class women, leaving the concerns
and cares of the lower classes behind. In the IWLM's case, at least, this is
an unfair, untrue assertion. Yes, the majority of the original founder members were either professional women, or degree holders, or both. Many
were deeply involved in other political movements. In one sense or another, they were all well educated. It was due more to their own ambitions
and particular skills than to their economic status that it was possible for
them to successfully co-ordinate the IWLM's activities and catch the public's attention as no group of women in recent times had.

Many of the IWLM founders attached the same importance that
Johnston had to the women's sharing of their personal experiences and
stories at those Monday night meetings. The simple process of the small
group of women talking about their lives was called "consciousness-
raising", a tactic that some of the IWLM founders had heard that American and British women's liberation groups had used to much success.
Some feminist scholars believe the tactic originated with American
women who had been involved in the civil rights movement in the sixties
and, frustrated with the men who were the leaders of the movement as-
signing them only mundane secretarial tasks, began concentrating their
energies on women's liberation. Consciousness-raising as it pertained to
women's liberation has been described simply as self-education through
group discussion, and it was based on the idea that women had to free
themselves individually in their own minds before they could begin the
heavier, practical, and concrete work for bigger societal changes. Mary
Maher is convinced that consciousness-raising was crucial to the group's
success because the same gathering of women at the IWLM meetings
would never have come together under any circumstances other than the

fight for women's liberation. For the many similarities between them, there were also strong differences that surfaced in different situations. Class was just one of them, and not the most divisive. Politics was another. The lengths to which each was personally willing to go to provoke change was another, and these ranged from Máirín de Burca's lengthy arrest record to other members' reticence to break the law at all.

Consciousness-raising created a bond of sympathy between these women with different educational backgrounds and political affiliations. They had tapped into each other's personal stories, and it was a wonderful feeling for each woman to discover that all these other women, regardless of how much money they had or how well educated they were, had experienced the same difficulties as themselves. More than one of the women describe a euphoric feeling that grew from this discovery of common experiences that they never would have known were common if it weren't for these conversations. It is not unusual for women to compare the feelings that their new understanding of the world created as similar to those of starting a new relationship or falling in the love; the change that takes place in the psyche is often that complete and profound. Essentially, consciousness-raising allows women to see their difficulties for the first time not as a result of personal failure, but rather as a result of the injustices inherent in political and societal systems of discrimination. It was through consciousness-raising that the now-familiar slogan "the personal is political" took on new meaning for most women.

More important, once women discovered that they weren't alone and that they were all experiencing the same injustices and struggles because of this discrimination, it was simply not possible to sit idly by and watch it continue without doing something to right the wrongs. And at the same time that the consciousness-raising sessions were opening each woman's eyes individually to the fact that she wasn't alone, the sessions were succeeding in instilling in each a sense of the necessity of a *concerted* effort to bring about practical improvements in women's conditions in society.

Because of their work in the newspapers the journalists in the founder group – Mary Maher, Mary Kenny, Mary McCutchan, Mary Anderson, Nuala Fennell, Rosita Sweetman, and Nell McCafferty – all seemed to have grasped the power that personal testimony had in inciting women to action, even before the first IWLM meetings. They knew better than anyone the comfort it gave women to hear individual stories from others who were going through the same difficulties. Whether it was a deserted wife struggling to raise her children on next-to-nothing, a woman with twelve children she couldn't support and another on the way because of the ban on contraception, or an unmarried mother shamed into giving her baby up for adoption, the journalists had received enough grateful letters from women for publishing such stories and showing them for certain that *they were not alone.* If someone else had the same problems as they had, somehow they didn't seem so scary, so insurmountable. This was yet another function that the women's pages in those days served – they were an extension of the consciousness-raising sessions that the journalists ran in Gaj's on Monday nights for all the Irish women countrywide who couldn't fit into the room above the restaurant.

If those who read the women's pages took heart from hearing others' stories, the IWLM founders also gave strength and confidence to each other. Marie McMahon was one of the youngest of the founder members, a typesetter who, like de Burca and Johnston, had left school at fourteen. She found the consciousness-raising sessions spectacular but was shy about discussing some of the topics that came up. Many of the IWLM founders can't remember much about the discussions, but one that has passed into legend required the women to take turns explaining the circumstances around when they saw their first penis! Like the content of the women's pages, anything having to do with sex or sexuality was still fairly new territory and many of the women found it hard to shake the foundations of their Catholic upbringings enough to be able to talk freely about such things. It just wasn't done. Often the consciousness-raising sessions would disintegrate when someone would seize up, refusing to discuss whatever topic was at hand.

But the other component to each Monday night meeting was one of practical planning. Some of the women just didn't see much point to the consciousness-raising sessions, so such practical matters seemed necessary to keep them satisfied that they weren't wasting their time. There were several women in the founding group who thought that they could talk forever without making any concrete strides for women's rights, like changes in the law – a common criticism of the weakness of consciousness-raising as a tool for political change.

Máirín Johnston's enthusiasm for consciousness-raising sessions didn't go unnoticed by the other women at the meetings. Perhaps because she was a little older than some of the other founder members at thirty-nine, she wasn't at all embarrassed about any of the topics that came up for discussion. Marie McMahon remembers that Johnston was an example to her that openness was not something to be feared, that in fact it could only help women to be less afraid to demand the civil rights that they deserved. But for women who had lived all their lives in a society that demanded restraint and even secrecy on so many issues, it was extremely difficult to accept the idea that it was beneficial to finally begin the kind of dialogue the IWLM founders started. For most of the IWLM women, this was one of the hardest obstacles to overcome and one of the first steps to women's liberation as they defined it. It simply took incredible courage to go so deeply against the grain of the society in which most of them had been born and raised.

Johnston seems to have drawn much of the courage that others admired, and her desire to be a part of social change, from her mother's strength of character. She remembers feeling some of the apprehension that the other founders mention about being involved in such a radical group as the IWLM, but she was able to see the bigger picture of what they were trying to accomplish. Controversy did not bother her; after all, Suffragettes had been very respectable women who had been out in the streets smashing windows to make sure they were heard. Compared to that, walking out of mass, writing newspaper articles and making television appearances actually seemed tame. Johnston had a very keen sense of the extremes to which it was sometimes necessary to go if you were really serious about provoking change. "I suppose there was a little bit of nervousness there all right, but because there were so many of us and there was the excitement, that did away with the fear," Johnston says. "I always admired women in Irish history who took great risks, so I felt I was being true to myself if I was taking a risk that was going to bring about some sort of change for the better and that I shouldn't be thinking of myself and what might happen or what might not happen. My mother had to live through a time in our history where everybody was afraid and yet she stood up for herself . . . so you just hold your ground and you win out in the end, because things do change."

5

Two Different Doctors

"The revolution can never be achieved by one person, only the masses." — Dr Moira Woods, in an *Irish Press* interview with Mary Kenny, 8 October 1970[1]

When her fellow IWLM founders speak of Dr Moira Woods, they inevitably mention her intelligence, her kindness, her dedication to many socialist causes, and her serene beauty, but not necessarily in that order. Moira Woods was exactly the type of person whom Máirín Johnston might have been just a bit wary of before Johnston's participation in the IWLM's consciousness-raising sessions. Woods was undeniably wealthy, formally well educated, lived in Ailesbury Road, one of the most elite areas of Dublin, and was married to another doctor. But it was Woods's idealism and activism that set her apart from most of the other women in the upper echelon. All the same, Máirín Johnston was less surprised, when she first met her, that Woods was so politically involved than she was that Woods experienced many of the same discriminations as working-class women did.

There is evidence that Woods herself felt she fit in better with Gaj's group and the other women in the IWLM than she did among her own neighbours in one of Dublin's wealthiest areas. She told Mary Kenny in an October 1970 *Irish Press* interview that she and her family were "not recognised" in the neighbourhood: "Just the other day I heard that I was harbouring the Viet Cong in my home."[2] Neighbours' children had been told not to play with hers because they came from a "Communist" household. During the summer of 1970, Woods invited some of the squatters who had lived in Pembroke Road and had been ordered out of their dwelling to live in her house for several weeks until they could find a new place, an offer which the neighbours undoubtedly frowned upon. But Woods had a vision for her neighbourhood, for Dublin, and for the world, a vision which those who had benefited the most from capitalism were the least likely to agree with – one of true integration, with all classes and nationalities mixed into one area.

London-born Woods is the daughter of a British colonial civil servant and an Irish mother. The family was in Burma when the Japanese invaded the country and was relocated to Australia as a result. Woods was a brilliant student and achieved very good marks despite, like Mary Kenny, being "difficult to handle"; she was expelled from several convent schools for her "insubordination". The last convent school that Woods had attended was in Kenya, where she saw the ugliest consequences of British imperialism in the way the students in the all-girls' school mistreated the African men who served them at mealtimes. It was around this time that Woods was becoming more interested in politics while simultaneously turning away from the Church – mostly, she said, because of its militarism. Woods's plan at the age of sixteen, Kenny wrote in the *Press*, was to hitch-hike her way across the Sahara desert, hop a boat across the Mediterranean and be sheltered by an Italian count whom she had already identified as one Arthur Galetti, the grandfather of a school friend.[3]

Plan B, which involved coming to Ireland to study medicine at Trinity College, worked out better. She continued to develop her interest in politics there by joining a peace group founded by Quakers. After graduating from Trinity she returned to England for one year to practise medicine, coming back to Dublin to teach physiology in Trinity. Although Woods formally belonged to no political parties, her views were obviously leftist. In Kenny's assessment, Woods was a "surprisingly devout" Catholic who viewed Jesus Christ as a pacifist and a revolutionary in his own right.[4] Kenny's choice of the word "surprisingly" reflected the tendency of some feminists to frown upon those among them who were pro-Catholic in any way. It was difficult for such feminists at the time to approve of any kind of support for a church which seemed to be doing its best to make sure some of the worst discriminatory attitudes toward women stayed just as they were.

One of Woods's main criticisms of Irish society was the economic inequality that she saw as a direct result of capitalism. She told her six children that although they were among the most privileged, their situation had nothing to do with natural virtue – they were just a good deal luckier than most other children happened to be. Woods's preference for providing people with as much unbiased information as possible and leaving them to make their own conclusions was reflected in her anger upon discovering that her children's civics textbooks were teaching them that Communism in all its forms was an "evil thing". It would have been better for teachers to go into the economic theory of it or its origins or even abuses instead of just teaching children capitalistic propaganda about "Communism" full stop, she told Kenny in their interview.

"It sounds all Constance Markievicz, but you see, once you have gazed on the stars – once you have had a glimpse of how bad the capitalist system really is, how it works against people, you can never look back again," she said.[5] Woods's opinions, delivered with such force and conviction, make it easy to see how her conservative neighbours might have been wary of her.

Kenny's lengthy profile on Woods was prompted by Woods's public appearance as a "judge" in the mock trial of President Richard Nixon, whose visit to Ireland during the first week of October in 1970 had sparked many protests and debates, mostly organised by anti-war groups. While the Gardaí had their hands full that week with all the "usual suspects" in Dublin activism like Máirín de Burca, who had been arrested during a protest for throwing an egg at the Presidential car, Woods was also out doing her part, donning a curly white wig and black robes to preside over the protest condemning Nixon for what she and the anti-war protesters involved in the Irish Voice on Vietnam saw as his crimes against the Vietnamese. Judging from the newspapers' accounts of the protest, Woods and the protestors executed a very effective demonstration. The *Independent* reported that 1,500 people had shown up at the American Embassy in Ballsbridge to burn the President in effigy:

Asked to give their verdict, the crowd shouted a unanimous "guilty" – the sentence was predictable. The effigy, which had been carried from the city strapped to a coffin emblazoned "US Imperialism", was dragged from the platform, doused in petrol and burned. After the demonstration a group of protesters began a picket on the embassy, which they plan to continue until the Presidential plane leaves Dublin this evening. A statement from the organising group, issued during the meeting, criticised the Irish government for its silence on the Vietnam war.[6]

Kenny was right when she observed in her profile of Woods that the medical doctor and mother of six who resided in Ailesbury Road was not the most obvious choice to preside over such a protest. But when one considers the diverse backgrounds of the IWLM founders and examines more carefully the atmosphere in Dublin at the time, Woods' activism seems less surprising. There were all kinds of Dubliners – students, the working-class, pacifists of all ages, civil rights activists, and, of course, women's liberationists – who felt strongly enough to take to the streets at the start of the seventies. In that context, it is not as far-fetched that someone like Woods would have been so involved in such groups.

Woods's fellow IWLM members recall her varied contributions to the women's movement and the value of having someone like her in the group. Like Mrs Gaj, Máirín de Burca remembers, Moira Woods had an aura of respectability that de Burca knew she herself lacked but that proved to be useful in many situations. Woods might have felt some hostility from her own neighbours, but in a wider social context, she had a degree of credibility as a highly educated, professional woman. June Levine wrote about Woods's help calming her nerves after the infamous consciousness-raising discussion in which the topic was the first time each woman had seen a penis. For Levine, as she described in her memoir, the experience had amounted to sexual abuse – some man had exposed himself to her while she was still a toddler in her crib, placing his penis through the bars and then scolding her for grabbing hold of it.[7] When the memory came flooding back to Levine in Gaj's, she was overcome with emotion and remembers Woods taking her out into the hall and speaking soothingly to her. Woods later became heavily involved in the creation of the Well Woman Centre, and others also speak of her gentle ways and kindness. Lyn Madden, a Dublin prostitute in the seventies and a good friend of Mrs Gaj and some of the other IWLM founders, thanked Woods in the acknowledgments to her own memoir. "Thank you to Dr Moira Woods, who saw me in her medical capacity, but by sparing the time to talk to me, gave me back a little respect for my body".[8] Hearing those who knew her well talk about her talents, one begins to understand that Woods probably possessed that rarest of qualities in a doctor – the ability to connect with people through conversation and sympathy and to incorporate this connection into the healing process.

To listen to her fellow feminists' recollections of her, Woods's intellect was indeed unparalleled. Marie McMahon finds it difficult to decide what to talk about when asked what she thought of Moira Woods and what she can remember of her contributions to the IWLM in its early days. To McMahon, Woods is very hard to classify. "Besides being by far the most beautiful person in the group to look at, which is an awful sexist thing to say," McMahon says. "She had a brilliant sense of humour. She was amazingly intelligent and brilliant at finding out, at researching. And she was extremely politically courageous." Mary Sheerin remembers discussing poetry with Woods when Sheerin had come across no one else in Dublin who had heard of one of her favourite poets.

"Mrs Woods is a remarkably beautiful woman," Mary Kenny wrote in 1970. "Indeed, she seems possessed of that ethereal quality, that illumination of the face, which comes to all those who believe. She is well in the Anglo-Irish tradition of beautiful, passionate, radical women who are willing to storm the gates of any establishment for The People".[9] What set Woods particularly apart from her fellow IWLM founders was the fact that she was technically more a part of the establishment herself than any of the other women were. But her background and her wealth never deterred her from criticising injustice where she saw it, even if much of that criticism was levelled at the capitalistic system from which she herself had benefited.

For all of the risks she took and for how unpopular she may have been with some of her neighbours, Woods still commanded a high level of respect. Like Mrs Gaj, she could be counted on to come to the aid of activists who had got themselves in over their heads with the Gardaí during a demonstration. Within the IWLM, she was naturally the authority on medical issues and had access to useful information about contraception and other aspects of women's health.

At times, Woods could be one of the more extreme women in the group when it came to the question of how far the IWLM should go in their protests. Enthusiastically taking on the role of the judge in Nixon's mock trial, she had proven her willingness to put herself on the front-lines, risks and all. When Frank Crummey had said that most of the women involved in the early days of women's liberation didn't much care about getting arrested, he was talking specifically about Woods. Mary Maher remembers that Woods had mentioned, at least in passing, a plan to set her coat on fire in church at one of the masses the IWLM was planning on attending and then walking out in protest at the Archbishop's letter against all contraceptive acts. Maher doesn't remember which one of the other founders talked Woods out of it.

Woods's commitment was both deep and varied. Late in the summer of 1969, during the height of the Civil Rights demonstrations, she met at Gaj's with Mrs Gaj, Frank Crummey and another Gaj's regular, Dr Paddy Randall. They knew there was going to be trouble and decided to travel by car to the North to offer supplies and medical assistance. Woods ordered huge, industrial-sized amounts of food and medical supplies to take to demonstrators on the barricades. She and Randall drove around offering medical assistance and food to anyone out in the streets who needed it. Woods had a rather more difficult time of it than Randall, as she was about eight months pregnant. When the invoices came some time later, she rang the suppliers and said there must have been some misunderstanding. Hadn't she told them that everything they'd sent for her order was a donation? When the time called for it, Woods wouldn't hesitate to make her own rules.

Dr Woods's commitment attracted criticism and admiration alike, but some IWLM founders who were less involved in other political causes saw some reason to be ambivalent about her and the other founders with strong ties to left-wing political causes like Sinn Féin, the Irish Voice on Vietnam, and the Communist and Labour parties. Like Woods, Margaret Gaj, Máirín de Burca, Mary Maher, Máirín Johnston and Marie McMahon made no secret of their involvement in any of these groups, and all of the IWLM founders knew what each other's politics were. But there was a wariness on the part of some of the IWLM founders, like Nuala Fennell, Mary Sheerin and Mary Kenny, who were less involved in other political causes. They felt that the newly formed women's liberation group had so much ground to cover that for half its members to be so involved in other political causes was a hindrance to the women's cause.

* * *

EIMER PHILBIN BOWMAN was another doctor who was at the IWLM's earliest meetings, but unlike Dr Woods, Dr Philbin Bowman was not involved at all in political activism. She heard about the IWLM meetings from her friend, the poet Eavan Boland. Boland, like Philbin Bowman, was present and active at the group's early meetings but is not considered a "founder" of the group by most other IWLM members, and does not consider herself a founder. Philbin Bowman's mother, Eva, was an accomplished academic and one of the top scientists in the country, and by the early seventies she was head of the Department of Chemistry at UCD. Eva never considered giving up work after Eimer and, later, her two siblings, were born, although her job became increasingly demanding. In those days, before the five-day working week, people worked Saturday mornings, so they only had Saturday afternoons and Sundays off. Throughout her own childhood, Eimer understood that her mother was unique, because she knew very few of her friends' mothers worked. But if her mother struggled with balancing a particularly demanding full-time job and raising three children, Eimer doesn't remember it. Eva had always appeared to be perfectly capable of being both a career and family-oriented woman, and neither seemed to suffer for the other. The family employed a live-in housekeeper from the earliest days after her mother went to work at UCD, so Eva had outside assistance in running the household and raising the children, not unusual in middle-class Dublin households then.

Philbin Bowman's deep respect for her mother is obvious, and she assumed that as a young woman she would be able to balance her own family and career as effortlessly as her mother seemed to have done. When this turned out not to be the case, it was much more difficult for her to face what she saw as her own inadequacies. It was not until she joined the IWLM and heard the other women's stories that she began to realise that her struggles were more a reflection of society's discrimination against women than of any personal shortcomings. Philbin Bowman's class in medical school was just over one-quarter female, but she was one of the first women to get married, which she did in her fourth year, at the age of twenty-three. By the time she graduated two years later, she was the mother of a six-month-old baby and was three months into her second pregnancy. It was 1969, the same year Dublin's first family planning clinic opened, but Philbin Bowman had not given much consideration to birth control. "I remember my mother saying to me once, 'If I was your age, I'd certainly be on the pill,' and I remember thinking at the time that was quite an intrusive comment from her," she says.

Following graduation from medical school, students were required to complete a one-year internship before practising as a doctor. At her interview at her teaching hospital for her mandatory internship post, Philbin Bowman discreetly avoided mentioning that she was pregnant. "I felt extremely vulnerable at the interviews and I knew that it was enough for me to have been married with one child for them to have little interest," she says. For the first time, she was aware that it would be very difficult for her to be able to satisfy the demands of completing her medical training and being a mother of two young children at the same time. As she expected, the hospital did not offer her a post. "I remember thinking, you're abnormal in the eyes of the medical world if you don't marry and you're not really acceptable to them in terms of a doctor if you have children. In other words, there's supposed to be a way to get this right but certainly I had got it wrong," Philbin Bowman says. She decided to apply to the health board hospitals outside Dublin for an internship post after her teaching hospital had turned her down, and was shocked to discover that only single women were eligible to apply. She had run smack into a marriage bar at the final hurdle, which she had never heard mentioned during six years of medical training. Her private teaching hospital turned her down because she was a mother; the public health board hospitals turned her down because she was married. Although she accepted several "locum posts" – filling in for colleagues on holiday – she found them too lacking in continuity to allow for any sustained learning experience. Initially, she blamed herself for terribly bad timing, but at the same time she had a nagging awareness that she was living in a country where the notion of contraception was still frowned upon, even for married couples. She began to realise that the obstacles she was running into had little to do with her and more to do with the system which was blatantly unfair to women.

During 1970 and 1971, with two infants and a medical degree but unable to practise, Philbin Bowman stayed at home, a full-time mother. When Eavan Boland told her about the new group of women liberationists, she was interested. She had never been involved in political organisations before in any capacity. "My impulse, or my interest, in going there [to the ILWM meetings] was completely personally directed, it had come absolutely out of my personal experience and the fact that I had come up against these obstacles that I had no idea were there," she says. She was staggered by the number of issues the other IWLM women who were deeply immersed in political causes brought up at the meetings. She eventually began to wonder if the IWLM was biting off more than it could chew as a group by not limiting itself to strictly "feminist" issues like contraception and equal pay. "I didn't dismiss any of these women," Philbin Bowman says, "it was just that it was a much bigger picture than I had imagined, and bit by bit you saw that much bigger issues fell within the ambit of it."

Philbin Bowman didn't participate in any of the IWLM's public activities or protests, and attended meetings sporadically, although she was present as an audience member at the group's 1971 appearance on *The Late Late Show*. She was used to the idea that medical professionals were not supposed to seek out publicity, and that was a hard mentality to break out of, even in the name of women's rights. She felt she had already drawn enough attention to herself in her failed efforts to secure her internship, and felt that she "wouldn't have been able to take the flak" that most of the IWLM's public protests involved. "You feel a sense of admiration for the people who did it, a slight sense of shame that you might be associated with them, and wondering how on earth you'd defend it. It was complicated," she says. Her feelings about the mechanisms and causes of discrimination against women were changing as a result of her participation in the IWLM and her discovery that so many other women had, in their own careers, run into similar roadblocks. These new revelations were both gratifying and unsettling to Philbin

Bowman, as they were to so many of the other women, and she struggled to adjust to the new filter through which she was seeing the problems she had encountered in her professional life.

Looking back now, Philbin Bowman regards her three years of full-time mothering in the early seventies as revelatory, and experiencing the role of a woman at home "through feminist eyes" determined her future career choices. In particular, she recalls the impact of reading Betty Friedan's *The Feminist Mystique,* which prompted her to apply to the Department of Psychology in Trinity College Dublin with a proposal for a research degree. Her thesis, later published, was a study of the sexual and contraceptive practice of single women without marriage plans who attended a Dublin family planning clinic. Several years after the IWLM disintegrated, Philbin Bowman solved the problem of possessing a medical degree without the ability to practise. In 1976, six years after graduating from medical school, she reapplied to her old private teaching hospital, which offered her an internship post. The marriage bar that had prevented her from securing a post at the public hospitals had been abolished in 1973. Her mother Eva moved in with the family for a time, helping to mind Eimer's still-young children while she completed her internship. Six more years of specialist training in psychiatry followed until finally – twenty years after entering medicine – she emerged as a psychiatrist. She now practises part-time, has a special interest in autism spectrum disorder, and works as a consultant in the Well Woman Clinic. "What motivated me [to work] there was that it was a woman's clinic. As a psychiatrist I can offer a service to women within a women's clinic setting that is not a psychiatric hospital or institutional setting, but a welcome, friendly, relaxed place."

Several of the IWLM founders, like Philbin Bowman, who had not had much previous experience in political groups and were less outwardly radical than members like Woods and de Burca, must have wondered sometimes how they had found themselves in the upstairs room of Gaj's every Monday night .The places from which the IWLM members were making their own ways to Gaj's for the Monday meetings were probably as varied as their own backgrounds – any one of the three major newspaper offices, an earlier political meeting, or a house with their own young children, whom someone else would mind for a few hours.

At the earliest meetings at Gaj's, once the restaurant had been designated as the permanent meeting place, the founders looked around and wondered who might happen to drop in that week, and what she might have to say. Women who worked in the Civil Service or in other offices in and around Baggot Street had heard about some of the meetings that went on in Gaj's, and as they walked by the restaurant on their way home in the evenings, some wondered what went on, with full knowledge that they themselves did not, either by choice or nature, belong to the same group of people in the same way. Inside the restaurant, the group itself was struggling to figure out exactly how it fit together. Many of the women knew each other well; others were meeting for the first time.

Once everyone had gathered upstairs, chaos ensued. One would have to be loud, confident and slightly bold to make one's voice heard over the din. It was slightly cramped, the warmth building as a few more people inevitably shuffled in late. There were jokes and rows. Someone would suggest a topic that everyone would, in theory, be expected to contribute to. The topic was usually something different or risqué enough so that nearly every woman in the room was plucked, despite the warm and generally friendly atmosphere, out of her comfort zone. And while some of the women who were more pragmatic and practical were frustrated almost from the very beginning with what they saw as the meandering course the meetings often took, it was the tapping into the personal stories and histories, and sharing these with one another, that formed the foundation upon which the IWLM built itself.

The young professionals heard from the housewives, who heard from the political activists. They did not always understand each other's views, but they did have a common goal, and as they drifted back off to their different lives at the end of the night, it was usually this they remembered. Since the latter half of the meetings was loosely designated for the planning of protests, topics for articles and things more concrete, most of the women went off feeling they were slowly working their way toward the same purpose together, even if a few terse words or an off-putting remark lingered.

Most significantly, they were naming the things that, although they may still have been invisible to most of society, were preventing them from being free, equal citizens – their own feelings, the country's deeply ingrained patriarchal attitudes, the oppressive laws. It was in this way, through (albeit hectic) conversation and debate, that the IWLM began its real work toward women's liberation.

Some of the women with less loyalty to the left were more reformists than revolutionaries. For them, even stimulating conversations like the ones that happened on Mondays at Gaj's were not enough. They believed that the changes that really mattered, like concrete revisions of the discriminatory laws, had to happen more slowly than the other women were willing to accept. Still, this was the first women's organisation in Ireland in which reformists and revolutionaries were able to engage in dialogue and work alongside each other, however fragile the equilibrium that held the group together may have been. During the first few months that the IWLM founders met regularly, they worked through some of their embarrassment in the consciousness-raising sessions, wrote relevant articles for their respective papers, and got to know each other better. It was then, as they started on their first tangible project – the creation of their aims in the form of a charter – that their real differences began to emerge and the strength of whatever force was binding them was truly tested.

6

Chains or Change

"Although there has been some piecemeal reform in the legal status of married women in this country, it can still be said that upon marriage a woman in Ireland enters into a state of civil death." — From *Chains or Change*, March 1971[1]

"Its value is that it compiles the whole range of grievances between two covers: widows, deserted wives, factory girls, education, job barriers, legal discrimination. It ends by enumerating five reasons why you're better off living in sin than marrying. We learned a lot ourselves putting it together, and I defy any woman to read it and not get narked about something." — Mary Maher on *Chains or Change*, from *The Irish Times*, 9 March 1971[2]

*C*hains or Change was the title of the IWLM charter – the first document to compile some of the most severe inequalities that Irish women endured. The founders researched, wrote, edited, revised, photocopied and stapled it all together within a remarkably short space of time. The front cover had to be no less than stunning; Mary Kenny took it upon herself to design it. Kenny had just the idea: true to a well-earned reputation for outrageousness, it included graphics that were a bit more than risqué for the times. It featured, as one of her fellow founders recalls, "a big bare tit".

Kenny's idea for the cover was probably not the most outlandish thing she could think of, but it reflected her preference for raciness. She wanted to reproduce Eugene Delacroix's famous depiction of "Lady

Liberty Leading the People" in the Parisian Uprising, bayonet in one hand, French tricolour flag in the other, and breasts defiantly exposed. The painting was lauded as a symbol of the power of feminine strength and firm conviction, with the lady as the clear leader of the rebellion. This was, in Kenny's eyes, the perfect image for all of society to behold, and associate, with the IWLM.

Her fellow IWLM founders were less convinced. With other less important matters, the group was willing to tolerate and even, at times, enjoy Kenny's vivaciousness and flamboyance. But *Chains or Change* was the product of several months of the group's hard work, and it was a powerful document in its own right. It was meant to symbolise and summarise the group's goals and ideals. In the best possible scenario, it would enrage the women (and men) who read it and incite them to action. Within the IWLM itself, which had been coping with the strain of containing such a diversity of political opinions and objectives, it was a reminder of the group's essential aims. And Kenny wanted to adorn the cover with an image that may well have killed the booklet before it even arrived at the bookshops and newsagents.

It was Marie McMahon, a typesetter and one of the youngest founders, who saved the design, and the day, with a new idea. In her files, McMahon had a picture of the Pope with his hands folded in prayer. She enlarged just the hands and redrew the rosary beads that were around them to look like chains, so that instead of the beads moving piously throughout the fingers, the chains were binding the hands together. The final cover of the booklet, in black and white, is somewhat crude in its starkness, but it is also effective. The design was meant to convey the restrictions that women felt under the law and mores of the culture. The IWLM founders knew that the hands were the Pope's, and for them the rendering of the rosary beads into chains also pointed an unmistakable finger at the Church as a major source of women's oppression. But since neither the Pope's face nor any other identifying characteristics were shown, besides a blurry depiction of the famous holy ring, it's safe to assume that most of the public never even realised the hands were supposed to be the Pope's. The founders' decision not to identify his Holiness was most likely another deliberate group choice to sidestep the predictable criticism that the IWLM was trying to destroy the Church's authority.

Looking at the demands the IWLM outlined in *Chains or Change* thirty-five years after its publication, none seems desperately revolutionary. The IWLM called for equal pay; an end to the marriage bar that kept women from working after they wed; equal rights in law; justice for widows, deserted wives and "unmarried mothers"; equal educational opportunities; and contraception as a human right. The five demands were born of the founders' own experiences, but the way the group presented each in the booklet reflects some of its fears about how each one was to be received by the public, as well as some of the internal conflicts it had to sort out in the booklet's creation. In that case, what was omitted is just as important as what was included.

For all of the IWLM founders, the demands for equal pay and the removal of the marriage bar were the most obvious and important. Almost every woman who had been employed in Ireland had experienced firsthand the maddening injustice of working alongside men, performing exactly the same jobs with the same or sometimes better proficiency, and receiving a fraction of the men's pay. Although the founders came from working-class to upper-class backgrounds, they all realised that for women, money was power, in the form of more *options:* options to raise their families as they saw fit and even to limit their families if they could afford to travel outside the Republic or send away for contraceptives; options to leave abusive husbands or support themselves if their husbands deserted them; options, in short, for better lives. Such options were harder to come by if women had limited earning potential, no matter how hard or how efficiently they worked.

Máirín de Burca was especially livid about the lack of equal pay legislation. From her early days as a shop girl she had gone to trade union meetings, years before the women's liberation movement formed, trying to get the union to ask for the same pay increase for women as they did for men. It was always, de Burca remembers, a one-pound increase for men and fifteen shillings for the women. She lost in the end – the union simply told her that they just wouldn't be able to get it. Like her experience with the kind, black woman in her Chicago neighbourhood as a child, that defeat left an indelible impression on de Burca.

The IWLM founders also made use of some of the most dramatic statistics to prove their points, such as the fact that Irish women were earning only 54.9 per cent of men's wages according to the latest figures from the Central Statistics Office. In 1938 they had actually been earning slightly more: 55.6 per cent of men's wages. The introduction to the section on equal pay and the marriage bar reflected the force and conciseness of the language used throughout the booklet: "Any investigation into the position of women at work in the Republic reveals one clear fact: Irish women are cheap labour."

The journalists, for their part, had been writing about the lack of equal pay long before the IWLM formed. As professionals, most of the journalists were very lucky – it was one of the few fields where equal pay was already a reality for women, rather than a lofty goal. The marriage bar did not seem to apply at the newspapers, either. Mary Maher was allowed to keep her job at *The Irish Times* upon her marriage, and was even given maternity leave when both of her daughters were born, which was absolutely unheard of at the time. If a woman had been fortunate enough not to be sacked upon marriage, she definitely would have been forced to leave when she became pregnant.

At the *Irish Press*, Mary Kenny had written an article titled "Equal Pay: The Facts" with the subheading, "We must be militant" almost a year before the IWLM's first meetings. Kenny used the article to acknowledge, and then systematically refute, the arguments against equal pay. "There are many arguments against equal pay," Kenny wrote. "All of them have been devised by men, defending their own interest." People asked why a single woman should make as much as a married man with a family to support, but Kenny countered by asking why a single man should make more than a single woman, as it was under the system at that time.[3]

The *Irish Times* women's page hadn't been idle on the issue of equal pay, either. Mary Maher had written a piece titled "Equal Pay: Women are sick of nothing but promises" a full year before Kenny's article, which also attempted to analyse the historical and social contexts that allowed the discriminatory system to emerge:

> Women cannot be blamed for their lack of training. Neither can
> they be altogether blamed for the apathy they've shown toward
> their own economic welfare. A population which has shifted from
> scattered self-employment and private domestic service to wide-

spread industrial and commercial work in only forty years had no historical sense of the worth of its own labour, or the value of united action.[4]

The *Independent's* Janet Martin wrote an article in September 1970 pointing out that most employers had a crafty way of getting around the issue of women's equal pay by adding a little loophole in the language. The employers she talked to said they were in favour of women's equal pay *for equal work*, but that very few women did exactly the same work as men. They cited the fact that women were absent from work more than men due to illnesses and that as a rule, women did not work at night. They neglected to mention that company policies often barred women from working overtime or on night shifts. Martin concluded her piece by asking, "How can a woman claim equal pay if she is not allowed to work the same hours or as long as a man?"[5]

Mary McCutchan wrote a related piece in February 1971 about a husband and wife, Michael and Phillis Fogarty, who were both labour specialists and the joint authors of a book titled *Women in Top Jobs*. The Fogartys were both advocates of the removal of the marriage bar, with Phillis Fogarty arguing that people's fears that the market would be flooded with women if the bar were removed were unfounded. "Its removal might affect directly only a handful of women, but it will change girls' attitudes to their jobs. They will no longer look on work as a stopgap between school and marriage – they can plan real careers," she told McCutchan.[6] On all three newspapers' women's pages, there were countless other articles related either directly or indirectly to equal pay – profiles of women who had lost their full-time jobs due to the marriage bar and had then been re-hired on a part-time basis for a fraction of their original pay; women who had been deserted by their husbands but who were still not allowed to apply for most jobs because of their marital status . . . the list of grievances was long and ugly.

In making the case for government reforms in the way "women in distress" – widows, deserted wives and "unmarried mothers" – were treated, the IWLM may have been less successful. Their arguments were still strong, reasonable and logically presented, but the fact remained that none of the IWLM founders themselves fit into any of those three categories, at least at that point in time. Officially, journalist June Levine was an "unmarried mother", but she had been married in Ireland and obtained a divorce in Canada, where she had lived through much of the early 1960s with her husband, a doctor. The "unmarried mothers" to whom the IWLM was referring in the booklet were mothers who had never been married, since divorce was not legalised in Ireland until 1996. Máirín Johnston was separated from her husband, but they still lived in the same house with their three children – she upstairs with her new partner, and he downstairs with his.

The "women in distress" section detailed the widow's plight by examining the arduous process the state put her through in determining what her allowance should be. Widows would receive a contributory pension only if their husbands had been able to make a set number of employment contributions. If they hadn't, widows had to go through a means test proving they had no other income, and even if they passed the test they received a maximum of only £5.00 per week for one dependent child, increasing to only £5.75 per week for two children. Deserted wives faced similar restrictions. Under the law, the impetus was on the deserted wife to prove that she had made every effort to reconcile with her husband, that he had left of his own will, that six months had passed since he had left, and that he had not sent her any money at all during the past six months. One guilty five pound note posted from England would have ruined the woman's chances of getting any assistance from the state at all. She was also required to be under fifty years of age and have at least one dependent child in order to qualify for the meagre state allowance, akin to the amounts widows received.

In 1971, single mothers did not officially exist in Ireland. That there were unmarried Irish women who had babies was a fact that was simply never mentioned in public. The article in *Chains or Change* detailed the obstacles, isolation and extreme social stigma that single mothers endured. There were those who had no option but to enter Mother and Baby Homes to have their child adopted. There were others who arrived pregnant in England every year to try to keep their babies, sometimes ending up as London prostitutes or in other miserable, demeaning jobs to support themselves and their children.

The booklet made no mention of the other group of single pregnant Irish women who went to England for abortions, returning to Ireland with excuses of business or shopping that had to be done abroad. This omission is itself indicative of the times and of the founders' own mentalities – abortion was a topic that had not even come up in conversation at the meetings or at any of the consciousness-raising sessions. The way most of the founders explain the absence of the topic that is today one of the most widely and passionately debated women's issues in the western world is simple innocence. In examining any of the aspects of the IWLM's work, it is vital to remember that in 1971, Irish women were fighting for the most basic of their civil rights. If most women did not even have legal access to contraceptives other than the pill, and then only under the pretence of having it prescribed by a doctor as a "cycle-regulator", then how could the IWLM possibly have asked for abortion on demand? Not one of the IWLM founders remembers the topic of abortion ever even surfacing and being rejected as too damaging to the group – it simply wasn't even on their radar.

It was the same with divorce, which was mentioned in *Chains or Change* only briefly as an addendum to deserted wives' predicament: "Because we admit of no divorce, we refuse to co-operate with the British on enforcing British alimony payments and therefore they refuse to co-operate with us in chasing up deserting husbands. It must again be stated too that there are Irish women who are not Catholics, whose antecedents were promised by Wolfe Tone and the leaders of the 1916 Easter Rising where Catholic, Protestant and Dissenter would enjoy equal rights as citizens of this country."[7]

There was at least one single mother reading the *Chains or Change* article on unmarried mothers who was unsatisfied with the IWLM's portrayal of her situation. Maura O'Dea (now Richards) was the founder of Cherish, the country's first support group for single mothers. The particular phrase that Richards took offence to stated: "We need a central organisation which will help and rehabilitate the unmarried mother. Ideally this organisation should be able to advise her to keep her child if she so wishes, help her find housing and employment and organise crèches and nurseries."[8] Richards wrote in her 1998 memoir, *Single Issue:* "Even within the Irish Women's Liberation Movement, and with the best of intentions, others were talking on our behalf and patronisingly suggesting we needed 'rehabilitation' rather than liberation. The idea of unmarried mothers acting for themselves had not entered their minds".[9] In light of such criticism, it is easier to understand the origins of some of the later accusations of elitism that some women who joined the movement over the next several months hurled at the founder members. At the same time, Richards' dissatisfaction with the IWLM's depiction of single mothers is an example of the value of some of the group's mistakes. It was the IWLM, and the publicity it harnessed, that forced people into at least admitting that single mothers existed in Ireland – now it was up to some of those single mothers themselves to come out and fight for their rights as they saw fit, as Richards did.

There were two other issues of great importance to most of the founders, which they downplayed in the booklet in order to make the IWLM and its aims more acceptable to the general public. They were the legalisation of contraception and the one-house/one-family issue. If a reader of *Chains and Change* had no other knowledge of the IWLM, they would never have suspected how big a part of the group's entire programme was the campaign to change the laws banning contraceptives. In fact, contraception was not even listed in the booklet's table of contents as one of the main topics – it was hidden under the heading "Incidental Facts", and the summary of the law was succinct:

> Although at the time of writing the situation is under review, artificial birth control and all printed material giving knowledge thereof is against the law of the Republic of Ireland. By a nicc trick of public hypocrisy, the contraceptive pill is permitted, since it is imported into Ireland merely as a "cycle regulator". Some 25,000 Irish women use it, ostensibly under the guise of a medicine to regulate the menstrual cycle. To employ any other device is to break the law of this country. The moral question is not here under discussion; the fact remains that Irish women who do not adhere to orthodox Roman Catholic dogma are technically criminals, and when caught, are punished by deprivation of their right to plan their families as they wish.[10]

The group offered no other opinion or analysis apart from the simple statement of the facts, which admittedly is powerful in itself. But the IWLM founders must have felt they had more freedom to express their views in the newspapers, through their journalism, with their condemnatory articles about the existing laws and the state's refusal to reform them.

The IWLM had discussed the one-family/one-house demand at length since its earliest meetings, but there were several women in the founding group who argued that it was too much of a departure from purely "feminist" issues to be included in the group's list of demands. Máirín de Burca remembers the rows over the demand, and as one of the most active members of the Dublin Housing Action Committee, she was one of the biggest advocates of its inclusion. Máirín Johnston agreed, with the logic that you couldn't liberate a woman from the kitchen sink if she hadn't a kitchen sink to be liberated from. But others were wary of getting too far off the track of *women's* rights issues and becoming too closely associated with leftist and socialist issues. In the end, one-family/one-house was included on the IWLM's official list of six demands even though it was left out of *Chains or Change*. De Burca, Johnston, and the other founders with strong ties to left-wing political groups had been able to persuade the majority of the group, at least, that the housing crisis affected women more acutely than anyone else.

The process of putting the booklet together had taught each of the founders what the group was capable of achieving if everyone pitched in – the journalists doing the bulk of the research and writing, the typesetter creating the design for the cover, and others aiding in the production with the endless photocopying and stapling. Although the final publication may look amateur by today's standards of fancy computer graphics and design, the booklet was truly a milestone in the history of the women's movement in Ireland. It marked the first time that anyone had compiled for publication a comprehensive list of the injustices the church, state and social code perpetuated against women. But it also sharpened the founders' awareness of the ideological differences between them and forewarned of some of the fractures that were already deepening and threatening to break whatever forces of cohesion were keeping the IWLM bound together.

That aside, even some of the founders themselves were astounded at the magnitude and pervasiveness of the oppression that Irish women endured when they opened the *Chains or Change* cover for the first time. Apparently, the public agreed that the booklet made for gripping reading.

A paragraph appeared on Mary Kenny's *Irish Press* women's page on 24 March 1971, under the title, "The Civil Wrongs of Irish Women",[11] apologising for the almost overnight sell-out of *Chains or Change*, and promising that more would be available at the booksellers' the following week. The number of people out there who were paying attention to the founders' little group was growing by leaps and bounds.

Paying the Price

"There was amazing solidarity at those meetings . . . the biggest thing I thought was that I wasn't on my own in this world."
— Marie McMahon

Marie McMahon had found the IWLM's consciousness-raising sessions as exciting as Máirín Johnston had. As much as she learned through the group's discussions, though, there was nothing like seeing the finished *Chains or Change* to force her into confronting the reality of the many wrongs that Irish women suffered. "The depth of the anger that women felt once we were together . . ." McMahon muses. "We couldn't sit on juries, we couldn't leave the country unless our husbands signed our passport, we couldn't collect our children's allowance. The list was endless. When we actually sat down and when it was actually put together, I was sitting there practically in tears at the injustice that we were living under." Just as consciousness-raising was simultaneously exhilarating and painful for McMahon, so too was compiling *Chains or Change*. They had created this document; now the IWLM founders had to face its truths themselves. Their critics, who were mostly women, hounded them about the consequences of the changes they were demanding. But no one knew the difficulties of advocating that kind of complete societal change better than the women who were pushing the hardest for it themselves.

The publication of *Chains or Change* was all about exposing the hypocrisies oppressing women at all different levels – the state, the Church, the educational system, the social codes that forbid even the acknowledgement of facts such as the existence of unmarried mothers in Ireland. The IWLM founders felt that it was wonderful that they were finally able to produce a document that named the most severe of these hypocrisies in one source.

Mary Maher, who at the time was married with one child and had another baby on the way, had written the closing article in the booklet titled "A personal summing-up by a working mother: five good reasons why it is better to live in sin", a document that listed five solid arguments against marriage. Number one pointed out that a woman could keep her job if she chose "living in sin" over marriage – anyone employed by the Civil Service, any semi-state body, the trade unions or the banks would automatically be sacked due to the marriage bar. Maher also exposed one of the most baffling anomalies in the state's treatment of unmarried mothers – an unmarried mother with a Civil Service job could have up to two children and still be able to keep her job, also enjoying a several months-long maternity leave with each child. "We make this point not to criticise the Civil Service for its responsible treatment of unmarried mothers, only to ask why they feel less responsible toward married women even before they have children?" Maher wrote.[1]

Maher also wrote about the tax benefits of staying single, and pointed out that a woman "living in sin" in an unhappy relationship was in a much better position to be able to leave the man without forfeiting all her rights to the home they may have built together. She concluded the article by stating that Irish women, upon marriage, were relegated to the status of property, and that the institution of marriage itself was something invented to preserve male superiority and a system of female chattels.

About half of the IWLM founders were married at the time the group was founded; June Levine was the sole divorcee, and Máirín Johnston was separated from her husband. Marie McMahon was one of the women, single at the time of the IWLM's founding, who speaks with a good understanding of the strains that could be brought upon a relationship by the transformations some of the founders went through. McMahon remembers that most men she knew, even the ones with whom she worked in the other leftist political groups, were anti-feminist. She had thought that if any men were likely to be supportive of the cause, they would be men who were fighting other social injustices. But she remembers trying to get "contraception as a human right" included in the manifesto of one left-wing student group with which she was involved and being sneered at by one of the young men, "Where would you be if your mother had used contraception?" McMahon remembers quite a few other men present nodding their heads. She thinks a good number of relationships broke up over women's liberation.

Other women in the group who were already married, like Dr Eimer Philbin Bowman, felt a bit uneasy at some of the meetings, wary of criticism from the others for submitting to an institution that they had publicly advised other women against. Philbin Bowman was just beginning to realise that her difficulties were a result of flaws in the system, and not her own fault or bad timing. But even as she found the meetings terribly exciting, they were troubling because they caused a new sort of dissent between herself and her husband. "I suppose you'd go along to meetings fearing they'd say, look, what are you doing being married, marriage does nothing for women. There was a dilemma for those of us who were married." Personal growth and change is never easy, and even as the IWLM was struggling to change the public's perception of women's wrongs, the founders' perspectives were changing as well.

Dr Philbin Bowman's husband, journalist John Bowman, was nonetheless supportive of her work in the women's movement, and some of the other founders remember their husbands or partners as advocates rather than obstacles. Máirín Johnston's partner helped create the banners – white stencilled lettering on black fabric that simply read "Irish Women's Liberation Movement", which the IWLM used in their most famous demonstration. Mary Maher's husband, trade union official Des Geraghty, shared most of the child-minding duties like changing nappies. In the journalists' pieces on the women's pages, they tried very hard to convey the idea that being an advocacy group for women's rights did not mean they were anti-men; in fact, men would benefit immensely from women's equal rights. As Nell McCafferty says today, what man in his right mind would be unhappy with the sexual freedom that legalising contraceptives would bring them? Only those, Máirín Johnston suggests, who didn't trust their wives and thought women would be unfaithful if they weren't afraid of getting pregnant by another man.

McMahon isn't the only one who remembers the dark side that many men showed during the early days of the women's liberation movement. IWLM founder and then *Irish Press* journalist Rosita Sweetman distinctly remembers a TD coming out of the Dáil on one of the IWLM's pickets there and saying to the women, "You should be fucked on your hands and knees like dogs because that's all you are."

"I remember that's the first time I thought, God, there's a real beast out there, and if you yank its tail, it'll squeal," Sweetman says. She also remembers snide remarks from men in pubs, asking her and her female friends why they weren't at home cooking dinner. McMahon still believes that the source of men's differing degrees of animosity was fear. "Their power was threatened, I'm convinced of that," she says. The worst of what men could call you at that time, as McMahon remembers it, was "lesbian", and some didn't hesitate to do so.

By 1970, the twenty-three-year-old McMahon had been going to Gaj's for years for the same reasons as most of Gaj's customers – the conversation, the craic, an interest in politics, and the fact that you never knew whom you might bump into. McMahon was also a member of the branch of the Labour Party that met in the upstairs of the restaurant, the same branch of which Mrs Gaj was a member.

Even though she was sixteen years younger than Máirín Johnston, McMahon and she shared similar events in their childhoods, which instilled in them at an early age a keen awareness of the social inequalities and injustices Irish women were forced to endure. Born in Leeson Street in 1947, McMahon lost her father at a very young age, as Johnston had, so young that, like Johnston, she had no clear memories of him. McMahon's mother, like Johnston's, was forced to raise her, two sisters and a brother on practically nothing. "I just remember raging, and part of it was the fact that I had to hand her my wages," McMahon says. "So I worked really hard all week and she wasn't subsidised by the state or anything like that." After leaving school when she was about twelve, McMahon took a shorthand typing course and started working as a typesetter when she was fourteen. After working for three or four years, McMahon's boss asked her, the layout artist and the printer if they would be interested in taking over, and McMahon found herself as a very young partner in her own typesetting business.

At this stage, McMahon says, the late sixties and early seventies, the city was alive with revolution. It was not just the women's movement that was building momentum – it seemed there were marches in Dublin every other day of the week, between the activities of the Dublin Housing Action Committee, the Communists, the student groups, the trade unionists and many others. Very few people would have been willing to typeset for some of the ultra-left groups, but McMahon welcomed work from these activists. She printed many of their newsletters and papers, sometimes adding her own editorial touches to the work. It was through typesetting for these political groups that she learned more about specific activist organisations in the city, and developed an even deeper interest in politics. She also got to know some of the leaders of the various groups very well.

Of all of the political activity going on in Ireland at the time, the two biggest injustices as McMahon saw them were discrimination against women and discrimination against the minority population in Northern Ireland. She describes herself as a feminist-Republican. "I'd say women were the closest thing to my heart, but I grew to be equally involved in the issues of Republicanism," she says. Differing attitudes to the emerging Troubles in the North were to make it a divisive issue in later women's groups, and although some of the IWLM members had very strong views on the armed struggle, the Northern question never posed a serious threat to the stability of the group. There existed an unspoken understanding between members that the North was not a topic open for discussion at meetings, and in any case the founders had enough on their agenda to fill their Monday night sessions without introducing such a potentially incendiary issue. Still, McMahon had joined the People's Democracy, a student-based civil rights group that began at Queen's University Belfast, and she often marched with them. Mary Maher had written an article on People's Democracy late in 1968, and some of her observations about the difficulties that the group's lack of structure created among its members could easily have applied to the IWLM three years later:

> People's Democracy is an amorphous body without constitution
> or membership . . . where the structure is so fluid that inevitable
> problems have already caused crises. The meetings observe a
> scant minimum of parliamentary order, with a chairman, anyone
> can come, anyone can speak, and everyone can vote. Not all of
> those who vote in favour of marches actually march themselves,
> which causes criticism from the left. Criticism from the right
> wing tends to argue that the more naïve and idealistic students are
> being manipulated by "outside" interests . . . [2]

McMahon was used to the excitement and spontaneity that being in such
a group allowed and, like the rest of the IWLM founders who were immersed in different left-wing causes, she saw no problem in running the
IWLM the same way. But the IWLM was soon to discover that the
harder it tried to remain structureless and leaderless in the name of democracy, equality, and throwing off the patriarchal mantle of organisation, the harder it was getting to reach a consensus and ultimately hold
itself together.

   McMahon wasn't one of the original five present at the Bewley's
meeting in the summer of 1970, but she was one of the wider circle of
about a dozen or so founders who started meeting very soon thereafter in
Mary Maher's house and Mary Kenny's flat McMahon struck up a strong,
instant friendship at Gaj's with Fionnuala O'Connor, an out-of-work
teacher waitressing at the restaurant. O'Connor is now an *Irish Times*
journalist who has written extensively about the North. McMahon and
O'Connor went along to some of those first meetings together. Others in
the group remember McMahon as simultaneously enthusiastic and quiet.

   "It was because I was trying to concentrate on what certain words or
expressions meant," McMahon says. "I learned a lifetime education in
those months." Like Johnston, McMahon struggled with some of her
own feelings of inadequacy at those first meetings because of her lack of
a formal education. McMahon knew she was in the presence of some
extremely articulate, confident women who worked in the media and as
political organisers and were more accustomed to speaking in front of
groups. But those who used her typesetting services comment on her
ability to catch errors of fact, grammar and punctuation that other experienced editors had missed. There is evidence that McMahon gave herself

considerably less credit than she deserved. Nonetheless, she built her own confidence through her membership in the IWLM, and was always one of the first in favour of extreme action and going as far as possible in terms of direct action strategies. "Nothing was too extreme; I mean, we were a raging inferno," McMahon says. "Once the flame was lit, it was just petrol going onto it all the time."

McMahon's initial sense of women's wrongs sprang from watching her own mother's struggle to raise a family alone with virtually no help from the state, but her grasp of the injustices Irish women endured came more sharply into focus as she grew up and became involved with other human rights and radical political groups throughout the sixties and seventies. Like the other IWLM women, she felt that equal pay and contraception were two of the biggest women's issues of 1970. Even at the typesetter's, before she was able to become a partner in the business, she had been paid less than the men doing the same work, so she knew unequal pay didn't just exist in the shops and factories. But she also talks about the everyday injustices that would wear her down and make her boil and fume at the same time – the types of things that weren't included in *Chains or Change*.

"There were things like they wouldn't serve you a pint in a pub; they would only serve you a glass. And women didn't have the same money as men, and a glass wasn't half the price of a pint, it was a lot more than half the price of a pint," she says. The list was endless, from not being called to jury service, to not being allowed to leave the country without a husband's signature on her passport, to not being able to rent an appliance without the same such signature. When the IWLM started meeting at Gaj's and McMahon was finally able, along with the other women, to find an outlet for the expression of her anger through the consciousness-raising sessions, it was a tremendous relief. But like the other IWLM women who had strong backgrounds in politics and links to many other activist groups, she had other commitments during the IWLM's short existence that required a lot of her energy. Feminism and Republicanism were always the two causes closest to McMahon's heart, but she was also passionate about doing her part to help end the Vietnam War, the issue that put her behind bars with Máirín de Burca at Mountjoy prison. And although the IWLM founders avoided political debates centring on issues like the North, it is obvious that the split in political ideologies was often lurking in the background when the group created its charter and planned protests. Politics ended up being a divisive factor within the group. Ironically, without the skills of some of the most politically experienced women like de Burca, Johnston, Woods and McMahon, the IWLM could not have organised its most effective protests as well as it had. The cost of the IWLM's ability to be effective in the short term was its inability to function in the long term.

McMahon was practically a full-time political activist throughout the seventies, and the depth of her commitment to different causes was not without cost. The final incident that crushed McMahon's spirit, and signalled to her that it was time to curtail her activism, was being arrested and brought to a Garda station under a bogus charge of prostitution in the summer of 1978. McMahon had been at Gaj's late one night with Lyn Madden, the Dublin prostitute who was a good friend of both McMahon's and Gaj's. Madden was on her way to work for the night down near the canals in Dublin's southside, and McMahon walked with her on her way home. Madden had reason to fear her husband, a violent man from whom she was separated, and as the two neared the canals, some of the other prostitutes told Madden they had seen his car in the area earlier that night. McMahon decided to stay with Madden for a little while to make sure she was safe, and the Gardaí on patrol arrested her for prostitution while ignoring Madden and the rest of the prostitutes along the canal. Mrs Gaj came to the Garda station to identify McMahon, but she ended up being formally charged with prostitution. McMahon believed it was simply a case of the Gardaí wanting to teach her a lesson; they knew her well from her previous arrests and court appearances related to political protesting, and they knew she was no prostitute.

"Believe it or not, of all the incidents and of all the things that ever happened to me in politics, that's the thing that had the most profound effect on me," McMahon says of the arrest. McMahon was convinced that the Gardaí were trying to blacken her name because of her involvement as a researcher in the production of an RTÉ radio programme with Pat Kenny, *Day by Day*. The programme in question dealt with prostitution, and one of the prostitutes had named a specific guard whose treatment of the prostitutes at the canal had allegedly bordered on assault.

Ever since then, McMahon claimed, the Gardaí had been out to get her. To McMahon, her arrest during the summer of 1978 along the canals seemed to prove her correct.

At least with the other times she had been arrested, the Gardaí had actually had legitimate reasons – as with the smashing of the bottles of cow's blood and the burning of the American flag at the US Embassy during the 1971 Vietnam protest. McMahon admits that it had been fair of the Gardaí to arrest her and de Burca on that occasion because they had both been perfectly guilty. But the arrest in 1978 was different – it was obviously symbolic, and it was obviously personal. The publicity of the arrest and the subsequent hearing also ended up being very damaging to McMahon in both her personal and professional life. At the time of the arrest, McMahon was subletting her typesetting office, and the land-lord insisted upon her eviction. He genuinely believed the publicity and assumed she was a prostitute, and he didn't want that kind of woman in his building, in spite of the fact that McMahon's business was flourish-ing at the time.

McMahon had also just moved into the first house she had bought, and none of the neighbours really knew her yet. Her address was printed in the paper and she heard of a petition being circulated around the neighbourhood to put her out of the house. The third thing McMahon lived in fear of was her mother's discovery of the scandal. As she re-members it, her mother did not find out right away, because there was a gap of several months between when the story of her arrest first appeared in the paper and the beginning of her trial. When the trial finally was set, McMahon was moved to tears at the sight of the people both outside and inside the courtroom who had come out to support her. Her fellow IWLM founder and great friend, Fionnuala O'Connor, took the train from Belfast to come to the trial. Other IWLM women like Dr Eimer Philbin Bowman, Máirín de Burca and Máirín Johnston also signed a petition protesting McMahon's prosecution. Other signatories read like a who's who of respectable public servants at the time, with the TDs Ruairi Quinn, Michael O'Leary, Dr John O'Connell, John Horgan, and Senator Gemma Hussey adding their names to the petition. McMahon's close friend and feminist colleague Róisín Conroy was instrumental in organising the women outside the court. Many other Irish women seemed to view the case as symbolic of the Gardaí's chauvinistic attitude toward women, and a symbol of the vulnerability of Irish women to arrest under false pretences. It was just another example of the discrimination women had to endure.

Even the judge, McMahon remembers, was looking for an excuse to dismiss the case. Nell McCafferty was there, and McMahon recalls her standing up in court and saying that if McMahon went to jail that day, she and all the supporters in the courtroom were going with her. The pregnant Fionnuala O'Connor added her voice to that promise as well. The judge found his reason to dismiss the case fairly quickly. When the garda who arrested McMahon was on the stand, the judge asked if he had told McMahon why he was arresting her as he was doing so. The garda said no. The judge asked why, and the garda replied that she had been too aggressive. The judge immediately dismissed the case.

The media generally hailed the outcome of McMahon's case as a victory for women. Máirín De Burca wrote an article of her own about the case for the magazine for which she was a staff member at the time, *Hibernia*. De Burca's article betrayed some of her own old dissatisfactions with the Gardaí, who had not followed proper police procedures when they arrested McMahon. "This is a nasty little tale," de Burca wrote. "The Gardaí come out of it with less than honour or decency. The lesson for all women is simple and is the time-worn message they have received from men throughout the ages: 'keep to your place, and your place is where we say it is'".[3]

As traumatic as the case was for McMahon, and despite all the disruptions it caused in her life, she was gratified and bolstered by all the support she received during the ordeal. Once the same neighbours who had tried to run her out of her new home had a chance to get to know her, they ended up as some of her closest friends. By the early eighties, when her son Tommy was born, everyone on the street was thrilled to have a new baby about. But none of the positive events subsequent to the dismissal of her case really lessened the stresses that the whole ordeal had placed on her. McMahon thinks of the case as the beginning of the end of her work in politics. She recognises her feelings now for what they were – the first signs of burnout from nearly a decade of fighting injustice on the front lines.

McMahon's work as a feminist and political activist throughout the sixties and seventies was dominated by risk and sacrifice, but she also realises how being a member of the IWLM helped her as a person. The consciousness-raising sessions and the creation of *Chains or Change* had both made her aware that the oppression she had experienced all her life, and that she had grown up watching her mother experience, was not women's fault but a product of deep flaws in society that perpetuated discrimination against women. Being part of a group of women who were confident of that fact in turn gave McMahon confidence in the fight for equality that she never knew she had in her, a confidence that over-flowed to all of her political activities. Whatever differences of opinion she had with her fellow IWLM founders, some of which ran ideologi-cally deep, she is grateful and extremely proud to have been part of the group that was responsible for initiating so many wonderful "firsts" for women in Ireland. And like Frank Crummey, McMahon saw herself as indebted to the friends she had made at all of the meetings at Gaj's. As many of them had demonstrated during her prostitution trial in 1978, they would always be there, supporting, picketing, and demonstrating in solidarity and genuine outrage at the injustice she was suffering. In her own personal life, that was the most important legacy of her involvement in politics and the IWLM – the fact that she knew she'd never really be out there on her own, no matter what obstacles she encountered.

There was at least one IWLM founder for whom the bonds that were forged during those meetings at Gaj's proved less strong. She was one of the most visible and vocal of the founders during the group's existence, publicly reversing her position years later on many of the issues she had written and talked about during the early seventies. Although most of the hard feelings that existed between the founders in the aftermath of the group's disintegration have ebbed in the thirty-five years since, Mary Kenny's story continues to puzzle the women with whom she fought so forcefully for liberation, seemingly in a different lifetime.

8

Hats and Hotpants

"I was in general very rebellious, and so therefore I was the sort of person who would have been looking for a cause of rebellion in any case." — Mary Kenny

Thirty-six years after the IWLM's first meeting, many of the founders remember exactly the same outfit that Mary Kenny wore to one of the meetings – green satin hotpants. She might have worn the hotpants at one of the earliest meetings that summer of 1970, possibly the one she hosted in her own flat right before the IWLM founders moved their group permanently to Gaj's. Everyone was used to Kenny showing up in outrageous clothes to match her outrageous personality, but on this particular day she was also smoking a long-stemmed velvet pipe, which only added to the picture. She also favoured hats with long feathers, although on the day in question the memory of her hotpants seems to have eclipsed everything else about her appearance. In some ways, Kenny's vivaciousness was a fun diversion; they never knew what they were going to see when she walked into the room. Her energy was electric and impossible to contain. But when it came to the question of handling the IWLM's image in the media and how the majority of Irish women would perceive the group, Kenny's flamboyance and unpredictability caused tension between group members. In a group that was supposed to be leaderless, she also attracted criticism for posing, intentionally or unintentionally, as a leader.

Kenny was born in Dublin in 1944. Her two brothers and one sister were much older than she, the closest in age being eleven years older than

Mary. After her father's death when Mary was five years old, she went to live with an aunt for the summer and ended up staying seven years. In her latest book, Kenny wrote that while she "thinks of herself as thoroughly Irish", she spent a great deal of her childhood with her aunt who had an Irish Protestant background and that some of the attitudes of the Irish Protestant ascendancy formed part of her early influences.[1] She attended convent school in Dublin until she was 16, when she was expelled for bad behaviour and inattention. In some of her earliest freelance writing in Dublin, for the magazine *Irishwoman's Journal*, which June Levine edited for a year, Kenny elaborated on the experience. She wrote about what happened in the school when she had fallen ill for almost an entire term:

> Suddenly, where girls had constantly disobeyed rules before, they now constantly obeyed them. All at once, where chaotic history classes presided over only by gales of laughter and giggles had been the norm, now they were a model of Prussian order. Imperceptibly, the atmosphere of the convent changed overnight from a seedbed of revolution to a bower of perfect calm. And then the establishment knew it! *That* perfectly dreadful girl was away. From then on, my days were numbered . . . "You are the bad apple which rots the whole barrel," Mother Superior denounced me. "The root of all evil." What an indictment! No wonder I am admired.[2]

Even at such a young age, Kenny seemed to already have possessed the charisma that attracted others to her and her ideas. Although her influence in the convent school was self-admittedly a disorderly one, she was already a leader among her peers. In the same piece, Kenny recalled her brother's consolation upon her expulsion that she shouldn't worry about it because it would be "good for the autobiography". He was partially right; Kenny was making good fodder of the experience, at least, for a short magazine article. She got over what must have been the considerable shock and embarrassment of expulsion quickly enough, and finished her piece by "thanking" the nuns who expelled her:

> They teach you humbleness when what you need is confidence; passive resignation when what you need is the ability to fight and lobby for your rights; "ladylike" attitudes when you need fundamental womanly courage and realism; conservative acceptance of

all orthodox intellectual views when you need boldness of mind
and intellectual muscle. And an attitude to sex which, the world
over, is recognised as turning girls either into nymphomaniacs or
frigid neurotics. Maybe I'm too hard on them. After all, by expel-
ling me, they did save me from this awful end – they admitted
they hadn't tamed me.[3]

Kenny acknowledges a strong rebellious streak as one of the defining features of her personality from an early age. "If there's a sign saying no
smoking, my basic instinct is to take out a cigarette," Kenny says today.
"And I don't smoke, actually. But just because I won't be told." After her
expulsion, she lived in France for two years as an *au pair*, where she wrote
some freelance articles and began to exhibit some of the determination and
commitment to reporting that would define her later career. When public
transport shut down during the student protests in Paris in 1968, Kenny
cycled around town doing interviews in order to complete her story. The
young troublemaker from Dublin was beginning to find her niche and develop her talent as a journalist abroad, barely out of her teens.

With a small collection of cuttings and a yearning for something different, Kenny applied for a job at London's *Evening Standard*. The editor
asked her for one good reason why he should hire her, and Kenny said,
"You'll never know what you missed if you don't." It was with this pro-
jection of confidence that Kenny went about her work in London from
1964 through 1969, when she returned to Ireland to begin editing the *Irish
Press* women's page. The idea of essentially working for herself was very
appealing to Kenny, and she would have much more control over the stories published in the paper. The *Irish Press*'s women's page would come
to bear the unmistakable stamp of Kenny's irreverence and her preference
for controversial topics. One senses when reading through the pages she
edited during her two years or so at the *Press* that the worst criticism she
could imagine anyone levelling at her page was that it was uninteresting.

Kenny returned to an Ireland that was ripe for change, and she arrived just in time to play her part in it. So many political movements
were gaining momentum in 1969, spurred on by the music of the Beatles
and the Rolling Stones in Britain and America and the Dubliners and
other balladeers in Ireland. Kenny had witnessed the energy of the
women's liberation movement in America on visits to her sister Ursula

who lived in New York City, and the young journalist was ready to take on the old order and help usher in the new as soon as possible. Kenny loved the collegial atmosphere that the staffs of the three women's pages enjoyed, and drinking at the Pearl Bar with the other journalists was one of her favourite pastimes. There was one night of drinking and conversation when Maeve Binchy got a graphic glimpse of the fragility of Kenny's bravado. Kenny had taken to smoking pipes, and not just any pipes – the most brightly coloured, long-stemmed, noticeable pipes she could find. After smoking one such pipe successfully, Kenny was getting awfully sick in the toilet as an amused Binchy looked on. Considering how preoccupied she was with image, Kenny probably would have been beyond mortified if anyone else had discovered her there.

"Taming" Kenny was a feat many tried and failed, certainly her family and her employer at the *Irish Press*, editor Tim Pat Coogan, among them. It was no secret that Coogan was an admirer of his *Irish Times* counterpart Douglas Gageby. Coogan had worked under Gageby when Gageby had edited the *Evening Press*. Comparing the patterns in coverage of the two papers under the editorship of both men, it is obvious that Coogan emulated some of Gageby's ideas, appointing specialist correspondents when Gageby did, making similar changes in layout, and, of course, starting a women's page soon after the *Times*. As Mary Maher points out today, the relationships between the newspaper editors and the structure of the Irish newspaper industry itself in the early seventies had more to do with the IWLM's advancement and the general growth of women's liberation than people often realise. Journalist Risteard O'Muirithille summarised Kenny's own effect on the *Press* in a 1983 *Magill* piece, long after Kenny had left the paper:

> Kenny made waves. She made them fast and she made them deep. With her hair dyed blonde, she wore hotpants to work, and sometimes she wore mini-skirts right up to here. She smoked a pipe and engaged near-celibate journalists in conversations that made them blush. She tried all the kicks of the sixties. One day, in a restaurant, she announced in a loud voice, "What I would really like to do is screw a priest." Those were heady days in the *Irish Press*, and Kenny was responsible for much of the head. For this was the end of the sixties in Ireland, and people were toying

with the possibility of letting it all hang out, but of course in a restrained Irish way. Mary Kenny let more hang out than most, certainly more than Coogan wished to see.[4]

O'Muirithille argued that Coogan himself had some of the same characteristics as Kenny, comparing Coogan to an unruly boy scout with a "need to
disrupt". When the boy scout met the expelled convent school girl, there
was friction. Still, if Coogan was trying to match the *Irish Times*'s spirit of
liberalism, Kenny could certainly help him do it with her writing. The friction that erupted between Kenny and Coogan could have been the simple
result of Coogan realising a little too late that Kenny was virtually impossible to restrain. Maybe they shared too many of the same qualities. Kenny
rarely worried that Coogan would really fire her; she knew as well as he
did that her women's page was selling far too many newspapers. But there
were occasions when she was called into his office over some story or another that had gone too far, or had at least caused a considerable stir. One
in particular was a story Rosita Sweetman had written that merely mentioned the subject of female masturbation. "I was called over to have sort
of a discussion in his Mussolini-type office," Kenny says. "You know, the
whole thing about the Mussolini structure was that everything was big in
order to make the human being feel small. And the poor man, I talked with
him for an hour and a half and he couldn't bring himself to mention that
article. He could not bring himself to do so," Kenny says, amused.

The other interesting facet of Kenny's work for the *Press* was the incredible freedom Coogan gave her to print what she wanted. As she remembers it, there was a period where no senior editors scanned her
pages before they went to press, so that they read her page for the first
time along with the public. That seems like a huge amount of trust for
the editors to place in someone whom they had reason to be so wary of.
For as long as Kenny was at the *Press*, Coogan probably always struggled with the extra revenue that her page was bringing in and the stress
of wondering if her next story really was going to enrage readers enough
so they would stop buying the paper in protest.

It was through journalism that Kenny met Mary Maher, Nell McCafferty, June Levine, and the other founders of the IWLM. When Maher and
de Burca began recruiting women for a women's rights activist group,
Kenny knew she had to be involved. It was probably just what she had

been waiting for in Ireland – she'd certainly published enough pieces about the women's liberation movements abroad, as well as many of the issues that ended up in *Chains or Change*, including equal pay, unmarried mothers and education. She was clipping along at a frenetic pace between her editing of the *Press*'s women's page, the protests and demonstrations, and her wild social life. She claims that she honestly cannot remember many specific details about her years at the *Press* and with the IWLM because she drank very heavily at the time. Mavis Arnold, who wrote for Kenny at the *Press* in the early seventies on consumer affairs, remembers that Kenny used to say she edited the women's page "in between pickets".

While each of the IWLM founders who edited women's pages did so with their own unique voices, Kenny's page was the most heavily infused with her own personality. She is the first to admit to having a healthy ego, which she didn't mind expressing in various ways in the "Women's Press" page. She even went so far as to have different staff members interview both herself and her mother for feature articles – one entitled "Mary – The Militant Feminist" and the other, "Meeting Mary's Mammy: June Levine talks to Mary Kenny's mother to find out what it's like having a problem daughter".[5] In her own interview, Kenny told reporter Clare Boylan:

> I want to change the world. I want to do a multitude of things – to provide a sort of service for my readers. One hopes to help them, amuse, inform, and to broaden their horizons. Basically one wants to provide a forum . . . just take, for example, all those women who don't believe in equal rights for women. They are living in a cultural ghetto. They have been conditioned as surely as any black man who defers to white supremacy. It takes a long, long time to change things and even if one doesn't succeed, one can pave the way for someone who eventually will.[6]

In the same interview, Kenny said that one of the regrets of her life is that she missed out on university and that she has always felt slightly inadequate without a formal education. Although, economically, she was from a much more middle-class background than Máirín Johnston, Máirín de Burca, or Marie McMahon, this was something Kenny had in common with those IWLM founders. It was also something she remedied in the 1990s, when she received her degree in French Studies from Birkbeck College, London University, as a mature student.

There were many other instances of Kenny placing her distinctive mark on her own page – there is the story she ran with no less than ten photos of herself posing in different hats for a feature about hat designer Pauline D'Alton. "I suppose it's very immodest of me to publish all these pictures of myself wearing Pauline's hats, but honest, there wasn't another model available," Kenny wrote.[7] One senses that her readers would forgive Kenny her immodesty because her sense of humour was often so delightful. In another story titled "One Girl All Alone on the Town",[8] Kenny wrote about the best places for a single girl to go out, making sure to mention the city's first drag queen, "Mr Pussy", who was then performing at the Baggot Inn. She also exhibited the wonderfully apt comic wit which so many of her colleagues in the women's movement shared; the same women whom critics of the movement claimed were so dour, serious and humourless. "At Shelbourne Bar they charge half price for women, which I consider to be a monstrous piece of discrimination that I am prepared to put up with," Kenny wrote.[9]

There was, of course, a more serious side to Kenny's women's page. She used her page to guide her readers through the activities of the women's liberation movement, at all times inviting them to get involved in any way they wished. She wrote about what she saw as the advances in Irish journalism and the role women played in it, as well as the changing nature of the women's page itself:

> The days of the women's page or magazine programme devoted exclusively to knitting patterns and recipes have gone. Problems of sex and marriage, politics and education, religion and social reform are now the dominant themes. The reports of women's page editors often have an accuracy and depth which is lacking in the report and comment in general newspaper or broadcasting coverage.[10]

Kenny ended that article by quoting Senator Neville Keery's recent speech to the Dun Laoghaire branch of the Irish Housewives' Association in which he called women journalists "the real radicals of journalism". Perhaps in response to criticism that she and the other women's page editors were using the newspapers too heavily to promote their own agenda, Kenny ran another piece soon after debating whether journalists should be active in politics:

Caught up in a maelstrom of public affairs, and perhaps frenzied by the heightened atmosphere which television cameras have lent to these events, the younger school of journalists feel it increasingly incumbent upon themselves to be "involved" in such important and moral affairs as public housing, local government, party politics and moneylending. They focus passionately and very often consequently much more effectively on the evils that they see around them. It is one of the reasons why so much of what you see and read today is so much more convincing and effecting than formerly, because it is written and broadcast by a newer, younger school of journalists who are dedicated much more to moral commitment than to the old-fashioned objectivity. In fact they have shunned "objectivity" as the most despicable, opting-out abstraction of all.[11]

Kenny here articulated Maher's shared belief that on their women's pages, which essentially were features, and not hard news pages, they were allowed to be as opinionated as they wished. In the same article, Kenny wrote that the day she joins a political party would be the day she resigns from journalism. To be fair, she wrote the article about six months before becoming a founder member of the IWLM, but that doesn't change the fact that although the IWLM was not an established, political party, it was undeniably a political organisation. Obviously, Kenny perceived the IWLM as being somehow outside the definition of a political activist group – either that, or her vow to resign from journalism upon joining a political party was either forgotten or never seriously contemplated. Kenny was not the only IWLM founder who did not look at the group as a political entity, though – June Levine wrote about how Máirín de Burca helped her see the political dimensions to the IWLM's work one night at Gaj's:

"They think you are getting us involved in politics and revolution, Máirín," I said to Máirín de Burca, the Sinn Féin activist, one night.

"They'd be right," said Máirín, "we *are* involved in politics. We're trying to change the things that affect people's lives, that's as political and revolutionary as you can get. What else do you think we're at?"[12]

Since the IWLM founders had consciously chosen *not* to model their group on any existing organisation, men's or women's, the difficulty some of them experienced in defining for themselves exactly what kind of a group they had helped create is understandable. They hadn't wanted to elect chairpersons; that would have been copying the patriarchal structures of male organisations. The only person who had a designated, fixed task was Margaret Gaj as the treasurer. Everyone else had the opportunity to do any and all of the other work – designing flyers for protests, researching and writing articles for *Chains or Change*, public speaking about the group's goals and any of the other necessary tasks. All the women, in theory, were given equal time to speak at the meetings, although many of the women as individuals were so boisterous that one can imagine the voices of the few quieter ones being drowned out. The drawback of this system of running the meetings was the ensuing chaos. In hindsight, Máirín de Burca can see that one of the biggest reasons for dissent within the group was the fact that, unlike established political organisations, the IWLM lacked a set platform of ideas and goals upon its creation. The founders literally didn't know, at least not specifically, what they were signing themselves up for when they started meeting – they worked out their goals and aims *as* they began their group, not before. So it was no surprise that some of them were dissatisfied with some of the decisions made. The advantage to this system, though, was the free emergence of spontaneous and original ideas that would not have been possible in a more structured group, even if it sometimes caused more disagreements than were usual in more established political organisations.

Similar to Kenny's and Levine's inability, at least at first, to see the IWLM as a political entity when most of the public probably saw it as just that, the founders were also finding it difficult to convince people that the IWLM was a "leaderless" group. Again, no one was assigned the task of public relations representative, but as the group gained more and more recognition (mostly of its own making, through the founders' own women's pages) that task had to be taken on. Taken on it was, and primarily by Mary Kenny. There's evidence that although Kenny was never a woman who shied away from attention, her public image grew out of her own control at times. Today, she claims she never intentionally sought out the spotlight or wished, at any time, to be labelled as a leader of the women's liberation movement.

And yet, there were other visible and media-wise women in the IWLM who did not receive nearly the attention that Kenny did. Kenny had already been a media force unto herself before the IWLM even began. It is not surprising, then, that whether she asked for it or not, she was perceived as a, if not *the*, central organising figure within the movement. RTÉ rang her in October 1970 to ask her about the official line in the women's liberation movement about the mid-length skirt that was gaining popularity that year. "Now, Women's Lib is not the Communist Party; there is no centrally-decided doctrinaire official line, and it would all depend on what point on the spectrum of Lib that you find yourself at . . ." she wrote.[13] For all that she repeated such statements, the fact remained that RTÉ was not ringing Máirín de Burca in her Sinn Féin office to ask her about the official position of women's liberation on anything, and de Burca had been much more instrumental in the IWLM's creation than Kenny had.

Later the next year, when the IWLM was in full swing, Kenny published an interview with David Andrews, then parliamentary secretary to the Taoiseach. Andrews accused Kenny of both leading and abusing the women's liberation movement in an "unscrupulous attack upon both the government and the system of society as we know it". He said Kenny abused her position as a journalist and used her position in the women's movement to publicise herself, finally stating, "I have no argument with you or with Women's Lib. I have an argument with you as a leader of Women's Lib," to which Kenny replied, "We have no leaders. I am an active member, like anyone else, but I am not a leader . . ."[14] But neither Mary Maher at *The Irish Times*, Mary McCutchan at the *Independent*, nor any of the other IWLM founders, journalists or not, had been the subject of similar accusations. Máirín de Burca knew that a group's most deviant members were also the most vulnerable to criticism. "If you want to denigrate an organisation, you go for its wackiest members, don't you?" de Burca says. "And I think she [Kenny] was used for that purpose without at all wanting to be, because of the way she was."

Looking back on her conduct in the women's movement today, Kenny acknowledges that some of Andrews's criticisms hit the mark. She admits that her flaunting of convention in such a public way was due more to her interest in advancing her career than the actual strength of her convictions. "I feel a bit phony about that," Kenny says. "I feel it was sort of an ego trip and it was another way of showing off." What most people who remember her from the sixties and seventies wonder the most about Kenny now is how she could have changed her views and ideology so extremely from then to the present time. Many of those who had seen Kenny as one of the most prominent pioneers of women's liberation were confused and angry when, later in her career, she began to recant much of what she had said and written during the movement's most exciting days.

As the seventies wore on, Kenny married English journalist Richard West and moved to England where her two children were born. Gradually but steadily, her writing changed until it became utterly unrecognisable as that of the same *Irish Press* women's page editor who in 1971 had stood up with Máirín Johnston and walked out in protest of the church's stance against contraception at the Haddington Road church, or who had led the women in protest against the ban on contraceptives by singing "We Shall Not Conceive" to the tune of "We Shall Overcome" outside the Dáil the same year. She repented the actions of her younger, wild days, and publicly praised the virtues of Christianity. As June Levine wrote in her memoir, many of those back in Ireland who had known Kenny in her women's lib days were disgusted with the self-righteousness and religious fervour that now defined her work. For those women who had looked to Kenny as a leader in the fight for women's equality, as well as for her fellow IWLM founders, there was more than a little resentment, and a sense that Kenny had betrayed them. Kenny felt that resentment very acutely upon her return visits to Ireland as the seventies drew to a close when some of her old newspaper colleagues wouldn't even speak to her.[15]

One only needs to compare Kenny's speeches and writing in the *Press* from the early seventies with just about any one of her columns today to understand the extent of her transformation. An April 1971 *Irish Press* article titled "Women's Lib – Its Crisis", which recaps the main points of a speech by Kenny in Buswell's Hotel, quotes her: "What Women's Lib wanted in fact was a total redefinition of sex roles; an end to stereotyping and a more creative approach to work, marriage and living." Her speech went on to criticise the capitalist system as one of the main reasons for women's oppression – an idea with which Dr Moira

Woods and Máirín Johnston wholeheartedly agreed – and suggesting that traditional capitalism had to change in order for women's situations to really improve. The economy was only interested in the productivity of every worker; women did not count as things were because they didn't produce anything worth money. In a socialist society, she said, raising children would be accorded the dignity in real terms that it merited.[16]

In May 2004, in the *Irish Independent*, Kenny's view of capitalism and its effects on women could not be more different: "Build a business. Make money. Make profits, indeed. Create employment. Enhance prosperity. This is what capitalism does. And by the way, it most particularly improves life for women."[17] Marie McMahon acknowledges that people mellow as years pass, and no one should be crucified for changing her mind. However, she feels that changing your mind and changing your whole framework of political beliefs, as she believes Kenny has done, are two different things. Like most experienced journalists, Kenny is skilful at avoiding questions she would rather not answer. When pressed for an explanation on her turnaround, she says simply that one can't go on being a rebel forever and that everyone changes as they age; she just changed more quickly than most. She makes a clear distinction between two categories of people who provoke change, based on Sartre's writings – the "revolutionary" and the "*revolté*". The true revolutionary wants to take power away from those who have it, acquire it for himself, and begin with a new system, Kenny says. The *revolté*, however, wants to keep rebelling against the prevailing power, but does not seek to take the power himself. Kenny classifies herself as the latter, and again, she attributes her attitude to her innate sense of contra-suggestiveness. There's no need, in her view, to challenge the Catholic Church any more in the same forceful way because it no longer possesses the great influence and power it had in the seventies. Kenny's fellow IWLM founder and journalist Nell McCafferty is surprised at Kenny's own explanation of rebelliousness for the seismic changes in her mentality. "Well Jesus, I thought she found God," McCafferty says dryly. McCafferty insists that if you really look at Kenny's writing carefully, she has actually remained more consistent with her youthful views than people have given her credit for.

While some of Kenny's fellow IWLM founders acknowledge, like McMahon, that people change as they age, they can't quite reconcile their memories of the old Mary with the new, or fully understand the reasons for her transformation. But then, Kenny herself isn't quite able – or willing – to explain those reasons either. Regardless of how she's changed, though, the IWLM women all remember her in those days with a degree of fondness, and perhaps a stronger degree of exasperation. Some of her logic now about the issues the IWLM concentrated on – chiefly contraception – seems a bit flawed. Kenny says that when she gets together with old friends they always talk about grandchildren, and that so many of the women who campaigned for contraception are now eager to have grandchildren. "I'm not saying it's necessarily a contradiction, but if we had all practised this contraception we were all on about, I suppose none of us would have grandchildren at all," she says. Her phrasing is eerily reminiscent of the comment that had so enraged Marie McMahon coming from a fellow (male) political activist about contraception during the women's movement. Hadn't Kenny been the most vocal one of all the IWLM founders in trying to change minds like his?

Kenny looks back on her own involvement in the IWLM as something of a paradox. The group had an "admirably good programme" and she's proud to have been a part of it, but she has very mixed feelings about her own conduct. Even with all the tension Kenny created within the group, Mary Maher says that the IWLM would have been a very boring gathering of women without characters like Kenny. "I suppose we did set out to shock in a way," Kenny says. "That was part of the fun of it, you know."

Whatever Kenny's motivations were during the seven months that the IWLM founders were doing the bulk of their work, it somehow seems a little less important now *why* she was there than the fact that she simply *was* there. She was criticised at the time and subsequently for her irreverence, impetuousness, flamboyance, egotism and sometimes even arrogance. But within the context of the IWLM, where cooler heads usually prevailed, it seems in hindsight as if Kenny fulfilled the exact purpose in the women's liberation movement that she needed to in order to help the movement continue. The IWLM was primarily a stepping stone in the larger Irish women's movement; the initial group that exhibited a new willingness – and fearlessness – to challenge the status quo. The supreme confidence and courage that the IWLM founders projected without the merest hint of apology is what Irish women and men remember them best for. It was this legacy of the IWLM's strength that eventually helped bring forth the many subsequent pressure and lobbying groups and women's organisations of the seventies and later.

Even if Kenny today remembers feeling fear, apprehension or embarrassment during her time with the IWLM, others remember only her enthusiasm for change. She was not a leader of the group in the sense that her influence contributed to its stability and cohesion – in fact, her conduct most often had quite the opposite effect. But she did "lead" the group in the sense that her own willingness to push the old boundaries of good taste and acceptable behaviour further than almost anyone else ended up as one of the IWLM's defining and enduring characteristics. In that sense, even if Kenny herself is a bit uncomfortable with it, her own legacy is linked with that of the IWLM and the beginning of the most remarkable era of improvement for Irish women in modern times.

When Kenny walked into a Monday night meeting at Gaj's in February 1971 and breezily announced that the group had been offered the chance to appear on the enormously popular *Late Late Show* with Gay Byrne, she was met with mixed reactions ranging from anger to excitement to no small amount of fear. Like a lot of moments from those years and from her time with the IWLM, Kenny claims she has no memory of orchestrating the media event that was to become the single most important night in the life of the young movement. That's not how most of the other women remember it, though – it was almost certainly Kenny's idea to tell Ireland about themselves via RTÉ's universally viewed Saturday night chat show, and who but Kenny could really have arranged such a thing? Another debate was about to begin within the group, this time over how to handle outside media coverage to its best possible advantage. The matter of *The Late Late Show* also highlighted the gap between the public's perception of Kenny's role in the IWLM and her actual one. One imagines it is very likely that Máirín Johnston's initial reaction to Kenny's announcement that night in 1971 was similar to her reaction today when she is asked about Kenny's influence on the group.

"Mary Kenny, God help us." It's unclear whether there's more exasperation or amusement in that "God help us," as she throws her eyes skyward, but then, Johnston probably doesn't really know herself.

Showtime

"*The Late Late Show* rose around 1963 when life was never better and the still water of Irish life was crying out for a good stir . . . nobody ever turned *The Late Late Show* off. The show was too unpredictable: you just never knew what you might miss. The show was too central: topics too close to viewers' lives were being discussed or people were being introduced whom everyone had always wanted to have a good look at . . ." — Colm Tóibín[1]

Shortly after the IWLM began meeting at Gaj's in late 1970, Máirín de Burca and Mary Maher started to wonder how it would be best to introduce the group to the public. They knew that they could print what they liked on the women's pages of the three national newspapers, but it was the other media outlets over which they had less control that were worrying. They had studied the American women's liberation movement and they knew how demonstrations organised by women could be falsely portrayed or blown out of proportion, with reporters focusing on women's militancy rather than on their messages. They also knew that in Ireland, where the divide between rural and urban women ran very deep, they had to be especially careful in the way they presented themselves. The IWLM ran the risk of appearing as a godless group of young city women who wore miniskirts and smoked and drank too much – not exactly the types of people everyone's mother could accept easily, much less listen to. There was always the danger of the IWLM's image eclipsing its message. A few individual group members only exacerbated that

problem with their personal conduct. It was a dilemma that was to plague
the IWLM from its creation to its disintegration.

Máirín de Burca and Mary Maher, for their parts, felt that it would be
best to wait one year or so from the IWLM's first meetings for the group
to really "go public" – begin opening meetings to the general public, advertise for more women to join, and perhaps plan more group publications and larger protests. Judging by de Burca's protesting record and the
number of causes with which she was so involved, one would think the
world couldn't change quickly enough for her. She was obviously willing
to break the law and risk a jail sentence if she believed in anything passionately. But as one of the IWLM members with the most political experience, she was also acutely aware of one singularly important aspect of
social change. She knew that even if you felt you were paving the way for
a lot of necessary changes, you had to find a way to convince as many
other people as possible, wholeheartedly, that those changes were needed.

"We were a rural society to a great degree at the time, but a lot of very,
very conservative rural women still felt hard done by," de Burca says.
"And there was no point in racing ahead because we were half a dozen
young progressive women in Dublin. You had to try to bring them along
with you, or what was the point?" Maher agreed – since the group had
originally come together with little more than the idea to "do something
about this women's thing", she felt it needed more time to solidify *exactly*
what it was, what it wanted to do, and what it was about. Producing
Chains or Change had helped it do that, simultaneously highlighting some
of the disagreements and problems between individual IWLM members.
But publishing a booklet together was one thing. Appearing on television,
and on the most popular television show in the country's history, was an
entirely different matter, and Maher and de Burca urged caution.

For most of the other IWLM founders, the prospect of introducing the
IWLM and its ideas to Ireland on *The Late Late Show* was nothing if not
wildly exciting. Máirín Johnston, Marie McMahon, Nell McCafferty,
June Levine, Mary Anderson, Mary Sheerin and, of course, Mary Kenny,
fell into this category. The rest of the founders had mixed feelings about
the show, but as it was, the majority of the women thought it was a fabulous idea, especially Máirín Johnston. "I don't necessarily agree with
Mary and Máirín that it was the wrong time, because when is the right

time? And how do we know that if we left it and continued to just talk and discuss, that the whole thing wouldn't have just fizzled out? Whereas going on *The Late Late Show* gave it an impetus that drove it forward. So I would say there is no such thing as the right time," Johnston says.

So the IWLM's majority voice had said "yes", loud and clear, to the *Late Late Show* appearance. Kenny arranged for the show's top researcher at the time, Pan Collins, to come to Gaj's one Monday and sit in on a meeting. The group was just finishing several months of work on *Chains or Change*, and when the date for the show was set for 6 March 1971, the founders saw the perfect opportunity to co-ordinate the launch of the charter so that it would receive the widest possible publicity. Organising the speeches that each woman on the panel would give into topics that coincided with the aims outlined in *Chains or Change* would reinforce their messages, making them even more salient. If the IWLM was going to make the most of this one incredible chance to tell the country about itself, the panellists themselves had to be articulate, composed and, above all, acceptable to all those women in the country who would be hardest to convince of the value of the IWLM's cause.

"Everything to do with *The Late Late Show* was to tame down Mary Kenny," Mary Maher says. "That's why we didn't go on ourselves." On the panel of five women who appeared that night, only two – Máirín Johnston and Nell McCafferty – were actually IWLM founders. The other three were, in their own words, the most "presentable" women the IWLM could think of – Senator Mary Robinson, RTÉ producer Lelia Doolan and historian Mary Cullen. One could almost see the haze-like aura of respectability that emanated from them. Each had an allotted period of time to address a specific topic. Johnston would talk about women's labour issues, discrimination in the workplace and the trade unions, areas in which she had had the most experience from the earliest age. McCafferty addressed the desperate situations of women in crisis – deserted wives, widows, and unmarried mothers. Mary Robinson, who would go on to be elected Ireland's first woman president in 1990 joined the panel to talk about how Ireland's many discriminatory laws against women were inconsistent with the Constitution. Television producer Lelia Doolan, one of the only women at the time in such a powerful position in the broadcast media, pointed out inequalities toward women in the Irish educational system and how the media's own portrayal of women reinforced negative gender-based stereotypes. Mary Cullen talked about the many difficulties inherent in being a working mother. Nearly all of the other IWLM founders were in the audience, prepared to jump into the fray if necessary. Audience participation was integral to *The Late Late Show*, and they knew they would more than likely have a chance to bring up other relevant issues. They expected to experience the unpredictability that defined the show, and they were as ready as they could be for live television.

Nell McCafferty is puzzled, even today, as to why the group thought it was wise to put her on the panel. She was, self-admittedly, not particularly respectable, and although she would have controlled herself on television, she had one of the foulest mouths of any of them. She was an outstanding public speaker, though, a skill she had acquired mostly through a combination of her work in the civil rights movement in her native Derry and in the IWLM's earliest days. She remembers giving one speech in Derry in the late sixties to an all-male audience with fellow activist Cathy Harkin crying with the fear of speaking in front of the crowd, and holding Harkin's hand through the whole thing. Within the year, at a protest on a lorry outside the GPO, one of the feminists from the IWLM was asked to speak. McCafferty had wanted Mary Maher to do it, Maher wanted McCafferty to, and Maher won. McCafferty made a speech she says she's sure was terrible standing on the lorry, but after that, she never feared public speaking again. But if the rest of the IWLM founders didn't seem to see her as a risky figure to put on the panel, McCafferty claims she saw herself that way. "Since I was from the North and associated with pepper bombs, petrol, Provos, and killing, why was *I* allowed on the *Late Late* panel?" she asks, genuinely curious. "They chose me, and I've never understood that. I was more outspoken probably than all of them, and probably cutting, and I had a Northern accent. They trusted me. Big compliment. I must have great charisma," she says.

All of the women remember presenter Gay Byrne, a legend in his own right, as the consummate professional. Byrne liked nothing better than controversial people and topics, so he was guaranteed a terrifically spirited discussion with the IWLM women on the show. Regardless of its opinion of the group for good or bad, the country was fascinated with women's liberation in all its facets. Since the show's creation in 1962 – originally intended to be a temporary summer programme – much has been written about the enormous impact it had when it was able to get an issue, as author Colm Tóibín put it, "on the crest of its wave", as was certainly the case with the women's liberation movement. Tóibín wrote about Byrne's own tremendous influence as the presenter of *The Late Late Show:*

> His talent was in knowing how fast the pulse of the country was beating and in knowing whose pulse he should be taking. In Ireland like nowhere else the airing of the problem was enough to cause a whole lot of trouble. Had he not come along with the instincts of a successful impresario and created a mass audience and then raised the issues he did, it is conceivable that dissent on the essential ingredients of Irish life would never have reached the ears of the majority of people in this country.[2]

Byrne's own perception of *The Late Late Show*'s influence on public attitudes didn't align completely with such lofty declarations of the programme's significance. "I have found again and again that television does not have a fraction of the influence which people seem to think it has . . . I do not for one moment believe someone's opinions necessarily are going to be changed overnight by having a discussion about something on *The Late Late Show*," he wrote in his 1972 memoir.[3] He added that he does believe television has had a slower, steadier effect in altering the Irish public's attitudes towards the church's influence, women's conditions, and sex, gradually prying and opening up these and other taboo topics for discussion. Byrne had kept tabs on topics and individuals that never failed to evoke immediate and heated responses from the Irish public over the years, and among them were the Irish language, the border, contraception, marriage and the divorce question, and – unsurprisingly – Mary Kenny.[4] Since the women's programme would include at least the last three of these, it was impossible for a show featuring the women at the helm of the IWLM *not* to make for riveting television.

Eimer Philbin Bowman believes there are advantages to the slower, steadier changes that Byrne wrote about; in a way that's difficult to articulate, the type of debate that *The Late Late Show* fostered allowed the entire country to grow together. *The Late Late Show* paved the way for gradual changes to happen because it deliberately questioned society's direction by posing new ideas and challenges to some of its staunchest

values for a few hours every weekend, and then went off the air and allowed viewers to ruminate on those ideas and challenges. That it was so
universally watched was also pivotal to the fact that the whole country
was, in effect, able to participate in the same debate. "I think it must be
like Greek meetings in the square, written large," Philbin Bowman says
of the show's influence. "And I think that is absolutely extraordinary. I
think, probably, we're fortunate in that way, and that's a healthy thing in
that you're debating within your own society." Currently in its forty-
fourth year on the air, Byrne left the show himself after thirty-seven
years. While still popular, *The Late Late Show* is no longer the crucial
cornerstone of the culture, the impossible-to-miss programme that it was
in the sixties and seventies. There are just too many entertainment
choices, both on television and outside the home, and few topics have the
ability to shock and entrance as they did back then.

Unfortunately, the best research efforts of the RTÉ librarians failed
to turn up a record of the studio ever possessing a copy of the show
broadcast on 6 March 1971 on which the IWLM appeared. June Levine
was one of the IWLM founder journalists who was on the programme as
an audience member that night and she later became a researcher for *The
Late Late Show*. Levine has written in some detail about the show in her
own 1982 memoir and although it is a tragedy to lose the intensity and
immediacy with which film can capture voices and movements in a way
that print cannot, Levine's writing remains the most complete account of
the event. She recalls that everything was going quite smoothly on the
show throughout the panellists' individual speeches. Byrne flipped his
way through a copy of *Chains or Change*, asking the women to expand
on some things, questioning others. The audience was entranced, expec-
tant and completely attentive. But the calm was not to last long. It was
when the audience was invited to join in the discussion, after each panellist had had her say, that emotions took over and the group's plans for
the show went right out the studio window.

One woman in the audience said that it ought to be possible to solve
the problem of unemployed men drinking all of their dole money in lieu
of giving it to their families without changing the Constitution, by setting
up local committees to whom wives could complain, and from whom
they could receive the money directly. Although they had succeeded in

keeping her off the main panel, few of the IWLM founders believed
Mary Kenny would stay quiet the whole night. She jumped in with an
answer to the woman's question: "Do you really think, seriously, that a
patriarchal society is going to do this? Do you really think that the men
in Dáil Éireann, the men who make the legislative situation in this country, care at all?" Kenny asked. "I think that they would drag their heels,
they would resist changes in any of these areas up to the hilt, because I
don't think that they give a damn," she said. Levine, who in the audience
had been "seething for ages", declared that in Ireland you didn't have to
be black to be discriminated against, you just had to be a woman.[5]

True to form, Kenny managed to create even more controversy that
night with her comments, albeit unwittingly. Her criticism that the men
of Dáil Éireann didn't care about women had touched the nerve of then-
Fine Gael TD Garret FitzGerald, watching at his home near the Donnybrook RTÉ studio. Fired up and ready to defend himself and his colleagues, he rushed to RTÉ to be let onto the show. The IWLM women
were less than pleased at the turn of events that had allowed a man to
hijack their programme, most likely for his own political gain, through
the tremendous exposure he knew he would receive the minute he
stepped on *The Late Late Show*'s stage. Byrne and the show's production
team could not have been more delighted with the drama inherent in such
a twist. FitzGerald took his seat, with Byrne introducing him to the
women as "one of your hated legislators", and admitted that Kenny was
right, the Dáil had not done much to push for the law reforms that the
IWLM was talking about. But he claimed that it wasn't because the men
of the Dáil were purposely against passing laws improving the lives of
women; the system, he said, responds to pressure, and "there hasn't been
pressure for civil rights from women".[6]

If there was a more sure-fire way for the politician to make the IWLM
women livid, he would have been hard-pressed to find it that night. If anything, FitzGerald's comment only strengthened the IWLM's resolve that
they had to do more. The founders would have been the first to agree that
it was Irish women's fault for not organising themselves and putting more
pressure on the government for the badly needed legislative reforms that
would make a profound difference in so many of their lives. But they
knew that Irish women needed help – their own experiences forming the

group had taught them how simultaneously exhilarating and terrifying the prospect of change could be. The IWLM founders knew that women had to free themselves in their own minds by taking the first and most funda-mental step – becoming aware of their own oppression and its true sources. Then they had to raise the rest of the public's consciousness about women's oppression so that they could begin the process of working for more solid reforms with the necessary support. The intangible mental changes were, in a sense, even more important than the tangible changes, and they were an absolutely necessary precursor to actual law reform. The IWLM founders knew this; it had been their intention with their women's pages, their own small consciousness-raising sessions, the production of *Chains or Change*, and now their appearance on *The Late Late Show*. They did not need Garret FitzGerald to tell them that more pressure from women was necessary, while he conveniently garnered some spectacular media attention for himself and his party.

Raised voices and reddened faces, on the parts of FitzGerald, women in the audience and Byrne himself, ensued with Byrne trying to calm everyone down again. He eventually succeeded, and FitzGerald once again took up his original defensive stance. He claimed that he and some of his colleagues were already at work drafting a bill dealing with many of the issues the IWLM had brought up on the show, like forcing desert-ing husbands to pay up to half of their incomes to the wives they'd left. The women quickly changed the topic, though, away from what they saw as fantasy legislation and back to existing legislation that was oppressive to women, namely, the Forcible Entry Bill. This was the same bill that Máirín de Burca and Mary Anderson were to be arrested for protesting against outside the Dáil five months after the IWLM's *Late Late Show* appearance, a protest which eventually led to their challenge to the out-rageously discriminatory Juries Act. To the IWLM, it was very clear that women with children were the ones bearing the brunt of the miseries of the housing crisis, and it was they who would also be the most nega-tively affected by the Forcible Entry Bill.

Mary Maher asked FitzGerald why his party wasn't voting against the Forcible Entry Bill if it was so concerned about women. Nell McCafferty, who, then and now, wields the sheer weapon-like forces of sarcasm and directness in speech to devastate her opponents, told FitzGerald she looked forward to seeing him join women in squatting in the first house the day the bill was passed, breaking the law in solidarity.[7] FitzGerald replied that he was with her one hundred per cent, but could not vote against the bill because of party difficulties; however, he would oppose every clause in the bill. FitzGerald's comments demonstrated perfectly what the IWLM women had argued all along and what Mary Kenny had voiced moments earlier – politicians may have claimed they had women's best interests at heart, but they seldom took risks that would put them outside the realm of the conventions of the majority opinion of their colleagues.

Máirín de Burca remembers being "a bit pissed off" about what she saw then in the group's appearance on the show as an impulsive move that might do more to hurt the IWLM than to help it. She, along with most of the other women, were so wary of the group being associated with Mary Kenny's "mad phase" that, at the time, going on the show seemed like an extremely risky proposition. Now, in hindsight, de Burca is willing to admit the advantages of the group's appearance on the show. "I suppose in the long run, it didn't do us any harm. Once it was out, it was out, and you couldn't haul it back in again," she says. Mary Maher, although she would have shared many of de Burca's feelings about the Kenny factor, is quick to point out today that without characters like Mary Kenny and Nell McCafferty, who possessed their own special brand of fearlessness and irreverence, the IWLM would have been "a very boring group". Maher reasons that every one of the founders really did fulfil her own role in keeping the group alive and working for the length of its short lifespan, including the more troublesome ones. Mary Sheerin, who was at the time a publicist for the Gaiety Theatre, saw the show then and now as a terrific boost for the group. "It was a great PR coup from the point of view of a launching pad," she says.

History has proved that to be true. Women all over Ireland who had been following the IWLM journalists' articles in the newspapers saw words made flesh that night, and it was thrilling. Writer Maeve Flanagan, a teenager at the time the show aired, wrote about its significance in her life in her own memoir:

> Women's liberation was more interesting on *The Late Late Show* than in the dreary old *Irish Press;* there was a panel, studio audience, shouting, roaring and laughter; there were living

breathing people debating passionately. Some of the women were very funny. . . . All these women were confident and articulate; they buoyed each other up; the adrenalin flowed. It was difficult to make the connection between these wonderful creatures and my mother. But the connection was there; they were saying the very same things she had said. . . . I listened more attentively to those women than I had ever listened to my mother or my father. My mother and father were only a man and a woman grappling fearfully with feminism and all its ramifications. These women were television stars; they had style; they went on protest marches; they carried banners. They were revolutionaries; they were afraid of nobody. They began to interest me.[8]

Flanagan had witnessed her mother, a voracious reader of Mary Kenny's women's page in the *Irish Press,* undergo a dramatic and complete metamorphosis as the IWLM gained more notoriety. Prior to the *Late Late Show*, Flanagan had directed a childlike resentment against any de-stabilising influence in her home and family at Mary Kenny. Ever since Kenny's page had started, Flanagan's mother had cut clippings from it, quoted from it, and generally started to behave very differently toward her own husband and her family. She cooked less. She talked about politics. She voiced her opinions much more forcefully on everything from politics to mundane household matters. Flanagan "hated that Mary Kenny; she was evil; she changed mammies".[9] There was something about seeing those women on television, though, that changed Flanagan's young mind about them. Watching the show with her parents, she was terrified her father would make them turn off the television and she'd miss what the women had to say. To read Flanagan's account of the impact of the show, the IWLM had succeeded in conveying both the urgency and the necessity of their demands.

Even then, though, Flanagan recognised how difficult, and even painful, it would be to really put all of the changes the IWLM was advocating into effect. Under the bright television studio lights, in the glow of the audience's and the country's attention, the women could not have been more confident and convincing. But they had each other for support – who did all the women watching at home have once the televisions were switched off?[10] Flanagan looked at the consequences of the changes the IWLM women were proposing in the simplest but most illustrative of ways – if her mother would rather do other things for herself than look after the children, cook the dinners, and take care of all the other necessary household chores, who would? Her whole world was in danger of being upended; the changes had already begun.

If Flanagan saw both the opportunities and the drawbacks in the IWLM's proposals, some other women who were watching that night chose to dwell only on the positive possibilities of what the group said. Maura Richards was struck, like so many others, by the confidence that the women exuded under the pressure of appearing on live television before what they knew was a vast audience:

> The Women's Liberation Movement had hit Dublin in a big way. June Levine, Nell McCafferty, Mary Kenny and other women got a lot of coverage from the media and I envied them the ease with which they smoked fags on telly and talked to Gay Byrne about sex and contraception and divorce and women's right to control their own bodies.[11]

Other women testify to the domino-like effect that the IWLM's appearance on the show that night sparked in Irish women for years to come, allowing them to take heart in that initial, courageous act. Margaret Roche, a former chairwoman of AIM (Action, Information, Motivation), one of the first lobbying groups for family law reform, had escaped a troubled marriage and was raising young children on her own through the seventies. She remembers seeing Richards on *The Late Late Show* some time after Richards had established Cherish in 1972. Richard's appearance had the same effect on Roche that the IWLM's appearance had had on Richards. Roche thought that if an unmarried mother was telling her story on the most popular television show in the nation, it was only a matter of time before separated wives and mothers like her would start appearing, too. Roche has since become very involved with the independent Anna Livia radio station in Dublin, and was on the air for a time herself with her own women's programme. It was initially women's influence in the newspapers and on television that made Roche realise that the importance of oral testimony, especially to women, was not to be underestimated. "You never know when you go on radio and make a comment, how you're challenging some woman's perspective in a kitchen in the country in rural Ireland where she's suffering dreadfully. Suddenly she hears somebody say something, and that challenges her way of being in the world, and maybe changes it for the better. You never know how the ripple effects ultimately take seed and start a change for the better for somebody else," Roche says. Roche sees the IWLM founders in particular as educated, sophisticated and very brave.

Alice Leahy is another Irish woman who attests to the lasting impression that the IWLM founders left on her and, she suspects, many other women of the times. Leahy is the director of Trust, the organisation for the homeless founded in 1975 and based in Dublin's Liberties. She remembers being very aware as a young nurse in the early seventies of the new movement even though, like Maeve Binchy, she was never the type of person to join social movements, or become committed to membership in organisations. "I wasn't one of those women in that particular group, yet I knew all those women," says Leahy, who used to eat at Gaj's regularly.

> I got to know all of those women and would see them as great supporters and friends, and a lot of them stuck their necks out, and I often wonder if they got the credit they deserved. People never come back to say, "We got support from them", because the support isn't about money, the support is just about somebody out there, and you know if you put your head over the parapet, you won't be on your own.

If they had had any doubts themselves about the immediate impact of their appearance on *The Late Late Show*, the IWLM founders need not have wondered after their first public meeting, which took place in the Mansion House the following month. Meanwhile, as the spring wore on, the group was entering the most active phase yet in its young life. The controversies over its proposed changes in the laws banning contraception and its opposition over the Forcible Entry Bill were both gaining momentum. Individually, each woman continued her struggle with her own role in the group and in the wider movement, as well as the effects of her activism on her personal life. Even if the founders did have each other for confidence and support, the IWLM's rise and decline were so close that they nearly overlapped – closer than anyone could have predicted.

Interior of Gaj's Restaurant, March 1980 *(© Derek Speirs/Report)*

Margaret Gaj in Gaj's Restaurant, early 1970s *(© Derek Speirs/Report)*

Nell McCafferty,
November 1979
(© Derek Speirs/Report)

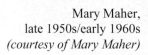

Mary Maher,
late 1950s/early 1960s
(courtesy of Mary Maher)

Máirín Johnston in St Patrick's Park, 1978
(courtesy of Mairín Johnston)

Máirín de Burca in the 1970s *(courtesy of Mairín de Burca)*

Mary Kenny participates in
a debate on "Abortion –
A Woman's Right to Choose"
in Trinity College Dublin's
Philosophical Society,
November 1979
(© Derek Speirs/Report)

Dr Moira Woods, 2 June 1982
(© Derek Speirs/Report)

Nuala Fennell at UN Convention of
Women in Nairobi, Kenya, June 1985
(courtesy Nuala Fennell)

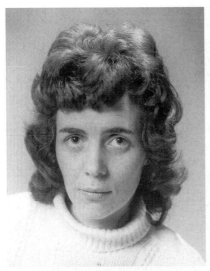

Mary Sheerin in the 1960s
(courtesy Mary Sheerin)

Eimer Philbin Bowman in March 1969
with her first-born child, Jonathan
(courtesy Eimer Philbin Bowman)

Marie McMahon, September 1978
(© Derek Speirs/Report)

Rosita Sweetman, late 1960s
(courtesy of Rosita Sweetman)

The scene at Connolly Station in Dublin following the arrival of the
Contraceptive Train on 22 May 1971; although most of the IWLM founders
kept a relatively low profile that day, Nell McCafferty is just visible on the
left of the photograph *(© Irish Times)*

Margaret Gaj and Frank Crummey in Gaj's Restaurant, March 1980
(© Derek Speirs/Report)

Frank Crummey and son outside
Mountjoy Prison in support of Marie
McMahon, March 1980
(© Derek Speirs/Report)

Máirín Johnston in May 1991
(© Derek Speirs/Report)

Nell McCafferty and Máirín Johnston at Nell's book launch,
November 2004 *(photo by Anne Stopper)*

Mairín de Burca's fiftieth birthday party; including, second row, from right: Margaret Gaj, Máirín de Burca, Mary Maher; back row, fourth from right, Moira Woods *(courtesy of Margaret Gaj)*

Maeve Binchy's sixtieth birthday party, 2001: Mary Kenny, front row, far left; Nell McCafferty seated on ground in front of Maeve Binchy; Mary Maher to immediate right of Maeve Binchy; Máirín Johnston, third row, second from right *(courtesy of Máirín Johnston)*

10

Finding Her Place

"If you know *who you are* and live your life according to your own convictions, refusing to squeeze into a mould cut by others, the whole concept of freedom and the change it involves in a woman's life becomes more welcome than threatening." — June Levine[1]

It took June Levine a while to figure out who she was, but once she did, hers became a powerful voice of change both through her work within the IWLM and in her journalism. Journalism was probably one of the most stabilising aspects in Levine's somewhat tumultuous life. She started working for *The Irish Times* as a cub reporter at age fifteen, and although she emigrated to Canada as a young mother in the mid-fifties, when she returned to Ireland ten years later she also returned to journalism. At the time of her return to Dublin, she was separated from her husband and found herself living as she had never anticipated – raising three children on her own in a society that was unsympathetic to women in her situation.

Levine is as much a Dubliner as anyone, but as a child she was unsure of her place in society. Her parents came from different religious backgrounds and decided to raise their children with an understanding of both. Levine was born in Dublin in 1931 in the Rotunda, when her mother was fifteen years old, and educated at the Zion school, the national school for Jewish children in Bloomfield Avenue. Levine's father was only seventeen at the time of her birth, and Levine has fond memories of living with her parents in her maternal grandparents' large flat in Pembroke Road. Levine's mother was a Catholic, and her father was a Jew of Lithuanian descent. There was even a brief period in her childhood when she went to synagogue on Saturday and mass on Sunday. "I can remember an awful lot of anxiety in my life when I realised that people were different and belonged to different religions," Levine told Máirín Johnston in a 1988 interview Johnston conducted for her book of profiles of Dublin women, *Dublin Belles*.[2]

Her parents eventually moved into a house of their own in Lennox Place and, although Levine remembers the struggles they went through once they were less attached to her mother's family, she was aware that independence was very important to her parents. One of her first distinctions between her mother's and father's families as a child was based on the differences in their traditional foods. Her Jewish grandmother could make several dinners from one fat hen; her Catholic grandmother's food was more polite, refined, genteel – white chicken breasts, buttered eggs, and brown bread.[3] Levine always had two sets of religious festivals – Hanukkah and Christmas, Easter and Passover. With Jewish friends, as a child, she kept the Catholic holidays secret; with Catholic friends, the Jewish holidays were never mentioned. After reading James Joyce's *Ulysses*, she felt a strong identification with the character Leopold Bloom as the outcast who never really fit in. To Levine, Joyce's most famous story is a marvellous portrayal of how people feel when they're not accepted.[4] "This is why the women's movement meant so much to me when I was still torn by all that conflict," Levine wrote. "It was only in the seventies that I realised that my people weren't Jews and they weren't Catholics. They were women. This was for me the resolution of that conflict."[5]

Like de Burca, Johnston and McMahon, Levine also left school at age fourteen. She took a course in shorthand and typing, which must have served her well in her first journalism job a year later. She remembers the shortages during the war, and the way her parents coped with them. Her father had a plot of vegetables that helped feed the family, and he made them wooden clogs when there wasn't enough money to buy shoes.[6] Her father could not have been happier when she married a

Jewish man, a young Canadian medical student, at age twenty. Six years later, the couple moved to Canada with their two children.[7]

Levine's marriage steadily unravelled over the ten years that she spent with her husband as a Canadian immigrant. She worked briefly for a newspaper in Saskatchewan until she and her husband moved to Arkona, Ontario, where the local Lions Club had asked him to be the village doctor. In the rural, isolated area, Levine longed for the activity and stimulation of the city. Upon their arrival into town, she was introduced only as the "doctor's wife" in the community hall. Everyone expected that she would naturally be assisting her husband in the surgery, which was part of the ground floor of their new home. The Lions Club would not be paying her a salary for her services.[8] She felt enormous pressure in being "the doctor's wife", and ran her house and the surgery like she was competing for housewife – or doctor's wife – of the year. Her bouts of depression, which she had experienced since the move to Canada, increased in length and intensity.

When she read Friedan's *The Feminine Mystique* in 1963, she identified with the author's articulation of women's restlessness and desperation; that terrible isolation many housewives felt of being trapped in a dead-end routine and the injustice of the opportunities that they had been denied. But Levine did not, at the time, fully recognise the problems that Friedan described as her own. The lessons of the book did not sink in enough to move Levine to take any kind of action in changing her own situation – yet. She felt she did not have the answers, and she simply was not ready for that kind of complete upheaval. The almost complete lack of options that women had in their lives, the low expectations and the impossibility of ever leading a life of worth for themselves, independent of a husband or children, were all things Friedan addressed that Levine had experienced. Her depressive episodes had reached the point where she was seeing a psychiatrist and receiving electroshock treatments in an effort to improve her mental health.[9]

Levine's condition finally deteriorated so that the best option, the only option, seemed to be for her to leave Canada, and her husband, and move back to Ireland with her children to her own family for a while. They called it a trial separation, but Levine was shocked at how badly her life had gone off track.[10] She'd had all the ingredients for the fairytale life – a professional, good-looking husband, well-behaved kids, nice house, clothes and furniture. She had followed the magic formula for happiness and success that women were taught practically from birth. Now, in her early thirties, she was on her way back to Ireland to sort things out and try to pull herself out of the black despair in which she was mired. Trying to find a flat as a single woman with three children in Dublin in the mid-sixties didn't do much to lift her spirits; the landlords always enquired as to the whereabouts of her husband, and many weren't happy with the answer: "We're separated." Finding work wasn't much easier, and Levine was refused several receptionist positions at doctor's offices.[11] She finally found a job selling cosmetics in a chemist's shop when a colleague from her teenage days at *The Irish Times* told her about *Irishwoman's Journal*, a new magazine "for the thinking woman" that was hiring.[12] Her colleague urged her to apply for a job, and although she was not at all confident that she was in any condition to perform her duties competently, she got the position and started as an assistant editor. Besides being pleased about being back in journalism, the job was her first step toward independence and, significantly, she was no longer an isolated housewife. She wrote under several different names for the magazine, which allowed her to be a sort of jack-of-all-trades expert on the issues – fashion, beauty, health, etc., with which the magazine was concerned.[13]

It was also a reintroduction into Irish life and the state of Irish women, from which Levine had been further removed than she realised during her years in Canada. She had been reading mostly Canadian and international magazines and newspapers, and she was surprised to discover that contraception was such a moral dilemma for Irish women. To Levine, it seemed like the most natural thing in the world for women, married or unmarried, who did not want to become pregnant to take the matter into their own hands and use some method or another to avoid it. Levine herself had always had access to contraception in Ireland and Canada through doctor's prescriptions, so it had never been a personal problem for her. She was also free of the moral guilt that so many Irish women felt, which was inseparable from their Catholic faith. She noted that, among other male journalists, the columnist Sean O'Sullivan wrote extensively about contraception, and was irritated that a subject that concerned women so deeply was being written about almost exclusively by men. The first, fresh crop of female journalists at the national newspapers was just beginning to muster the confidence to write opinionated articles about such issues. That it was the men of the church, male doctors and, at the beginning of the contraception struggle, mostly male journalists who were making the judgements and decisions made Levine deeply angry. She directed most of that anger toward women themselves for continuing to allow others to monopolise such an important debate instead of speaking up for themselves. "That this could be permitted seemed to me a philosophy of slavery and even in my lack of feminist consciousness I felt great impatience with women who played such a silly game," she wrote.[14]

She began to understand Irish women's attitudes toward contraception better through some of the letters she received at the *Irishwoman's Journal* in the late sixties. One woman wrote that she had asked her priest if she could take the pill. He had told her no, and she had stopped taking it. She lived in fear of getting pregnant again. Such letters helped Levine realise just how deeply matters of sex and sexuality were bound up with shame and taboo. These attitudes had the effect of separating women so completely from their own sexuality that many did not take responsibility for their own sexual actions or their consequences. She also began to realise just how deep were the wounds caused by the hypocrisy with which women were treated in Ireland. She met unmarried women who had given babies up for adoption out of a combination of desperation and social pressure.[15] Many had never told their families, or even friends, of their situations, and were on the lookout for single men in an effort to start their lives over. Levine never met an "unmarried father", and points out the hypocrisy underlying that simple fact – where were all the men responsible for the pregnancies of unmarried mothers? Often, they were already married with families of their own. And yet, marriage was the ultimate goal for young Irish women and Levine had met her share of bright young women who would go to great lengths to avoid the ultimate social shame – the state of spinsterhood.

Gradually, through her work as a journalist and her own interactions with Irish women, Levine's eyes were opened to the injustices that were embedded in Irish society in every oppressive attitude and law to which women were subjected. She had been away from home for quite a while, coping with her own deteriorating marriage. But now that she was back in Ireland and working toward her own independence, while raising her children as a separated mother, she began to feel a deeper sense of anger both at women's oppression and their own unwillingness, or inability, to do something about it.

It was around this time, as Levine was finding stability both socially and professionally, that she met Mary Kenny, just as Kenny was starting to think about returning to Dublin herself from her first steady journalism job at London's *Evening Standard.* Kenny had been trying to get some freelance work in Irish publications in order to facilitate her return home and her possible break into Dublin journalism. What Levine remembers about their first meeting, when she was arranging for Kenny to send an article to her for editing at *Irishwoman's Journal*, is Kenny's confidence. She was also ambitious and career-oriented in a way that very few Irish women were at that time, and Levine was not accustomed to meeting women of Kenny's age that were anything like Kenny.

"As she rode off on her bike," Levine wrote of that first meeting in Dublin in the late sixties, "I knew at last that the big mistake to make in life is to go around asking for permission. Whether permission was sought from other people, society or one's voices didn't matter. To ask for permission was to be shot down."[16] When Kenny became the first editor of the *Irish Press*'s women's page shortly after and Levine left her editorship at the *Irishwoman's Journal,* Levine began freelancing for Kenny. It was Mary Kenny who invited Levine to her first IWLM meeting, telling her that it was about women's liberation. Levine remembered asking Kenny, "Liberation from what?"[17] Levine attended the earliest meetings in Mary Maher's and Mary Kenny's flats before the group relocated to Gaj's. By the time the group began its meetings and its consciousness-raising discussions, Levine was struggling with anger over women's mistreatment, an anger that she simply didn't know where to direct. Within the IWLM, she found both direction and an outlet for her anger and she was one of the group's most enthusiastic founders.

Like Máirín Johnston, Levine was nearing age forty when the IWLM was founded, a little older than most of the other founders. Both women were also separated from their husbands and had children who were no longer infants. They'd had altogether different experiences from some of the other founders with formal educations who were younger and either single or recently married. Levine had feelings of inferiority similar to Johnston's about her lack of a university education, which had surfaced while she had lived in Canada with her physician husband. She shared the same attitude as Johnston as to the importance of educating oneself:

> Something started to happen in my head. It was as if some little cog went into motion and disturbed the rest of the machine. I wanted to learn about things, to have some education, to be able to join in conversations wherein were dropped the names of writers, poets, scientists, politicians, names other than my beloved Shaw, O'Casey and O'Connor. I didn't dare care about a degree, since I'd left off my formal education in primary school, but I wanted the knowledge.[18]

Levine had enrolled briefly in a degree course at the University of London, Ontario, even though the university hadn't wanted to take her at first, possibly because she had left school at such an early age and they doubted her qualifications. She had told them she'd pay the fees and work hard if they would let her sit in on the classes and mark her papers, and she received first class honours for her course work.

Levine and Johnston also shared similar feelings about the importance of consciousness-raising sessions. Prior to the founding of the IWLM, Levine couldn't find any discernable source or basis for her anger and despair. That was almost more frustrating for her than the actual feelings themselves. And whereas she had yearned for an education for knowledge's sake, it was not until those consciousness-raising sessions at Gaj's that she found the answers she had really been looking for about her dissatisfaction with her own life. She found that it was often the most basic questions within the consciousness-raising sessions that had the largest impact on her own way of thinking. Most of them began with the word "why" – why were women devalued, abused, undermined, chained to the service of others, taught to be dependent rather than independent, and treated like slaves? Why did they so often distrust themselves, their instincts, each other? Why did they believe in their own powerlessness? It was through these questions that the IWLM women began to identify the root sources of discrimination against women, and began that process of putting words to their oppression, creating the language they needed to articulate their feelings and problems to the rest of the world. Levine, like the rest of the founders, found that exhilarating and, to an even greater extent, a tremendous relief. Like everyone else at those meetings, she was gratified to learn that her problems were not hers alone – there were reasons for her dire unhappiness in her life with her husband, and many of them were not her own fault. Even more significantly, her own sense of powerlessness, or lack of control, over her own life and well-being was ebbing with every IWLM meeting. If there were causes for the discrimination and oppression she had experienced, there had to be solutions, too. She felt that with this group of women, she had a good chance of finding them.

Like every other founder, Levine had her own set of conflicted feelings about her membership in the IWLM. The other founders remember being a bit harder on her with personal criticisms than they had been on almost anyone else in the group. Although Levine was making huge changes in her own life since she'd returned from Canada, her old preoccupations with personal beauty and image that had intensified in her quest to be the perfect housewife were difficult for her to free herself from. Whereas the other IWLM women, especially the youngest ones, wore blue jeans, bandanas and little or no makeup, Levine was still mixing and matching accessories and cosmetics and spending much of her time and attention trying to copy the latest hairstyles. Her old notions of desirable femininity as tied to fashion persisted through the consciousness-raising discussions, where other founders tried to tell her that she was just buying into another man-made myth that women existed only to please men, both in appearance and behaviour. She couldn't be truly liberated herself until she realised that, they argued. At times, their prodding was less than gentle. Marie McMahon recalls some very personal insults that bordered on cruel about Levine's appearance.

But Levine's ideas about fashion, like her discontent, had deep roots that she was just beginning to understand and, along with the other founders, hers was a personal journey of realisation that she had to take step by step as it unfolded. McMahon also remembers that as time went by and the women got to know each other better at Gaj's, they genuinely began to understand the reasons behind each other's problems and quirks. In doing so, they were a little easier on each other by the end of the group's life span. In her memoir Levine recounts how her husband's expectations for her appearance made her extremely self-conscious, and she must have told similar stories in Gaj's. There was one day in Dublin, before the young couple moved to Canada, when Levine had been out in the city centre buying fruits and vegetables from the outdoor vendors in Moore Street. It had been a typical rainy Dublin day, and she had worn a grey flannel skirt and jacket with black stiletto heels and a bright print silk scarf, no umbrella. By the time she got home to her husband who was minding the baby, she looked like every other woman in the city – hair soaked, stockings muddied, but otherwise in good spirits, until her husband reproached her: "Who saw you like that? Do you know what you look like? To think of my wife being seen like that . . ."[19] Levine was humiliated – she had broken the rules in the women's magazines, displeased her husband, and was certainly not the picture-perfect wife at that moment. It was not until much later, after her marriage had ended and the IWLM was founded, that she realised that the things her husband had said to her were exactly the sort of things that broke women's spirits, kept them in "their place", and reinforced their fear and powerlessness. In her own case, they also contributed to her deep depression.

Although some of the IWLM founders remember Levine putting up with what was perhaps more than her fair share of criticism from the group, they also recall that, like Mrs Gaj, she was one of the women others would seek out for advice. Nell McCafferty was one founder who had just recently moved to Dublin and was still trying to find her own way in the city. She had no clue about cooking for herself, and one night Levine happened to ring Nell at home in the midst of Nell's complete mystification over how to prepare a pork chop for her dinner. Levine told her to get in a taxi, pork chop and all, and make her way over to her house, and they'd sort it out.[20]

The young *Irish Press* journalist and IWLM founder Rosita Sweetman also remembers Levine as a very nurturing influence. "She'd worry about whether you'd had lunch and if you had warm enough clothes and she always had a lovely home and looked after people who were having a hard time," Sweetman says. Sometimes if a conversation was floundering and just appeared to be going in circles, Levine could, with the skill of a journalist, pare the discussion down to its core and present it to the rest of the women in a simpler, more understandable way – not a skill to underestimate in a roomful of women where there were often three and four separate conversations going on at a time. Levine could give the group focus when it needed it the most. And while none of the founders really ever tried to brush off their share of the group's tasks, Levine was always one of the first ones to throw herself headlong into whatever needed to be done. She was not above any of the work, no matter how mundane – she saw it all as important to the IWLM's goals. Levine was one of the founders who spent many tedious hours leading up to the group's appearance on *The Late Late Show* photocopying and stapling copies of *Chains or Change* together for distribution.

Her writing also reflected her enthusiasm for better treatment for women like herself who didn't fit the mould of acceptability – unmarried and separated mothers, deserted wives and others. She wrote as force-fully as any of the other journalists in the group about the importance of women taking matters into their own hands and much of her work, like theirs, was crafted to incite women to action. In her last issue as editor of *Irishwoman's Journal*, in June of 1969, Levine had written about Berna-dette Devlin, the civil rights activist from Derry who had exhibited the strength of conviction and fearlessness that Levine felt should be an ex-ample to all women, north and south:

> Fear of freedom and the responsibility which freedom lays upon the individual is the reason why so many slaves remain slaves. I believe it to be the main reason why Irish women are second class citizens and smile ironically at the fact that it was from the op-pressed North of our country came the clear feminine voice of youth ready to stand as a free woman and accept responsibility for all of her people . . . let her be an example to women all over the country that: it *can* be done, *it has been done*.[21]

Levine was one of the first founders to publicly acknowledge, decades after the IWLM's break-up, her own obliviousness to the existence of other women's organisations at the time of the IWLM's formation. Some of the founders genuinely weren't aware of the other groups of women that were working for reforms; others knew about them but realised that they wanted to start something different from every organisation that had preceded it, although they might not have had a very clear idea about exactly how to structure the IWLM. Levine gave a speech to University College Dublin's Women's Educational Resource and Research Centre conference in May 1995 about her own insular attitude as a member of the IWLM:

> Until comparatively recently I believed that the . . . members of that group [the IWLM] . . . were the women's movement of Ireland. Well, no they weren't – because recently I was asked to research the forthcoming edition of the *Field Day* anthology which writes Irish women into history. I discovered that three years before we came on the scene a group of Irish women had got together to pressure the Fianna Fáil government into a First Commission on the Status of Women . . . [22]

University College Cork sociology professor Linda Connolly believes that the IWLM created, albeit unintentionally, the illusion that it was a mass movement because its media profile gave the impression that it was a far larger and better organised group than it actually ever was. Because the IWLM was able to grab the media's and the country's attention like no other women's group had ever done, people perceived and remembered it as the first modern women's rights group to emerge in Ireland. In reality, there were several other groups of women, some of them in existence for decades before the IWLM, which had been working in much quieter, subtler ways. These groups had neither sought nor attracted media attention; the media would not have had much interest in them as they worked for a better deal for women on much less controversial topics than contraception and the removal of the marriage bar.

One such group was the Irish Housewives' Association (IHA), a consumer group founded in 1942 out of middle-class housewives' discontent with the social problems and difficulties for Irish women that resulted from the effects of the Second World War. Certain foods and fuel were scarce and the IHA was concerned with issues of poverty and children's needs. From the group's founding right up to the time when the IWLM hit the scene, the IHA preferred to work for change through the establishment – writing letters to the government and the press, lobbying TDs and senators, and approaching state, semi-state, professional and trade bodies for support. Hilda Tweedy was its chairwoman from 1959 to 1962, and she recalled that the IHA was wary of the IWLM from the start:

> They [IWLM] very much thought that anything that went before them was old hat and establishment and so on. There was quite a lot of shall I say misunderstanding. But I myself always felt that I didn't always agree with the methods taken to highlight the issues were the best way of going about it because I thought it was rais-ing antagonism and the backlash from that would put back some of the work that we had been working on for years.[23]

The Irish Countrywomen's Association (ICA) was similar to the IHA in its goals and tactics. It was founded in 1910 as the "Society of United Irishwomen" by middle and upper-class Protestant women. Poor living conditions, high infant mortality rates, large under-nourished families, and an abundance of serious illnesses were all part of the rural Ireland that was "crying out for improvement" at the time of the ICA's found-ing.[24] Providing running water and electricity in all rural homes was high on the ICA's original agenda. But the ICA women also realised that if they wanted to improve Irish women's quality of life, they'd have to find ways to make life about more than simply surviving from day to day for women. They wanted to make rural life more attractive for young women, and to show them that there were possibilities for them to enjoy themselves. Besides introducing farming, horticulture and beekeeping to women, they taught music and drama as well in an effort to bring some colour into the lives of countrywomen.

The leaders of the IHA, ICA and other women's groups like the Women Graduates' Association and the Widows' Association came to-gether in 1968 to form an *ad hoc* committee on women's issues that grew into the Commission on the Status of Women (CSW), the first Govern-ment-sanctioned collective. The CSW's task was to make suggestions on how to ensure a more equal participation of women in the political, social, cultural and economic spheres, taking into account the costs and other im-plications of such changes. The CSW was made up of seven women and six men and was established in March 1970, just a few months before the

IWLM came together. The Commission published its first report in October 1971, just after the IWLM's disintegration, on equal pay. The report included recommendations for changes concerning the marriage bar and restrictions on women's employment, and called for the building of training facilities for women and the provision of twelve weeks' maternity leave. The Commission had received submissions from forty-one separate women's organisations in the process of compiling its report, the tone of which was moderate. The Commission had recommended December of 1977 as the date for the implementation of equal pay. As a direct result of Ireland's joining the European Economic Community, however, the date was eventually brought forward by two years.[25]

It was not the IWLM founders' style to use a moderate tone, or to be content with waiting five years for laws to be enacted, or to go through established government channels to try to change society. Its focus was much more on opening agendas outside the establishment and forcing people to talk about injustices like unequal pay. The IWLM wanted women to know, first and foremost, that a better, fairer existence was possible, and to be able to recognise their status as second-class citizens who were being denied their full civil rights. In the IWLM's view, the way to go about that was not by working on reports behind closed doors for years at a time, but rather by appearing on television shows, writing controversial articles, and making waves in the most public way possible. Politicians in power needed radicals like the IWLM founders on the outside to force their agendas and help bring about the creation of such bodies as the CSW through which they could work; radicals needed people on the inside, like then-Senator Mary Robinson, to carry out the slow, often tedious work of actual law reform to get legislative results on the inside.

Even though the IWLM had disintegrated by the time the CSW published its interim report in October 1971, both Mary Maher and Mary McCutchan wrote about it, and what they viewed as women's role in translating the Commission's theoretical suggestions on equal pay into a reality. Maher explained that she bore no grudge against the thirteen Commission members who "slogged away compiling the thing", but appealed to Irish women to take action themselves:

It will not be their fault that the Interim Report's recommendations, or even the eventual Final Report's recommendations aren't
implemented. It will be our fault. And the time to start avoiding
the blame is now. The only people who can make this report a reality are the women it concerns. It will require great organisation,
sure-footed negotiating, and a large dose of militant spirit. But it
can be done; by refusing to accept less than equal pay – oh, all
right, less than the step-by-step 5% if you insist – and refusing to
accept the marriage bar, by demanding a hearing on our opinion
of job evaluation. We had better start moving, though. Considering that only 44% of us have even bothered to join a union, sisters, we have a lot of work to do.[26]

Mary McCutchan wrote a similar call to arms on her women's page the
same day, proving that even though the IWLM founders had stopped
meeting in Gaj's by that time, the journalists would individually carry on
the group's message in the newspapers. The women's pages were still
places where they could do their best to encourage women to channel
their dissatisfaction into action:

The compilers of the report are not starry-eyed. They realise that
two nebulous, but elephantine obstacles to full equality in employment are the attitudes of men – and of women themselves . . .
so women, it is up to us. No government did anything without
pressure; the Commission has stated and put the weight of its authority behind the case for equal treatment in the world of work.
Now it is up to women, in trade unions, in the women's organisations (represented on the Commission), in small pressure groups
such as theirs fighting for women's liberation, and as vocal, active individuals to get the fair deal that is their right.[27]

Máirín de Burca concedes that she and some of the other IWLM founders were probably a bit arrogant about the IHA, ICA and the CSW. The
IWLM was less conservative and less concerned with respectability than
its predecessors, both in its demands and in its preferred tactics. The
IWLM women had not needed Garret FitzGerald to tell them during his
impromptu appearance on *The Late Late Show* that Irish women weren't
exerting the kind of forceful, concerted pressure on the government that

was necessary for it to take notice and actually put reforms into motion. The country needed some sort of jump-start to rouse itself out of complacency in its mistreatment of women. The IWLM women were doing their best to provide exactly that, and if they could achieve their goals, they would drag Ireland, kicking and screaming if necessary, into the second half of the twentieth century.

High on the success of its appearance on *The Late Late Show,* the IWLM was already planning its next big event in the spring of 1971 – its first public meeting. They would use the newspapers again to advertise. The first five founders in the original group in Bewley's had not known what to expect from their efforts. But now they had some grasp of the momentum that had been gathering throughout the seven months they had been meeting. They were onto something big, much bigger than they had anticipated in the beginning.

Standing Room Only

"I remember breaking with my family, I remember breaking with my class, and I was completely on my own. And I remember thinking, how am I going to get to this meeting in the Mansion House. Because it was a huge thing to get over there or even to walk in. I remember shaking and nobody would come with me. So I went and I remember going up to the door of the Mansion House and there were these very fierce-looking women . . ." — Róisín Conroy, feminist and artist, on attending the Mansion House meeting, 14 April 1971

Mary Sheerin was nervous that the Round Room of the Mansion House in Dublin, which she had reserved, was much too big for the unknown number of women who might show up for the IWLM's first public meeting on 14 April 1971. Following the wave of publicity they had generated by their appearance on *The Late Late Show* the month before, the IWLM founders had little choice but to organise a public meeting, inviting anyone who was interested in hearing more about them. They had no idea exactly how to go about the expansion of the group, but they knew there would be at least some women who were willing to come out and listen to them.

Sheerin had always thought of herself as a "background" member of the group, consciously avoiding the limelight. Tasks such as the booking of the Mansion House for the meeting were her *forte* – administrative and behind the scenes, but useful work. Her philosophy about social change was actually the opposite of most of the other IWLM founders' – she felt it was better to try to bring about changes from within the system, rather than from outside the establishment. But in 1971, the establishment was just taking the first steps toward implementing real changes for women. Even though Sheerin was not personally willing to break the law in the name of women's liberation as some of the other founders were, many of the IWLM's philosophies appealed to her.

Sheerin was born in Cabra in 1939 and remembers her parents' sacrifices to make sure she and her sisters got a good education. They would take turns walking their children the mile and a half each way from home to the Holy Faith school in Glasnevin because it was a good school. There were always books in the Sheerin house, and the family made great use of the public library. Sheerin's father Hugh, originally from Westmeath, had fought in the War of Independence. He was interned in Athlone jail for six months during the war before escaping, and he never lost his allegiance to de Valera. Mary grew up with the *Irish Press*, which was owned by the de Valera family, coming into the house all the time, believing that "de Valera was the most wonderful person that ever lived".

Sheerin's first recollection of being treated differently because she was a girl concerned education and the amount of the corporation scholarship that she received for secondary school in Dominic Street. For boys, she recalls, it was something like £100 or £110, and for girls it was only £15. So from a very early age, Sheerin was aware that it seemed more important to educate boys than it was to educate girls. Neither Sheerin nor any of her sisters initially went on to university, it still being quite a strain on the family finances in those days. Instead, she and her sisters joined the civil service after secondary school.

"It was a very depressed era in Irish society, and the Irish economic situation and all that, so you didn't expect very much really," Sheerin says. "I knew one thing, though, and I knew it from the time I was in primary school. I knew that the only way out was through education."

Sheerin remembers her eldest sister, Eileen, introducing her to the works of different authors, including one of Sheerin's favourites, Guy de Maupassant. She always enjoyed writing and when she went into the civil service at age nineteen as a clerk typist, she found the work boring.

In those years, though, Sheerin says, women didn't think in terms of a career; the aim was just to get a job. Expectations both for and of women were universally low in Ireland. She was working in the Department of Agriculture when an examination for typists in the OECD (Organisation for Economic Co-operation and Development) came up in Paris. She applied, was accepted and spent an illuminating five years working there and mixing with people from all different cultures. It was in Paris that Sheerin read the godmothers of feminist literature, including Betty Friedan's *Feminine Mystique* and Kate Millett's *Sexual Politics*, as well as other literature she hadn't had a chance to delve into in Ireland.

Coming back to Dublin was difficult for Sheerin. She returned to her old job in the civil service and hated it so much that she only stayed a fortnight. She'd always wanted to break into journalism, though, and she got a secretarial job at a publishing company on the stipulation that she'd have the opportunity to publish some of her own writing. It was also around this time that Sheerin got her first short story published in the *Irishwoman's Journal*, during the year in which June Levine was the editor. It was Levine who mentioned to Sheerin in late 1970 that there was to be a meeting in Mary Maher's flat about women's rights. Sheerin had been acquainted with Maher beforehand, but did not know most of the other women she met there that night.

By the time the IWLM started meeting at Gaj's, Sheerin was working in the Gaiety Theatre's public relations department and still writing bits and pieces for Levine. While she found the meetings exciting and stimulating, and enjoyed the sense of making progress and being involved with such a dynamic group of women, Sheerin did not find the consciousness-raising sessions as life-changing as many of the other women. But she realised early on in her IWLM membership that every one of the founders contributed and took different things from the group, and their differences were often their strengths. "We were a very diverse group of people, and that was no bad thing," she says. "Because if everybody was exactly the same, I don't think it would have got perhaps to the level it did."

Of the issues that the IWLM had included in its main aims, equal pay had specific resonance for Sheerin, who never married and never had any notion of depending on a man for financial stability. At the public relations firm where she worked doing projects for the Gaiety Theatre during her IWLM membership, she remembers fighting for her individual right to the same pay that the men she worked with were receiving. "It was ludicrous the way women were treated, the way women had to resign upon marriage. Women were doing exactly the same jobs as men and usually a hell of a lot better, and purely because of their gender, were paid less money. That was absurd," she says.

Sheerin remembers discovering that a man who was doing exactly the same job as she was in the firm was earning significantly more money than she was, and asking her supervisor for a raise. In fairness to her boss, she says, he increased her salary right away without argument, even though the Equal Pay Act had yet to be passed. At the same time, sixteen-year-old male couriers were automatically put onto a pension scheme in Sheerin's company, whereas for women, no matter at which level they were employed, there was no pension scheme at all. The expectation, she explains, was that women would get married and therefore have no need of a pension plan of their own. "There was this thing of marriage, you know, as an economic venture as much as anything," Sheerin says derisively. "I mean, you might as well be back with Jane Austen."

Sheerin remembers the way her firm rectified the situation. If women were still with the company at the age of twenty-five, they were eligible to become part of the pension scheme. She remembers a woman who, having just reached that age, tore up her pension form because she did not want to be seen as a spinster. The woman felt that signing onto the scheme was the symbolic equivalent of dooming herself to a life with no man. Sheerin remembers this event as the moment of her realisation that sometimes women could be their own worst enemies, a conundrum that all of the IWLM founders ran into at one point or another during their work in the liberation movement.

"The thing is that the policy was there, finally, and so that was something," Sheerin says of the pension scheme. "So if you like, you could say that the IWLM gave the impetus to initiate these changes and social justice and equality within a small area."

"A small area" was exactly how the massive Round Room of the Mansion House appeared on the night of 14 April when it was packed to the rafters with women and a smattering of men. Sheerin need not have worried about being over-ambitious when she made the arrangements for the meeting. The estimates on how many actually attended the meeting that night vary from 800 to slightly more than 1,000. Mary Maher has said if they had known that many women were going to show up that night, they might have been too intimidated to start the group in the first place. It was the first real indication that women all over the country were hearing something with which they identified in the IWLM's messages, and the founders were simultaneously pleased and stunned at the incredible energy and high turnout in the Mansion House. The problem was, they hadn't given much thought as to how they were going to attempt to organise all of these women who wanted to "join" the movement. There were literally hundreds of women asking where they could sign up, and the first thing that came to the founders' minds was postal codes – why not organise the women into branches by postal code so they could start their own meetings in their own immediate communities?

The Mansion House meeting was, to Marie McMahon, the most gratifying culmination of the IWLM's efforts to that point, the great crescendo of the movement. "The Mansion House to me would have been the equivalent of the Russian Revolution," she says. "We had succeeded in raising awareness, and we had organised this marvellous fantastic meeting and every woman at that meeting was a raging inferno of anger and frustration," she says. More than even *The Late Late Show,* when the founders had been unable to see the women they were reaching, McMahon looks back on the Mansion House meeting as a "blood transfusion" for the IWLM. It was the moment when the group realised just how many women were out there raging in the same way that they themselves were. The founders discovered an even broader solidarity with many, many women outside the confines of their meetings at Gaj's.

Before the Mansion House meeting, the IWLM journalists had done what they had grown accustomed to and were very skilled at – using the newspapers to publicise the group's main events. The following brief appeared in *The Irish Times* on the day of the meeting:

> If you have been wondering when you could join, or indeed whether you really would like to join, then sisters, tonight is the night. Women's Lib is going public in the Mansion House at 8 pm, admission free.

The purpose of the meeting is to inform people more fully of the aims of the movement and to form branches throughout the country. After a short opening statement, the meeting will be open to questions and discussion. Everybody interested in Women's Liberation, male or female, is invited to attend, and you really don't have any right to criticise, condemn, or dismiss the movement unless you go along tonight and hear what is being proposed. Perhaps your own comments and suggestions may change its course or alter an attitude, so liberate yourself with a baby-sitter and get there tonight.[1]

The IWLM journalists had also seized the opportunity in the aftermath of *The Late Late Show* to explain the goals of women's liberation in greater detail, when they could be sure more people were paying attention. Mary Maher had used the women's page immediately following the show to clarify exactly what the IWLM was and what the founders were trying to do. She emphasised that they had been meeting since the previous October and as yet had no Constitution, spokeswoman or leaders:

We're not asking anyone to join us; we are just hoping that Irish women will join each other, to form groups in whatever situation they find themselves in . . . to discuss the concept of liberation and how it applies to them immediately. To discuss, and to take action . . . women's liberation is a part of human liberation, and the object is to find a new definition of freedom for a future society that will differ dramatically from the present one. The movement is philosophical as well as practical. Finally, Women's Liberation is unlike other women's campaigns in that it does not conform to accepted notions of the polite and lady-like way to face battle. . . . The Women's Liberation Movement is political, courageous, imaginative, insulting, impudent, and it has won more notice and more recruits than any other women's civil rights movement has. At least, this has been the case in other countries. It's up to all of us to see what we can do here. And now.[2]

The panel of women that the IWLM had selected to speak at the Mansion House meeting included Dr Moira Woods, Máirín Johnston, Mary Maher, Hilary Orpen of RTÉ, solicitor Ivan Kelly, and Nell McCafferty, who acted as moderator. McCafferty also remembers Mary Robinson being present as a legal advisor. "I was allowed to facilitate, and do so with grace and authority," McCafferty says, echoing the same surprise she felt at whatever arrangement or agreement had passed between the founders that had made it possible for her to appear as a panellist on *The Late Late Show* the previous month. "I was quite a serious chairperson. I must have said the odd f-word . . . no, I wouldn't have said fuck in public then. But I must have made a few remarks," she smiles, ever-present cigarette dangling from her lips.

Another *Irish Times* writer, Elgy Gillespie, covered the meeting that night. As promised in the women's page advertisement for the meeting imploring women to come out, the IWLM panellists took the first part of it to reiterate their goals and demands once more. McCafferty offered the microphone to any women who wanted to speak, and the floor truly became the audience's. The queue that immediately formed grew longer and longer as more women, some for the first time ever, decided they wanted to talk about themselves and their own experiences and struggles. From the floor came stories, questions, comments and suggestions, as Gillespie details in her summary:

> Viewpoints ranged from the extremely personal to the intensely political: answering a young girl's question as to whether the movement was intended to be political, Mrs Johnston replied that, in the end, the price of a loaf of bread was political, and that women must concern themselves about living conditions such as the housing shortage "because men won't . . ."

> About 60 speakers in all, including several men, addressed the audience during the three-hour meeting and a queue had to be turned away at 11 pm. Points which were stressed repeatedly included the right to contraception, the need for women to join trade unions and fight for equal pay and conditions, and the need to participate in political action to effect change. Injustices to widows, unmarried mothers and deserted wives were aired; two speakers stressed that the work mothers did in raising children was of vital importance and unrecognised in society . . ."[3]

Gillespie wrote that among the cheers and applause that followed many of the speakers that night, there were also jeers from the movement's critics, calls of "Shame!" and "Where's your modesty?" Róisín Conroy even remembers sitting behind a woman who was partially in disguise, someone who was obviously opposed to the movement and kept blowing a whistle to disrupt and distract the speakers. Mrs Gaj was in the audience and spotted a male politician whom she strongly suspected was there purely for his own political benefit rather than out of any heartfelt concern for women's rights. She caught up with him at the door and cornered him, pinning him to the wall. She told him she knew what he was up to, and he had a lot of nerve. He apologised profusely and, Mrs Gaj recalls with relish, on many occasions afterwards.

The stories the IWLM founders heard that night from the audience members who stepped up to the microphone were familiar ones. The women spoke mostly of struggles related to lack of money due to the many discriminatory laws that the IWLM had outlined in *Chains or Change*. Some of the problems they heard about mirrored their own. "They were the word made flesh," McCafferty wrote of the audience members who took to the microphone. "They embodied the inequities, and more, of our demands. Few women claimed that they were doing this on behalf of other women. Practically every woman was speaking on her own outraged behalf."[4]

The specifics of what many of the women said that night have grown fuzzy in the minds of most of those in attendance, overshadowed by the dramatic and extraordinary announcement of one previously unknown woman. Helen Heaphy stepped to the microphone: an attractive young woman with a mature air whom McCafferty remembers as conjuring the glamorous image of Sophia Loren in gypsy mode.[5] Heaphy asked how many people in the audience were unmarried mothers, and was met with laughter and light heckling. Then she continued: "Because I am one myself and I am very proud of my little daughter." There was a second of stunned silence, followed by thunderous applause and a standing ovation lasting an eternity that was, in reality, several minutes long. "People were crying with emotion that she had the courage to stand there and say it," Marie McMahon says. "It was amazing." McCafferty wrote about the Mansion House meeting and the significance of Heaphy's statement thirty-one years later in *The Sunday Tribune:*

The silence of centuries had been broken. Until that night, 99% of unmarried mothers had been forced to give their children up for adoption, or hide them in a tangled family relationship where granny became mother, and mother became sister to the child. We clapped, cheered and made a holiday in our hearts . . . Nothing that was said that wonderful night -- or possibly since – can equal the impact of Helen Heaphy's simple statement.[6]

It was one of those moments when history splits in two, into "before" and "after" sections. Before Heaphy's statement, no one had ever publicly declared herself an unmarried mother in Ireland. Now, just by Heaphy's utterance of those few straightforward sentences, it was somehow less of a stigma. Someone had actually had the courage to talk about this previously unspeakable state of being, and that first articulation of the matter began the process of normalising it. Maura Richards has since been mistaken for making the statement that night because she became one of the most visible unmarried mothers in Dublin in the years following the Mansion House meeting as the founder of Cherish. In fact, Richards had not been at the meeting that night, she recalls, probably because she could not get a babysitter for her own small daughter.[7] Helen Heaphy has not spoken publicly since.

Mary Flynn attended the meeting that night, a young woman just out of college and curious about how she could get involved. She signed up for the Donnybrook branch and was surprised by the terms the IWLM used for the new groups they were creating that night. Most of the organisers were talking about "cells" instead of branches, which reminded some of the women – not pleasantly – of Provo-type language. "Later I discovered it was the normal left-wing way of organising things, particularly the far left, which was to then try and organise people geographically in local groupings," Flynn says. She could not help but be excited about the energy that the meeting had generated, and no small part of the great buzz was in the sheer and unexpected number of women who had shown up. "It was the first time like-minded women were able to come together, and in a supportive atmosphere kind of vent their frustrations and air their views that were at the time very much against the conventional wisdom and views of the day," she says.

The IWLM founders agree that the Mansion House meeting was one of the group's finest moments. But there are those who see it, also, as the beginning of the end for the founder group. What had until then been a group small and intimate enough to fit into Mrs Gaj's room above the restaurant was now a much larger gathering of hundreds of women from all over the city. In one respect, that was terrific, and everything the IWLM had hoped for – proof that they were touching women, moving them to come out and take action themselves. But it also created some instant and serious problems. How was a group like the IWLM that, as Maher had explicitly stated in an article just a month earlier, had no leaders, spokeswomen or Constitution, supposed to handle these massive new numbers of members? If the IWLM founders had proclaimed the movement free from the constraints that a leader or leaders would place on the group, who was in charge? Who would decide the best course of action for the branch groups, and where were the branches to turn if they had questions?

Charges of elitism toward the founders, from some of the branches, surfaced almost immediately after the Mansion House meeting. At the same time the women in the branches were enthusiastic and willing to take action; they just weren't sure exactly how to go about it, how to harness their energy and channel it into tangible results. They knew one thing, though – most of the women, while looking to the founders for guidance, did not want to be dictated to. Even amid the chaos of the Mansion House meeting, it was somehow decided that night that a representative or delegate from each of the branch groups would eventually attend one of the Monday night meetings per month, with the first expanded meeting to be held a few weeks later.

At that meeting, the socialists among the founders like Máirín de Burca, Máirín Johnston, Mary Maher and Moira Woods fought a hard battle in convincing the delegates to accept all of the IWLM's aims as of equal importance to the women's liberation movement. The political divides that had threatened the stability of the founder group were multiplied within the branches. As within the founder group, the one aim of the six that caused the most argument between the founder group and the branches was one-family/one-house, because it was seen as a socialist demand that was too far removed from feminist concerns. Some of the delegates were already beginning to question just how much authority the founder group should have over the branches. They wondered if they had to accept all of the founders' ideas in order to be part of the liberation movement.

It did not help matters that the founders were proposing another demonstration at that meeting that many of the delegates had objections to for the same reason that they resisted the one-family/one-house demand – it was too far away from what they saw as strictly "women's issues". The founders wanted to organise a women's liberation contingent for the May Day March with the labour concerns and the trade unionists. To the socialists among the founders, this seemed like a natural cause for the women's liberation movement to take up. It would only help women to get involved with labour, in the hopes of encouraging more women to join trade unions and to gain the unions' support in lobbying for equal pay and better working conditions. But those against the march worried that the women would get swallowed up in the protest; that the march organisers would be able to use them to increase their numbers in a "rent-a-crowd" capacity without giving much attention to what they saw as more important women's rights issues. As it turned out, about 300 women, some of the founders and many of the women from the branches, chose to march that day under their own homemade banner.

About three weeks after the Mansion House meeting, right before the May Day march, Mary Kenny wrote an article urging women not to give up on the movement because they weren't quite sure what they wanted their place in it to be or how they should go about joining it:

> Some of the Dublin postal districts have now organised themselves into new groups or branches of Women's Lib; others are just starting off talking about it. Quite a lot of women are attracted to it in a vague way but aren't sure how much they could be committed to it, or what they really want. Well, it takes a lot of talking, meeting, thinking out your own feelings, developing your social or political or psychological ideas before you can commit yourself and that's how it should be.
>
> Some of the study groups that have met are just uncertain about what way they want to change the inequalities or the attitudes ob-

taining in Irish society or how they would like to go about it. A tremendous amount of women are downright shy, for example, about things like pickets or demos. (It's awfully hard to go out on a demo for the first time; admittedly, you feel like a frightful eejit, but after the first one, it's dead easy.) Other women are just curious.[8]

Kenny's article was more a rallying cry to women than anything, as she proclaimed that the women's liberation movement "may indeed hail a new era for Irish women who in the past have by and large chosen a passive public role". She recounted some of the group's demonstrations, including one particularly brash protest outside Leinster House (during one of Mary Robinson's attempts to get a reading of her contraceptive bill) when a few frustrated IWLM founders including Máirín de Burca and Fionnuala O'Connor climbed in a window that turned out to be the men's toilet. This was the same occasion on which Kenny treated the crowd to her famous rendition of "We Shall Overcome", substituting "We Shall Not Conceive" for lyrics as the women were "escorted" out of the building.[9] Rather than let the famous Kenny bravado falter for an instant, she re-emphasised the movement's need for the aggressive strategies that often came in for criticism. "It's true that all tactics are not approved of, but on the other hand, when everyone is approving of you, it means you're not getting anywhere," she wrote in defence.[10]

Women needed that kind of encouragement, it seemed. Although the atmosphere in the Mansion House meeting had been exhilarating, many women who had signed up there were, as Kenny acknowledged in her article, unsure of what their own roles in the movement should be. Much of the energy that the Mansion House meeting had created dissipated very quickly in its aftermath. "Mass movements cannot be built on euphoria and then re-structured into highly disciplined autocratic organisations," journalist Pat Brennan wrote of the women's liberation movement as the seventies drew to a close.[11] Mary Flynn remembers that the branch groups like hers in Donnybrook were energised by their initial interactions with the founder group. "I think in reality when it came down to it, the question of what can you do locally, I don't think there was much that people did," Flynn says. The extent to which each branch got involved in the movement themselves, both in conjunction with the founders and independent of them, depended very much on its individual members. If the founder group was built largely on personalities, the branches followed that trend, although none of them was able to reproduce the kind of initial energy and attention that the founder IWLM group had. Some of the branches were much more active and ambitious than others. The Clonskeagh group plastered stickers reading "this is insulting to women" over advertisements in its area that it thought were sexist. The Sutton group focused specifically on the issue of children's allowances being paid only to men and was one of the first to publish its own magazine.[12]

Although Flynn has great respect for the IWLM founders and their place in history, she does recall the flaws that existed and the practical difficulties that became more obvious as soon as the movement grew so rapidly after the Mansion House meeting. "Despite having set up a mass movement, they weren't really prepared for the challenges and changes that that might bring," she says. Any one of the founders would agree with Flynn, but they would point out that while they had hoped from the beginning that their work would make many other women want to get involved in the fight for women's rights, they had not intentionally set out to organise and run a mass movement. Mary Maher had meant it when she had written in the immediate aftermath of *The Late Late Show* that the IWLM founders weren't asking women to join them; they were asking women to join each other and work for their own liberation in whatever ways suited them best. Not everyone was cut out for the barricades; there was no magic formula or handbook for participation in the women's liberation movement. It was not a group that was moulded from any one model of social change, but rather grafted together by women with experience in left-wing politics, the media, and some knowledge of the American and British women's liberation movements.

Even if the IWLM branch members were some of the women who were in the best position to recognise the flaws in the way the founder group handled the movement's immediate proliferation following the Mansion House meeting, there is still a high degree of respect for that first group of women and their accomplishments. "I suppose the actual Irish Women's Liberation Movement was this kind of meteor that burst across the sky and had just such enormous impact," Mary Flynn says.

"And it almost seems sad to be kind of digging into it and looking at all its faults and everything, and they were there. But it was the one movement that really started breaking open this restrictive corset that Catholic Ireland constructed after independence."

By the time the branch groups were each just starting to find their places in the wider movement, even more unrest was brewing within the small circle of IWLM founders. Their idea for the most daring and controversial public demonstration on the most *risqué* issue of the day was in its infancy, and was to cause deeper divisions within the group even as it earned the women international attention. Some might have sensed it amid that spring's frenzy of activity, while others were less prescient, but the IWLM's days as a cohesive group were rapidly approaching their end.

Odd One Out

"They were the short, sharp prod that this society, this male-dominated, church-ridden society, needed. And they did prod, and they were listened to and they did have a big impact. It's just, what comes after?" — Nuala Fennell, on the IWLM

Nuala Fennell, the one IWLM founder who later campaigned as a candidate for a mainstream political party and won a seat in the Dáil, wasn't at all interested in politics in the early seventies. Three young children, ageing parents, and her work as a freelance journalist was more than enough to keep her busy. Her time was precious to her, and her personality was such that she wasn't really a "joiner" of groups. If she devoted her energy to a cause, it was going to have to be very important to her, and worth her while.

Fennell was born in Dublin in 1935, and attended Dominican College in the city and, later, the Public Relations Institute of Ireland. In 1970, she was beginning to break into journalism as a freelancer and was struggling with the eternal dilemma of the working mother – balancing the tasks of running a household, raising children and career responsibilities. Fennell had been writing pieces for Mary Kenny at the *Irish Press* on a wide range of issues – families, children, community, book reviews – as well as doing some work in radio along the same lines. Kenny had asked Fennell several times to come along to a meeting of a small group of women who had just started getting together to discuss women's liberation. A few weeks after the first IWLM meeting in Mary Maher's flat, when Kenny and Fennell were out on assignment for the *Press* together, Kenny asked Fennell again if she'd come to her own flat for a meeting that night. This time Fennell decided to give it a try, probably at least in part to appease Kenny enough so that she'd leave her in peace for a while about women's liberation. After the first meeting she went to, Fennell thought that it was at least worth it to keep going back and contribute to what was happening.

Even as early as the first meeting, though, Fennell found the group disturbingly unstructured. While all the women were very bright and articulate and she found the meetings stimulating, she already had the sense that many of them were "just sharing experiences" and that there was more practical work the group could be accomplishing. Like Mary Sheerin, Fennell was less affected by the consciousness-raising sessions than many of the other founders. She was one of the members for whom the planning sessions at each meeting were the most important. In spite of her frustrations, though, she kept attending meetings out of a feeling that she could make some difference, some beginning stride toward correcting discrimination against women. She would not have fit into any of the other established, more conservative women's organisations like the IHA, but she was also an odd woman out in the already eclectic IWLM.

Fennell was undoubtedly from a more bourgeois background than most of the other founders, and she wasn't at all involved in left-wing politics. In terms of political ideology, in fact, Fennell's mentality could not have been further from that of the majority of the other founders. She was not a regular at Gaj's as many of the others were, and she did not find attractive the idea of manning the barricades and picketing in the streets or outside the Dáil. Although she recognised the injustice in many of the laws concerning women, she still had great respect for the legal system and was not keen on the idea of breaking the law to attract attention to women's liberation. The most that she had in common with some of the other IWLM founders was a professional interest in journalism, but she didn't often socialise in the popular newspaper pubs with colleagues, male or female, like Maher, Kenny, and McCafferty did. Kenny and Levine, as well as other journalist IWLM founders Mary McCutchan and Rosita Sweetman, were also much less politically experienced than

de Burca, Johnston, Woods, McMahon, Maher and Mrs Gaj, but somehow they all seemed to ascribe to the group's ethos more closely than
Fennell.

For all of her differences with the other IWLM founders, Fennell had
the same sense of just how bad some women's lives were from the mail
she received at the *Irish Press,* and along with it, the same sense of urgency for change. "When I went into it, I knew women's situation was
pretty dire," Fennell says. "I didn't have to discover it through women's
lib." So unlike some of the other IWLM members who were shocked at
the large turnout at the Mansion House meeting, Fennell wasn't surprised at all. She knew how many women were out there who were desperate to share their own stories of injustice and to hear others who had
experiences like their own; to finally realise that they weren't alone in
their suffering. But the other founders remember that Fennell often tried
to distance herself from the idea that she personally experienced discrimination and oppression as a woman; she always stuck to the line that
she was working for reform on other women's behalf.

From the beginning of the group's formation, there had always been
tension between Fennell and some of the other founders who felt that she
took a detached attitude toward feminism, not acknowledging that she
herself was subject to the same restrictions that all Irish women experienced. "I had a very good home life, and my parents were very loving, I
married a fabulous man to whom I'm still married, and had a very interesting job," she says. "And I probably didn't apologise for that." Fennell
also felt that she was in the minority as a group member with three very
young children to look after and that some of the other founders were not
very forgiving of the fact that she sometimes had to miss meetings because of her family responsibilities. Johnston, Levine, Maher, Woods,
Mrs Gaj, and Dr Eimer Philbin Bowman also had children ranging from
infants to adolescents, but that's how Fennell remembers it. Dr Philbin
Bowman, curious about Fennell's connection to the group and not having been introduced, asked Mary Kenny at an early meeting who Fennel
was. Kenny replied with some flip comment along the lines that Fennell
was her link with middle-class suburbia who kept her in touch with the
issues that Kenny, in her hotpants, miniskirt, and pipe-smoking days,
would know nothing about. Although there was much in Kenny's man-

ner to suggest a put-down in her comment about Fennell, there is also
some evidence to suggest that Kenny was purposely looking for women
who were outside the circles of left-wing and radical politics to be involved in the IWLM; she had, after all, actively recruited both Fennell
and Levine. Kenny was always eager to seek out women with a variety
of different personal experiences and backgrounds to write for her
women's page, and maybe she sought this kind of intellectual mix to
pique everyone's interest both within and outside the IWLM. Then
again, given her preference for controversy, maybe she simply wanted to
add greater potential for dissent and commotion into the group in the
form of a few unexpected recruits.

In June of 1971, barely two months after the Mansion House meeting
and about nine months after attending her first IWLM gathering in
Kenny's flat, Fennell sent her IWLM resignation as an open letter to the
newspapers. Some of the IWLM members, to this day, think that Fennell
resigned specifically over the Contraception Train that had been organised in May. Fennell was unhappy with the media attention that surrounded the Train and felt that the conduct of certain members of the
group had been particularly disgraceful. But she insists it was a combination of factors that she'd been struggling with since the very first meeting
that led to her leaving the group. Among the most important reasons she
left was her feeling that the IWLM was accomplishing little in the way
of solid, practical reform for the amount of time its members were
spending in meetings and on demonstrations. The lack of a strict organ-
isational structure was another factor. And some of the members' more
colourful antics also concerned her, specifically because she felt their
flamboyance was alienating some of the very women IWLM claimed it
was trying to attract. To Fennell, some of the personalities in the group,
particularly Mary Kenny's, were obscuring the messages and the issues.

Even though most of the IWLM members knew Fennell wasn't
pleased with the way the group was functioning, some were surprised at
the strength of the language –and accusations – in her resignation letter.
McCafferty, who is famous for her own colourful turns of phrase, said
she was startled, then and now, at the force of the language Fennell used
in her letter. In it, Fennell labelled the IWLM founders as "elitist" and

"intolerant", claiming they were using Women's Liberation as a front for other various political groups:

> I believe and have always believed in a woman as a person, free, independent and equal to a man, if this is her choice. I worked on and helped prepare the booklet *Chains or Change*, but I can no longer work for these changes with the elitist and intolerant group who are using Women's Liberation as a pseudo-respectable front for their own various political ends, ranging from opposition to the Forcible Entry Bill to free sedatives for neurotic elephants.
>
> At a recent seminar it was clearly stated that if any member, whatever her previous views, was not against the aforementioned Bill, then she was not in Women's Lib, and to this I can add authoritatively that if you are not anti-American, anti-clergy, anti-Government, anti-ICA, anti-police, anti-men, then sisters, there is no place for you either.[1]

Fennell continued her letter, citing Mary Kenny's as the "one sane voice" left in the group due to Kenny's recent warning that it could be suicide for the Irish Women's Liberation Movement to lose its identity by disproportionately fighting the causes of the other political groups to which its members were loyal. Fennell conceded that, in her view, most of the founding members truly believed and understood the problems and frustrations that women felt, but that Kenny's plea was too late – "Women's Lib has not only lost her virginity, but turned into a particularly nasty harlot, and in all fairness it is on this level she will be dealt with by the majority of Irish men and women." It was that particular phrase that stuck in McCafferty's mind as uncharacteristically vulgar coming from Nuala Fennell. And there was one other criticism that Fennell had included in her letter that some of the other founders resented: "For me, it would be funny if it weren't sad, being discriminated against by the group for being middle-class when they are all unquestionably that and trying hard not to show it."[2]

Marie McMahon, Máirín de Burca and Máirín Johnston wondered how anyone could really say they had come from middle-class backgrounds. Had Fennell managed somehow to overlook, or conveniently forget, some of the most defining characteristics of the women she had worked alongside for the better part of the last year? Several IWLM founders, including McCafferty and Johnston, countered Fennell's criticisms with letters of their own to the papers. McCafferty attacked Fennell's attendance record at meetings, saying that her absence had led Fennell to issue a statement saying exactly what the movement itself had been saying for months. "No political philosophy, be it right, left or centre, has taken over Women's Lib. The aims of the movement are entirely intended to lead towards the new society and equality of life in which there would be true liberation for all people," McCafferty wrote.[3] Máirín Johnston pointed out that Fennell had been present at the meeting when the group voted on the inclusion of the one-family/one-house demand, and had not voiced any opposition to it. The IWLM's naming of that aim was so closely linked to its opposition of the Forcible Entry Bill, which proposed to place much tighter restrictions on squatters and was so obviously linked to the housing crisis, that Johnston didn't understand how Fennell could have agreed with one and not the other. Johnston also argued that the IWLM was never intended to be a conservative group; by definition it really couldn't be anything other than radical, considering its goals and the fact that it was out to provoke seismic changes in society.[4]

However bitter the feelings were on both sides at the time of Fennell's resignation, the years have mellowed all of the women and replaced old tensions with a good deal of quiet respect. When Máirín de Burca says the disintegration of IWLM was a nice way to break up because people found their own niches and went on to do important work in different organisations, she mentions Fennell's co-founding of AIM, the first lobbying and resource organisation of its kind whose purpose it was to help women by providing legal advice and assistance, and Fennell's 1981 election to the Dáil. Marie McMahon would have seen running for public office as crossing over to the enemy's camp in her younger days, but she now recognises and admires Fennell's consistency in her commitment to helping women, whether through the establishment or outside of it, throughout her career. And Nell McCafferty points out that even though Fennell was disturbed by the IWLM's opposition to the Forcible Entry Bill at the time because she saw the group's involvement with that issue as evidence that it was getting too tangled up in mainstream, left-wing politics, the fact that she went on to co-found support groups like AIM for women in distress demonstrated her deep commitment to helping women with practical needs. In 1974, Fennell was instrumental in setting up an offshoot group from AIM called Women's Aid, opening the first refuge for battered wives in Dublin. Fennell had borrowed a derelict house from a business acquaintance, and along with a crew of helpers, fixed it up herself, scrubbing toilets and floors, painting and restoring so it would be ready for the first women and children arriving. McCafferty points to the irony in the fact that Fennell, who had resigned from the IWLM at least partially because of its resistance to the anti-squatting Forcible Entry Bill, technically became a squatter herself in setting up the shelter that year.[5]

Fennell herself also acknowledges her time with the IWLM as a learning experience. "I came out of it with the knowledge of all the problems that existed," she says. "And the amount of work that had to be done." When she founded AIM in 1972, she had a clear vision of the ways in which she wanted it to differ from the IWLM. Like the IWLM, though, AIM was originally very small (about twelve women); the first meetings were held in Fennell's husband's office in Clarendon Street. Deirdre McDevitt and Bernadette Quinn were among the early IWLM members who were also co-founders of AIM with Fennell. A few men belonged to the group as well, the issue of male membership one that the IWLM had never been able to reconcile.

"The first thing was that it would be structured," Fennell says of the differences between the IWLM and her vision for running AIM. In order to be accepted, she says, it would not have been possible to even use the word "women" or "woman" in the name of her new group because of the negative connotations that the public had begun to associate with the women's liberation movement as a bunch of extremely militant radicals out to destroy society's foundations. It was also a massive relief to Fennell to be working with women who were all anonymous, with no journalists or known personalities to distract from the practical work and the group's purpose. No one even knew that AIM was meeting for the first year of its existence, and Fennell liked the peace and focus that came from working below the media's radar. She was also content to be working towards solid goals that she felt would actually make a visible difference in women's lives. "Nobody could change the world unless you change the laws," Fennell says. "Even then I was a very firm believer that you change the laws and then change follows and flows from that," she says. This belief was, at its core, another of the main reasons why Fennell could never have continued to work with a group like the IWLM for very long, even under the best possible circumstances. Most of the IWLM founders had exactly the opposite philosophy – that legal reforms would never be possible until enough of the population demanded them. In order for enough people to exert that kind of pressure on the government, radical groups like the IWLM needed to reach as many people as possible with as many persuasive and articulate arguments as they could manage in order to urge the public to raise its voice.

AIM has come to be recognised as one of the most effective women's pressure groups ever to come out of the women's liberation movement. The group was highly influential in securing some of the most important legislation for improving the conditions of women's lives and expanding their rights throughout the seventies. The Social Welfare Act of 1974 which transferred the legal right to the Children's Allowance from only the father to either parent or guardian, and the Family Home Protection Act of 1976, which prevented one spouse from disposing of the family home without the consent of the other, are among the two most important laws that AIM's lobbying was instrumental in helping get passed.[6]

It was also a relief for Fennell to be at the helm of her own organisation that was firmly focused on this one particular area of women's rights. To hear Fennell talk about her problems with the other IWLM founders' involvement in left-wing political causes, one could easily conclude that her biggest concern was that their commitment in other groups would distract their attention from the women's rights issues they were supposed to be focusing on. "No, it wasn't the attention," she clarifies. "That's not where it was at. It was the energy. *Big* difference. The energy, the commitment, the work. The practical approach. Enlarge our *Chains or Change*; let's have our political action campaign specifically on four or five issues. There were enough issues in that magazine to have kept us going for years. That was where I differed from the others," she says.

Even with all of the IWLM's flaws and the frustration that Fennell felt was a significant feature of her experience as an IWLM founder, she recognises the group's impact in improving women's conditions and its significance in the larger context of the women's movement. But when she speaks about the group's legacy, even in her praise, she still maintains a distance from her own membership, always using the word "they" instead of "we" when referring to the group's activities. Even though she knew, by June of 1971, that she could no longer work within the IWLM, she also knew she had to play some part in the fight for women's equality. "There is quite a responsibility if you tap into a vein of discrimination and disadvantage. You can't just walk away from it. You have to do something about it," she says.

That Fennell had created AIM and Women's Aid in the seventies was impressive to many who knew how much work she had put into those two groups and how important her work had become to so many women. But Fennell, unfailingly pragmatic, still felt there was more she could do for Irish women through other avenues she had yet to explore. By the mid-seventies, Fennell had proven that she had the drive and the stamina it took to lead and organise, and people around her knew she had the potential to do well in politics. As the end of the decade neared and all the political parties were much keener to recruit women candidates, though, she decided to run in the General Election as an Independent in the spring of 1977. June Levine helped Fennell during her first political campaign, going from door to door in Fennell's constituency (South County Dublin), and cooking for the Fennell family when Nuala got too tied up with campaigning to make the proper time.[7] Fennell did very well in the election, better than anyone really expected, but not well enough for her to win. That wasn't to come until 1981, when she earned a Fine Gael seat in the Dáil.

Some of her old colleagues from women's lib and the women of the media were publicly less than supportive of Fennell during her first years as a politician – they would hold her at least to the standards that they held every other male politician to, if not to a higher one. (Perhaps if she had chosen a more left-wing party than Fine Gael, they might have been more supportive?) By 1983, Máirín de Burca had been freelancing in journalism and had worked as a staff writer for several magazines and newspapers, and she criticised Fennell in a *Magill* article that year for waffling on important issues. A photo of Fennell with several journalists during the lunch and tour of the Dáil that she had organised exclusively for the women of the press carried the caption, "Women journalists and their prey", an editorial decision that in all likelihood was not de Burca's. The main point of de Burca's article was that Fennell had no actual answers to the questions any of the women journalists posed that day. Mary Maher was there, and asked about Fennell's input into the recent budget on the behalf of women. "Condensed and interpreted," de Burca wrote, "her reply was 'none'".[8] De Burca's frustration with Fennell's non-answers to the journalists' questions was clear throughout her piece, and she had no patience for what she saw as an invitation extended by Fennell to the women of the press as just another political device; a glorified photo opportunity. "It was on the question of divorce that prevarication was raised to an art form," de Burca wrote. Fennell favoured an all-party committee to examine the question, even though she was on record as having said she was in favour of divorce and there had been an all-party committee on the Constitution fifteen years previously that recommended abolishing the divorce bar. Fennell insisted that another committee might produce consensus on divorce within the political parties.

De Burca was not the only fellow IWLM founder who asked Fennell tough questions that day or criticised her in print. Nell McCafferty asked the most sensitive question of all – what were Fennell's thoughts on the proposed amendment that would protect a foetus's right to life under the Constitution? Fennell replied that she didn't believe the amendment, if passed, would make any difference, and the reason she supported it in that case was because it was a party pledge.[9] The proposed abortion amendment and the chill of the media were the two plagues of Fennell's entrance into politics, as journalist Pat Brennan discovered in a 1983 interview with Fennell:

> For Nuala Fennell, her first year as a junior-minister has been anything but easy. Her first nine months in her new job were over-shadowed by the divisive [abortion] referendum campaign. Then, there was her disastrous first press conference when, flush with enthusiasm for her appointment, she attempted to share her triumph with her feminist colleagues in the media. She met a tougher and more hostile reaction than most male politicians – Charles Haughey and Garret FitzGerald included – have ever encountered.

"OK, I didn't expect any privilege, I didn't expect anything extra, but I certainly didn't expect to be treated so much worse," she says of that occasion. "Many of them wrote very bitchy things. I felt they showed a terrible lack of understanding of any woman who rises out of the ranks and goes into a new area. . . . It was so soon after my appointment and I found it quite amazing that they didn't act on the feminist support structures they had so often preached."[10]

McCafferty today does not recall singling Fennell out specifically for harsher criticism than any other politician, male or female, although some of the ink she spilled on Fennell and the abortion referendum was scathing enough. McCafferty wrote an article right after the amendment was passed lamenting the inability and ineptitude of women's rights organisations, feminist politicians and journalists to better represent women's right to control their own bodies in the course of the amendment debate:

There are obvious scapegoats, and it were better to name them than store up bitterness that will further divide us. Nuala Fennell, Minister of State for Women's Affairs, and Gemma Hussey, Minister for Education, behaved dismally. . . . Nuala Fennell was the first woman to publicly face the filthy flak . . . when she ran for the Dáil, in 1977, as an Independent on a women's rights ticket, she faced a whispering campaign that she was pro-abortion. She had never talked about it, much less thought about it, no more than most of us had. Abortion had not occurred to us, just as divorce had not occurred to us in 1970 when the women's movement was launched. But the whisperers equated feminism with abortion, and Nuala Fennell was a feminist, therefore she was in favour of abortion. She immediately denied the charge, giving public weight to the shadowy substance. It might have been accurate for her to state that she had not thought about abortion . . . Nuala Fennell and Gemma Hussey turned their backs on women's life outside the Dáil and put the party and their political fortunes first.[11]

McCafferty chooses to remember her kinder inclinations toward Fennell. She says that during Fennell's 1977 campaign for the Dáil, she wrote a partisan article (which journalists were allowed to write at that time on the morning of the election) praising Fennell to the skies. "And Gemma Hussey said that was worth a thousand votes, which I hadn't realised," McCafferty says. "And she and Gemma Hussey, they were caught between a rock and a hard place on abortion. My memory is I was quite tender with them over it . . . but I also criticised them. But they were terribly caught," she says.

Fennell herself made some of her difficulties known in achieving any legal reforms for women upon her entrance into politics, although she is quick to point out today that for any of her frustrations during her years in office, she never experienced anything like the frustration she felt with the IWLM upon her resignation. On the day in 1983 that the Taoiseach, Garret FitzGerald, appointed Fennell Minister of State for Women's Affairs and Family Law Reform, the *Irish Press* published an article by Fennell in which she complained that the Dáil wasn't interested in legislating for women's issues and that women could achieve more outside the Dáil.[12] Now that she was formally part of the establishment, it seemed, she better appreciated some of the advantages of working outside the system, as she had done for years. For Fennell, whether she was founding pressure groups, setting up women's shelters, or taking her seat in the Dáil in the decades following her resignation from the IWLM, the battles continued.

13

Learning Feminism Backwards

"I think I had a strong sense of the *logic* of injustice against women, so I could fight on that. But on a personal level, feminism only really came to me when my own marriage broke down and I actually lived some of the things we were fighting for. And suddenly I was deserted, and it was totally horrendous." — Rosita Sweetman

Rosita Sweetman was one of the IWLM founders who, in 1970, had the most to look forward to. At twenty-two, the young journalist had recently joined Mary Kenny's staff at the *Irish Press's* women's page, where she was writing about the North, the women's movement, and other social issues – the most exciting topics of the day. She was learning about the mechanism and depth of discrimination against women along with the other IWLM founders through the consciousness-raising sessions, production of *Chains or Change*, and the group's protests. But it was not until almost two full decades after the IWLM's disintegration that she really understood how it all applied to her own life. In 1970, Sweetman had a personal view of feminism that was similar to Nuala Fennell's – she had a good job and had never encountered any serious obstacles of which she was aware based on her gender.

Sweetman's mother and father had a tradition each Christmas of giving each other a book as a gift. The day before her mother died, she had listened to the whole of *War and Peace* on tape. Sweetman's father, a barrister, had always been interested in writing, so it seems natural that Sweetman herself would have had inclinations towards journalism and authorship. Sweetman suspects her father would have loved to have been an author himself if he'd had the time and energy, and he was very encouraging when she started writing as a young woman. Her mother proofread all of the books Sweetman wrote later in life. Neither parent ever perpetuated the idea, so firmly entrenched in many other families in the sixties, that daughters were only for marrying off.

If Sweetman inherited a love of literature and writing from both of her parents, she was also bestowed with a sense of confidence from an unlikely source in the Ireland of the sixties – the nuns at the Sacred Heart school that she attended in Dublin. "In some ways having a convent education is bad, but in terms of your own self-esteem and what you could do . . . they didn't think, just go out and get a husband, which was sort of the only alternative at the time," she says. "In that way, that education was an advantage because they did bring us up to believe that we'd at least have a career, even though it was 1965 . . . if you wanted to be a writer, they'd say that was wonderful."

Sweetman's first job out of school in her late teens was at Amnesty International in London. She heard that the BBC was looking for runners, jobs that literally entailed running scripts and prompts from a producer's office to a journalist in a neighbouring studio. That was her first foray into the journalism profession. Toward the end of the sixties, her father saw an opening for a research assistant for RTÉ's current affairs programme *Seven Days* back in Dublin and encouraged Sweetman to apply. She got the job, and worked with legendary RTÉ producer and writer Lelia Doolan, who appeared alongside the IWLM on *The Late Late Show* as a panellist in March 1971. Sweetman found journalism exciting in that it made her much more aware of the great social changes that were going on all over the world. As RTÉ was covering the student protests in Paris and the women's and black civil rights protests in America, Sweetman had a tremendous feeling that a new era of freedom was being ushered in and old barriers were being broken down. She was thrilled to see that the same kind of change was well on its way in Ireland, too.

"It was huge, like black and white television changing to colour television," she says. "Colour started to come into it. There was this amazing feeling of the world opening up and change being possible like there hadn't been in a long time," she says. At the same time that Sweetman was working at RTÉ, Mary Kenny was assembling her crack team of writers for the *Irish Press* women's page, and the more opinionated and daring the recruits the better. Kenny asked Sweetman to come and work for her after she had written a few trial pieces for the paper. Professionally, Sweetman saw herself as living in quite an equal world already, like many of the other journalists in the IWLM who had every opportunity to cover the same kinds of stories as their male colleagues. "I didn't feel discriminated against," Sweetman says. "I felt I was running the world. I guess I felt really privileged."

Sweetman's articles reflected both her own pioneering attitude and Mary Kenny's doctrine that she instilled in her staff – the more extreme and daring the stories, the better. The more a writer questioned the establishment and pushed a story, the better. The more provocative an article, the better. With that in mind, Sweetman produced some of the most cutting-edge articles under Kenny's editorship. She remembers one two-part series about the appalling conditions in a Dublin juvenile detention center, for which a warden smuggled her into the building after midnight to get a more accurate idea of what it was really like, free from officials' restrictions. Her article details the poor nutrition, harsh treatment, and dirty facilities the children endured, all in the name of reforming them of their delinquent behaviour. She concluded her series by quoting an anonymous official, probably the same one who gave her access to the building undercover: "Take any child from its home and give it a few months in a prison, with totally inadequate food, untrained and disinterested wardens, grim prison surroundings, the company of severely delinquent children – he's not going to end up loving the society that sent him there. He'll end up hating it. I certainly would."[1]

Sweetman was also one of the first journalists in the Republic to concentrate on the effects the growing violence in the North had on women. She wrote a poignant, detailed article on the wife of an IRA man who had died making a bomb that had exploded prematurely. She profiled a women's peace organisation in the North, which purposely incorporated Catholic, Protestant and Presbyterian women, who were trying to prove that it was possible for a small group of people, at least, to put their differences aside in the hopes of ending the violence. She gave a firsthand account of what it was like to be on a Belfast street during a riot.

Working with Mary Kenny, Sweetman heard about the absolute latest in feminist literature. Kenny would always have the newest book, whether it was by Kate Millett, Germaine Greer, Shulamith Firestone, or any of the other godmothers of the women's movement. The books would promptly be passed around the office, and she encouraged her writers to interview the authors themselves. "Every time someone got a new book . . . it'd be straight into the office or straight down to the pub," Sweetman says. "The material travelled round really fast, nobody was holding onto it." *Irish Independent* journalist Mary Anderson even used to compile reading lists and circulate them for buying and borrowing at the IWLM meetings.

Having Kenny as a boss also made Sweetman realise that she might not have been as insulated from discrimination against women as she had thought. Kenny wrote an article early in 1971 expressing her view that even in journalism, which she admitted was one of the few professions that accepted the principle of equal pay for equal work, women could only rise to a certain level. At the time of Kenny's writing, women could not be sub-editors, typesetters or photographers. None of these restrictions was written into management agreements or union rules, but they might as well have been for how closely they were followed. Kenny claimed that such restrictions, which she must have experienced quite acutely as a self-identified ambitious career woman, amounted to ". . . a barrier of male prejudice which is maintained on the vaguest and yet most unyielding grounds".[2] It would have been difficult for any female journalist to read such a strong condemnation of the patriarchal power structure in her profession without reassessing her own career opportunities, and Sweetman was no exception.

Similar to Marie McMahon's recollections, Sweetman cites the process of putting *Chains or Change* together as another milestone that shocked her into recognising Irish women's situation for what it really was – one of severe repression under the law. And as Sweetman became more active herself in some of the IWLM's demonstrations, she began to see firsthand how abusive were the confrontations that the women putting themselves on the barricades experienced. Sweetman remembers the protest outside the Dáil during Mary Robinson's March 1971 attempt to get a reading of her bill that would repeal some of the laws banning contraceptives as especially ugly. While there were several male senators who were genuinely supportive of the women's liberation movement, there were also those in the Dáil who went to lengths to malign the movement and its members. Sweetman heard more vulgarities that day from the movement's critics than ever before, from both inside and outside the Dáil, and it was a cruel and abrupt realisation as to how strongly the opposition felt.

"That was when I started to really see a different sort of discrimination," Sweetman says. She began to respect the great power of the IWLM's demonstrations or "street theatre", with all the attention the group was getting, and she was most impressed with the Contraceptive Train. She was part of de Burca's reception committee at Connolly Station that day. "Standing at the station and seeing them come down the platform towards the gates . . . my heart was pounding and I was thinking, the revolution is coming and there is absolutely no doubt about it," she says.

Sweetman travelled extensively following the IWLM's disintegration, working as a journalist and writer in Tanzania, Peru and Bangladesh. Her husband was a development economist, a position that required the couple to move often. In Tanzania, Sweetman started a women's page at the daily newspaper. Most of the wives of her husband's colleagues spent their time taking advantage of the amenities at whatever posh hotel they were staying at, and very few of them worked. Sweetman had other ideas about how she wanted to spend her time, and she was curious about women's conditions in other countries. In Latin America, she discovered that there were many consciousness-raising groups having discussions that were reminiscent of the IWLM's.

Sweetman's first book, *On Our Knees*, was published in the mid-seventies and concentrated on Ireland's changing attitudes towards sex and sexuality. The book consisted mostly of excerpts from interviews Sweetman had conducted with a cross-section of people, North and South, including everyday citizens, members of the clergy and social workers. She followed *On Our Knees* with a novel, *Fathers Come First*, about a young Irish woman coming of age. In 1979 she wrote another non-fiction book in a similar format to *On Our Knees* titled *On Our Backs*. She was in a constant state of shock writing *On Our Backs,* she says, because she was encountering an almost unbelievable amount of ignorance through her interview subjects on so many matters of sexuality and contraception. She concluded that there was very little social support for people, the consequences of which were dire. "People just flung into relationships, flung into marriage, flung into pregnancy, no proper contraception, no proper education, and then no support when the babies come along and no support when the guy turns into an alcoholic because he's twenty-three and suddenly has a wife and children to support," Sweetman says. "Just violence and drink and ignorance. I was in a bad state when I was doing that book. It was so painful."

The book was not all doom and gloom, though. Sweetman interviewed Frank Crummey, whom she had probably met at Gaj's, focusing on his crusading role in getting Dublin family planning clinics established. Crummey told Sweetman one of his favorite stories about smuggling condoms, which he referred to as "French letters", over the border during the early seventies:

> It was still illegal then to import contraceptives so it was my job to smuggle them across the border. We had some great fun. One day I was stopped in Balbriggan by these Gardaí doing an arms check. I had 40,000 French letters in the station wagon and insisted they were all for my own personal use. I said I had imported them, I was going to use them, and if they booked me I would challenge them under EEC regulations. "Ah go *way*," they said finally.[3]

On Our Backs had a big impact upon its publication, so big that *The Late Late Show* had scheduled an entire programme in September 1979 to devote to the book. June Levine, who began her job as a researcher for the show in 1974, had made no secret of pushing her strong agenda for addressing feminist issues on the programme. Levine would be in the audience supporting Sweetman. *The Late Late Show* had lined up between twenty and thirty panelists, all people whom Sweetman had interviewed for the book, and she was thrilled that the issues she had devoted so much time and research to would be aired and discussed in front of the large audience that the show guaranteed. Through an unfortunate accident of bad timing, though, the show was cancelled because of the Pope's visit to Ireland that weekend. "They said nobody would want to talk about contraception or sex because everybody's in a fever of holiness. So that was that," Sweetman said. She and the panellists were never rescheduled.

Sweetman's consciousness about women's issues was raised, bit by bit, throughout the seventies, starting with her articles for the *Irish Press* and her membership in the IWLM. She feels that she took a roundabout route to a deeper, more meaningful understanding of feminism that she was only just beginning to discover in her days with the IWLM. As she articulates it, she "learned feminism backwards". Intellectually, she understood and had a strong sense of the injustices against women – it would have been impossible to be involved in the IWLM and not have experienced that kind of realisation. But on a personal level, she only really came to understand a deeper kind of feminism when her own marriage broke down in the late eighties and she actually lived through some of the struggles that she had been fighting in her youth on behalf of other women. With two young children to raise on her own, Sweetman went through an agonising period of isolation and vulnerability. She had written about such women, but now she was feeling what it was like herself to be a deserted wife and a single mother. It only made matters much, much worse, that her husband had left her for her sister. It was, she felt, a double betrayal that robbed her of the support of some loved ones that may have helped her immensely. "I'm not glad I had all the pain, but I'm glad I had some underpinning intellectually when it came so that I was able to gradually get myself back together again and start fighting," she says.

Of all of the IWLM's activities that helped her learn and grow as a woman, Sweetman is the most grateful for going through the experience of consciousness-raising. She thinks it enabled her to form friendships with other women more easily, a skill she needed badly in the aftermath of the disintegration of her marriage. "It just broke down those barriers so even when the kids and I were totally at rock bottom and penniless and totally deserted by everyone, I felt that because of the women's movement and because I had learned a little bit how to open up that I was able to do that."

14

All Aboard

"It [contraception] is the cutting edge of what women think about themselves, I think. And those women back in the early seventies were tackling that in a very brave and exciting way. It frightened a lot of people but I think even women who might have been serious Catholics and thought contraception was the worst thing in the world had a grudging admiration for what they were doing."
— Caitriona Crowe, feminist and librarian, from *Hoodwinked*[1]

"Arrest me, I'm on the pill!"

"Women are only baby machines"

"Welcome home, criminals"

— Slogans from protesters' signs at Connolly Station, 22 May 1971, greeting the Contraceptive Train

The IWLM founders who went on the Contraceptive Train in May 1971 knew, even at the moment they were pulling into Dublin's Connolly Station with contraceptives of every shape and size imported illegally from Belfast, that they were making history. More than *The Late Late Show* or the Mansion House meeting, the Contraceptive Train was a protest extravaganza that attracted not only the attention of Irish journalists, but also much of the foreign media. The IWLM founders who were most instrumental in organising the train deliberately planned it for 22 May, World Communications Day. Apart from grasping what an important moment it was to become in the Irish women's rights movement, even the most fearless and flamboyant of the IWLM founders on the train had one overwhelming thought as they approached the customs officials with their illegal contraceptives that day: what will our mothers think? Any fears they had of going to jail paled in comparison with the wrath they might incur from their mothers if they were seen on television or in the newspapers carrying contraceptives into the country, especially if they were among the unmarried. But the IWLM founders had been fighting the laws banning contraceptives, in some cases long before the group formed, and the Contraceptive Train was the climax of their previous campaigning.

The journalists, of course, had also been hitting the issue hard in the newspapers in the year leading up to the Train. In scores of articles at the tail end of the sixties and the early seventies, the women's pages reporters and editors presented both the hard facts about the laws banning contraceptives and personal stories from the women – and men – affected by those laws. The main ban on contraception was enshrined in the 1935 Criminal Law Act, which made the importation, distribution, and sale of contraceptive devices a criminal offence. Publications with advertisements for contraceptives were banned in Ireland or seized at ports of entry by customs officials. The contraceptive pill, which had not yet been invented in 1935 when the law was written, was available in Ireland upon a doctor's prescription, officially as a "menstrual cycle-regulator". Many Irish women took advantage of this loophole in the law, resulting in a disproportionately high number of Irish women who claimed they suffered from irregular periods in comparison to other societies.

The articles on contraception that the women's page editors had been running only increased in number and length after the IWLM identified contraception as one of its main demands, a human right that Irish women were denied just as they were denied so many of their basic civil rights. As 1970 drew to a close, though, the Catholic Church gave the women in the IWLM an even better reason to fight harder for a change in the laws. In early December 1970, Dublin's Archbishop Dr John McQuaid had written a letter declaring that every action which proposed to make procreation impossible was in itself "unlawful" – i.e. sinful and immoral in God's eyes. "In other words, any such contraceptive act is wrong in itself," McQuaid wrote.[2] There were many, many married Catholic women in Ireland who desperately wished they had choices available to plan their families with their husbands. There were women who couldn't use the pill (the only legal form of contraception prescribed by doctors through the guise of cycle regulation) and were forced to break the law if they sought those choices. And then there were the masses of single Catholic women who were brought up to believe that it was a sin to have pre-marital sex – but after McQuaid's letter it seemed that it was clearly a "double sin" to use contraception.

The IWLM cited Ireland's ban on contraception as a violation of a basic human right – the right of women *and* men to be able to plan their families. The newly formed Irish Family Planning Association (IFPA) even identified Ireland's laws against contraception as a violation of the UN Declaration of Human Rights; however, it was not until the UN's 1979 "Convention on the Elimination of All Forms of Discrimination Against Women" that the organisation explicitly identified contraception as a human right. It is likely the IFPA was citing Ireland's specific ban on advertisements and educational information about contraceptives as a violation under Article 19 of the UN's 1948 Universal Declaration of Human Rights, which guarantees the right to "seek, receive and impart information and ideas through any media, and regardless of frontiers". It is interesting to note that even the authors of the UN's 1979 Convention on women's rights chose not to use the actual word "contraception" when referring to the subject:

> State Parties shall take all appropriate measures to eliminate dis-crimination against women in all matters relating to marriage and family relations and in particular shall ensure . . . the same rights to decide freely and responsibly on the number and spacing of their children and to have access to the information, education and means to enable them to exercise these rights . . . (Article 16,1.e)

From the beginning of their struggle to legalise contraception, the IWLM founders also saw the laws as disproportionately discriminatory against poor women. Máirín Johnston, always true to her working-class roots, was keenly aware of this underlying inequality. "You could limit your family if you had enough money," she says. Indeed, if women had the train fare to get to Belfast they could purchase condoms, spermicidal jelly and other contraceptive devices. If they could afford a doctor's visit and the cost of the prescription (and, more importantly, knew which doctors would be sympathetic to their plight) they could get the pill.

Ireland's first family planning clinic, The Fertility Guidance Clinic, was opened in 1969 in Merrion Square in Dublin. Several others were subsequently opened in Mountjoy Square and Synge Street and, by the mid-seventies, in Limerick and Galway. The clinics found another loophole in the law: it was illegal to import, advertise and sell contraceptives, but not to actually *use* them, so they decided to "give away" condoms and accept "donations" in return.

However, even geography affected a woman's access to contraceptives. Rural women who lived far away from any of these few clinics and for whom it was difficult to travel to the UK were at the mercy of their local doctors for prescriptions for the pill. The clinics were not funded by the state and relied on private contributions and outside grants, and thus were constantly struggling. In any event, since the advertisement or advocation of contraceptives, as well as the contraceptives themselves, were illegal, most Irish women were egregiously ignorant about contraceptive methods and the variety of contraceptives on the market outside of Ireland. Class even played a role in this aspect of the ban on contraceptives. Cheap, mass-circulation British newspapers like *Reynold's News* carried small advertisements for contraceptives and were banned, while more expensive publications that also carried contraceptive ads like the *Spectator* and the *New Statesman* were not.[3]

Once Archbishop McQuaid made it clear that, in his interpretation at least, the church opposed the very *idea* of contraception, the women's page journalists began hitting the issue even harder. A few weeks after McQuaid's statement, *The Irish Times* ran an article on the women's page titled "Contraception: The Two Basic Problems". The introduction to the article explained that it was written by "a Dublin priest". In it, the unnamed priest attempted to ease some of the guilt that he had seen married couples struggle with over the church's opposition to birth control:

There are circumstances, in cases of birth control, as in all other spheres of morality, which can lessen, and at times even remove, the guilt of those who break the law. This is not a denial of the law, nor a refusal to inform one's conscience as to what that objective moral law is, but simply a realisation that there is no such thing as an immoral act which is *always* mortally sinful for *everyone*. No theologian could say this. The Archbishop did not say it. Yet the tragic fact is that this is what a great many good Catholics seriously believe their church to be saying.[4]

The *Independent* had published an article on contraception on its women's page a few months earlier, before the Archbishop had attracted even more attention to the issue with his letter. In it, reporter Janet Martin went to a meeting of the brand new Irish Family Planning Rights Association (IFPRA), later to change its name to the IFPA. The twenty-six year old Senator Mary Robinson (then Bourke) was present and vocal. She announced her plans to introduce a private member's bill in the next Senate term asking for the repeal of the existing legislation. Martin also wrote about the policies of Dublin's first "Fertility Guidance Clinic" in Merrion Square, whose existence was possible only because of a grant from the International Planned Parenthood Association and a dedicated staff. Martin reported that the clinic referred women who were unable to take the pill to the Royal Victoria Hospital in Belfast where a British Family Planning Association unit operated and where they could be fitted with a mechanical device.[5] If some of the other issues the women's page journalists had been writing about – lesbianism, unmarried mothers, etc. – had been unspeakable before, reading about the specifics of contraception and contraceptive devices had to be equally shocking, if only because of the laws that prohibited the distribution of any information on them. The papers were able to get around those laws as long as reporters did not advocate the use of contraceptives or give too much information about them – just as many women found ways around the laws banning contraceptives themselves. For the more sheltered and conservative women, learning the specifics of how other women were able to bypass those laws must also have been simultaneously illuminating and scandalous.

Mary Kenny at the *Irish Press* was not to be outdone on such a controversial issue as contraception. In the autumn of 1970, Kenny inter-

viewed two women together who were each staunch advocates of opposite views on contraception and let them debate the issue, printing large
excerpts from the transcript on her women's page. Kenny's own opinion
on contraception was clear from her interjections. Meena Cribben felt
that contraception was "murder by anticipation", and believed Irish
women must allow the pope to interpret natural law for them. Kenny
challenged her by pointing out that this was unfair to Irish women who
were not Catholics: "I thought you could be Catholic, Protestant, Agnos-
tic, Dissenter, Jew, or for that matter Zen Buddhist and still be Irish,"
Kenny said. Monica McEnroy was a forty-year-old nurse, mother and
doctor's wife who had been a vocal campaigner for contraceptive law
reform for more than a decade. McEnroy said she was not going to engage Cribben in a debate about the morality or immorality of contraception, but that she merely disputed the government's right to step in and
say it would not allow women the medical means of limiting their families. She also accused Cribben of wrongly equating contraception with
abortion, an association that many who opposed contraception were
quick to make. McEnroy and others in favour of legalising contraception
went to great lengths to make it clear that it would not be the first step
down the slippery slope to legalising abortion, as many contraception
opponents argued.[6] Janet Martin of the *Independent* had also interviewed
McEnroy for her October article on contraception, when McEnroy had
been harshly critical of the Irish Countrywomen's Association's failure
to take a stance on contraception: "The ICA claim to represent the opinions of 25,000 women in this country, and yet they would rather write
letters to the newspapers about black spots on tomatoes," McEnroy told
the *Independent*.[7]

Archbishop McQuaid's letter confused many Catholic women even
further and heightened their struggle between the "immorality" of contraceptive use and the practical and financial difficulties of raising huge
families. But it also made the issue itself more acceptable for discussion,
and the IWLM journalists took advantage of that. They instinctively recognised that they could harness the same psychological phenomenon that
is often responsible for the enormous popularity some books and films
enjoy after being banned – the surest way to spark interest and attention
in something is to prohibit it. The Archbishop himself had made sure that

contraception was at the top of the list of controversial topics of the day. The IWLM journalists began simply to devote more space on their pages to the topic and let the nation air its views. They interviewed legislators, doctors and ordinary women. What they heard from women was a lot of frustration and angst. *The Irish Times* conducted a poll in December 1970 of their women's page readers, asking how many favoured a change in the law and asking them to identify themselves as Catholics, Protestants or some other religion. The results were unsurprising, representing the paper's liberal readership – of the 429 responses, only five were against repealing the ban on contraception. The *Times* reported that two of the letters in favour of a change were from Catholic priests who had signed their names. Many readers included letters of comment with their replies to the poll, which had asked only for a "yes" or "no" response. *The Irish Times* devoted the whole women's page to excerpts from the letters one day in the week following the poll. One letter in particular encompassed the IWLM's argument that the contraception issue was, first and foremost, a class issue:

> Firstly, while the state laws regarding contraception are undoubtedly a denial of a basic human right for those of us who are not Catholics, they do not seriously interfere with the better-off and better-informed, who find it easy enough, if inconvenient, to get round them. It is the less-well-off who are penalised. . . . Because of the ban on information, "the pill" has become synonymous with contraception in this country. Diaphragm seems to be a dirty word and the IUD unheard of. While the pill is undoubtedly convenient and efficient, it is not suitable for all women, and is certainly the most expensive method.[8]

Contraception was at once one of the IWLM's most delicate and important demands because, along with class, it symbolised so many of the other issues with which women were struggling at the time. "It's not all to do with contraception, unfortunately, is it?" the writer Leland Bardwell said in the mid-nineties of the contraception debate of the seventies. "It's to do with ignorance and knowledge and the ability to use them and drunken husbands and all kinds of problems" (*Hoodwinked*).[9] The IWLM founders were well aware of the complexities entangled in the contraception debate, and they knew they would have to tread more carefully with this issue than any of their other six demands. Of their goals, legalised contraception was the only one that was strongly related to sex and sexuality, distinguishing it immediately as the riskiest of topics. It was also the one issue that was directly linked to religion and which the Catholic Church had always vehemently opposed, a position that was all the more apparent due to the Archbishop's blatant denouncement of any proposed law that would repeal the ban on contraception. If the Archbishop was to be believed, the legalisation of contraception would be a major contributing factor to the complete disintegration of the moral fabric of the country. There were many in Ireland who did see it that way, and the women's page journalists heard from them as well as from supporters of their campaign to change the laws. Just a few weeks before the Contraceptive Train, in May 1971, Mary McCutchan at the *Irish Independent* published an unsigned letter from a woman who echoed the Archbishop's sentiments and dissatisfaction with the women's liberation activists:

> Dear "Independent Woman": Looking at the woman's page you would hardly suspect that Ireland is a Catholic country. For months you have been brainwashing married women to have careers outside the home and pressing for a change in the laws relating to contraceptives with, once, even a suggestion that we take "a new look" at abortion. I believe it is all part of a plan to prepare the ground for "permissive" legislation, directly contrary to the teaching of the Catholic Church.

> First we were told we should bring our laws into line with those of EEC countries, next we must do the same if we want a united Ireland. Now there is a sudden concern for the "rights" (i.e., to contraceptives) of the Protestant minority in the South.

> What right have pressure groups in Dublin, however vociferous, to dictate to the rest of the country? What makes you think the country as a whole wants the laws changed? If they are changed the press and television will be largely to blame for the consequences.

> If any work is more important than rearing children to know, love, and serve God in this life so that they may be happy with him forever in the next I challenge "Independent Woman" to name it.[10]

The autumn of 1970 saw the first round of women's page articles dealing with the specifics of the contraception laws, the establishment of Ireland's first family planning organisations, and the church's renewed articulation of its opposition to the very idea of contraception. The nation was on the cusp of an even stormier debate on the contraceptive issue as both sides intensified their arguments, and the IWLM's internal deliberations on how to publicly handle the issue mirrored the escalating controversy rippling through the nation. A second barrage of articles appeared on the women's pages in March 1971, coinciding with the IWLM's appearance on *The Late Late Show* and Mary Robinson's attempt to get a Senate reading of her Contraceptive Bill that would loosen the restrictions on the availability and sale of contraceptive devices. Officially, and in an effort to make it more acceptable to the public, the bill was lauded as the first effort at changing the constitutional position of the family in Ireland. Of the women's page pieces that appeared that spring, the articles authored by Mary Kenny again stood out as some of the most forceful. Kenny dedicated her regular Monday column, "Mary's Monday Miscellany", to the contraception question the week before Robinson's first attempt to get a reading for her bill. To begin with, Kenny reiterated the IWLM's insistence that people are mistaken in equating contraception law reform with a range of social evils, exactly as the woman who had written in to the *Irish Independent* had done. "It [contraception] does NOT instantly pave the way for divorce, abortion, euthanasia, mass prostitution of 11-year-old children and epidemic VD," she wrote.[11]

Kenny's article further explained the culture of fear surrounding the contraception debate, indicating the criticisms that she and the other IWLM founders were experiencing for daring to challenge the Church's teachings and the status quo:

> The fears which encircle the debate are also extraordinary. . . .
> Many people privately see the plain rights and wrongs of this bad
> law, but are afraid to say so publicly. My own mother has begged
> me not to show public support for change in this law – not because
> she disapproves of my views but because there are such deeply in-
> grained apprehensions in Irish people about anything which
> touches church affairs, however obliquely. You'll lose your job,
> your reputation, you'll make enemies of the powerful, you'll get

tarnished with the dead label of being an anti-cleric is the insinua-
tion. And this is precisely the mentality which restrains people
who otherwise support a change in the law . . . there is no need to
be afraid of witch-hunts in Ireland today.[12]

In her writing and on the barricades, Kenny's bravado never faltered.
Today, she remembers it differently, revealing some of her own fears
that her admirers and critics alike, and even most of her fellow IWLM
founders, never suspected. Just as Maeve Binchy remembers Kenny's
brush with sickness in a pub toilet due to her pipe-smoking one night at
the height of her popularity, she recalls Kenny's nervousness about
walking out of the Haddington Road church in protest of the church's
stance against contraception during the last week of March 1971. Contraception was all over the newspapers, Mary Robinson was fighting for
the reading of her bill, and the Archbishop issued yet another letter condemning contraception, which was to be read at all the Sunday masses
on 28 March. The IWLM was out in full force to oppose it, and many of
the founders (some whom had not crossed the threshold of church doors
in years) attended several masses at different churches so they could
walk out in protest. They went to the Pro-Cathedral and picketed the
Archbishop's residence later that evening. It was around this time that Dr
Moira Woods was threatening to set her own coat on fire in church,
which one of the other founders successfully talked her out of.

Máirín Johnston attended the Haddington Road mass along with
Kenny and several other IWLM founders. Johnston remembers that her
own nerves got the better of her. Kenny was the first to stand up during
the reading of the Archbishop's letter with a shout of "I object!", or
something to the same effect. Johnston stood up beside Kenny and
mumbled that she, too, objected to the church's position on contraception before they both hastily left the church. It was a bit of a "wet her-
ring" in terms of an effective protest, Johnston remembers. "I think I felt
a bit foolish after because it would have been better for us to have a debate, he up on the pulpit and us down below," Johnston says. "But we
didn't, and I think if I'd been braver and stood my ground, I think I
would have been prouder," she says. The brief, anonymous *Irish Times*
article the following day about the protests at the various masses con-
jured the image of a much calmer and articulate Johnston. "This is a mat-

ter that should be decided by women alone. Why should men dictate to us how many children we should have? We are leaving this church in protest," the article quoted Johnston.[13] The same article mentioned that most of the women who had protested at the masses were married, and that many of them were mothers. A statement released by the Irish Movement for Peace and Justice, also quoted in the article, revealed that the IWLM was not the only pressure group who recognised the plight of the working-class in relation to contraception. "Contraception in Ireland is a matter of class and not creed," the group said simply in response to the Archbishop's letter.

The articles on contraception that the IWLM journalists had been publishing well before the issue was thrust squarely into the public arena in late 1970 revealed their insistence for a change in the laws, but one in particular that was published a year before the Contraceptive Train almost predicted the group's most daring and famous public protest. Ironically, it was written by Nuala Fennell, one of the IWLM founders who most disapproved of the group's flamboyant media events and resigned just weeks after the Contraceptive Train. Fennell had written an article for Kenny's *Irish Press* women's page about the women from the Republic who took the train to Belfast specifically for contraceptives. Using one of Kenny's preferred journalistic tactics for putting one individual's experience on the face of a mass problem, Fennell tells the story of a twenty-two-year-old housewife. The young woman had little money, a small son, and an intolerance to the pill. When she had gone to her doctor for advice he had referred her to a family planning clinic in the North.[14] It was well-known that women often took the train to Belfast for contraceptives. But Fennell remembers that there was a contradiction between the aversion many women and men claimed they felt toward contraceptives and the lengths to which other women like the one she interviewed experienced in the desperation of trying to obtain them under the restrictive laws. Fennell was on a radio programme shortly after writing the article when a "sanctimonious" male interviewer asked her what was in women's minds as they were breaking the law, travelling out of the country to get contraceptives. "He was talking on the national airwaves about the morality of it, when it was interesting that to the women, it was just a practical need," Fennell says.

The original idea and decision to stage the Contraceptive Train came about shortly after the massive Mansion House meeting in April 1971, and after the branch groups had been established. In early May 1971, many members of the branch groups were present at a large meeting in the North Star Hotel when the idea was put forth. A few hands went up in favour of it, and then a few more, until eventually the majority of the women had voted for it. Nell McCafferty, newly installed at *The Irish Times* and still deeply involved in the civil rights movement, recalls that the train had been her idea, gleaned from a march in the North about a year previously "with the lefties" – members of People's Democracy and the Labour Party. The march went from North to South, and at the border student activist Cyril Tallman held up a copy of Edna O'Brien's *Country Girls* in one hand and a Durex condom in the other, saying both were banned in the south. McCafferty was unimpressed, even a bit disgusted. "I left the march that day, and I said I'm not standing for this. Partly I was thinking, God, a condom, this is really going to give us a bad reputation, and partly I was thinking, bloody men and their sex – they don't wave condoms in Derry but they wave them at the border. But the following year when, remember, we're all talking about contraception, that's when I got the idea, let's reverse the journey from Dublin to the North. It was based on that civil rights march in the North. How did I change over in one year?" McCafferty says.

Although McCafferty asks the question with genuine curiosity, it is not very difficult to understand how she had grown to see the importance of contraception as a human right over the course of that one year from 1970 to 1971. She had begun to recognise the similarities between women's struggles for human rights in the south and the civil rights movement in the north. As Nell saw it, one of the best things that could be done for the North was to change the South by loosening the bonds between church and state there. "The North is a Protestant state for Protestant people, and the South is a Catholic state for Catholic people and the Protestants in the North used to say, we won't go into a United Ireland with the Pope. And I thought, in my clever way, we'll change the South, and they can't accuse us of that," McCafferty says. To her, it was becoming increasingly clear that one of the best ways of bringing about the kind of change that would help the civil rights movement in the

North was through the women's movement in the Republic. Contraception went straight to the heart of those binds between church and state; the laws banning contraception were designed to reflect Catholic ideology. Do away with the laws, McCafferty thought, and demonstrate that the beginning of the separation of church and state was really happening, and you were on the right track in both the Civil Rights movement *and* the women's liberation movement.

Even though the majority of both the IWLM founders and the branch members present at the North Star meeting voted in favour of the train, the debates within the group about its most ambitious protest were far from over. Every one of the women knew that contraception had sparked such a sensitive debate because of all it symbolised – the teachings of the church that were still so sacred to so many and which Catholic parents nationwide reinforced in raising their children, and the most taboo subject of sexuality. On the other side, to the IWLM founders, legalised contraception embodied the brand new idea that women had a right to control their own fertility in spite of these first two. In her March 1971 article on contraception, the last of its kind to appear in the *Irish Press* before the train in May, Mary Kenny wrote that the idea of a pluralist society with objective civil laws was still very far away because of all of these other issues that were inextricably tied to contraception in people's minds. But just because the IWLM founders were perhaps more aware of the intricacies of the controversy surrounding the contraception debate did not mean that they themselves were unencumbered by them.

Máirín de Burca was perhaps the most conflicted member of the group in her attitude toward the Contraceptive Train. De Burca, whose arrest record showed that she was usually highly in favour of all forms of public protest save violent ones, made a personal decision not to ride on the train herself because she was a single woman and as such felt that she had no need for contraception. She was a strong supporter of the campaign to repeal the laws banning contraception, but personally ascribed to the belief that sex was to be shared exclusively between married adults. "I know it dates me for saying it, and nowadays it sounds silly, but at the time it was a real issue," de Burca says. Similar to her reservations about the group's appearance on *The Late Late Show*, she was also concerned about how the train would affect the IWLM's image in the eyes of Irish women all over the country. She thought that some women, especially rural women, would see those on the train as a herd of god-less, single, promiscuous women from Dublin who were out to stir up all kinds of trouble by launching a direct assault on the country's moral fi-bre. "You put people off if a single woman goes up and comes back with contraception. Everybody was going to say, it's immoral. She's planning to have sex and she's not married," de Burca says.

De Burca voiced her concerns at subsequent meetings and group dis-cussions about the train, making no secret of the fact that she thought it would be better for the group and the cause if only married women actu-ally took the train journey and brought the contraceptives back into Dub-lin. Ultimately, like all of the decisions the IWLM was to make, the choice was left up to each individual to participate in the ride or not. There was a large number of single women, of course, who ended up taking the journey to Belfast, among them Mary Kenny, Marie McMa-hon, Mary Anderson and June Levine. Mary Maher, who shared de Burca's concerns about the train just as she had over *The Late Late Show*, was in the hospital on the day of the Contraceptive Train, giving birth to her second daughter. Although de Burca had chosen to stay be-hind, she organised the reception committee at the Connolly Station plat-form for the women's return. She did her job very well – the interna-tional and the Irish media were there, and some camera crews had even gone on the train and filmed the women buying contraceptives in the chemist shops in Belfast. There was also a large crowd of supporters, including women who had not gone on the train because of work, those who had declined for reasons similar to de Burca's, and family members and friends of the returning "criminals". Some of the women who had chosen to stay behind, whether married or single, simply were not ready to involve themselves in such a display of making the sexual matter of contraception so public.

Of the founders and branch members who went on the train, forty-seven in all, each has a different story about their own personal experience that day. The passage of three and a half decades has done little to dull the excitement and tension of the day for some; for at least one, though, shame at her own behaviour is the overriding memory. Before their morning de-parture from Connolly station, Nell McCafferty had printed handouts with instructions on what the women should do when they returned to Dublin with the contraceptives as they went through customs that evening. The sheet listed all the possible contraceptives the women could buy in Belfast including condoms, the pill, IUDs and diaphragms. Free legal aid would be available to everyone. McCafferty's list of suggestions for confronting the customs officials included the following:

1. Declare nothing and risk being searched.

2. Declare contraceptives and refuse to be searched.

3. Declare contraceptives and refuse to hand over.

4. Declare contraceptives and hand over with protest of infringement of your constitutional rights.

5. Declare contraceptives and throw over barrier to sisters waiting beyond. Many people who couldn't come today will be demonstrating at Amiens Street in solidarity with our action.

6. Declare contraceptives and sit down in anticipation of customs action.

7. Declare internal contraceptive. Allow search from Female Officer only and shout "April Fool" before entry.[15]

For all of the excitement and careful planning, McCafferty was somewhat disappointed with what she saw as a relatively small number of women who actually went on the train – only enough to fill two carriages. Their first stop was the nearest chemist shop to the Belfast train station. Confusion ensued. McCafferty and as many women as possible jammed into the shop, with camera crews and reporters in tow. When McCafferty asked for a package of contraceptive pills, the chemist asked for her prescription. She asked for a coil, loop, Dutch cap (diaphragm), anything she could think of or vaguely remember that seemed appropriate, and he kept asking for her prescription. She called for June Levine, and "our redoubtable Jewish saviour sailed like a galleon to the front of the scrum".[16] Levine was unquestionably more experienced with such matters, having used doctor's prescriptions before for contraceptives and thus having a better knowledge of the specifics and the terminology of the devices by which many of the women were now stymied. McCafferty was not at all satisfied with the idea that they would be taking their stand at Dublin customs with just condoms and spermicidal jelly, the only two items that, as she and the rest of the women were now discovering, did not require a prescription:

> Uninformed I was, but stupid I was not. I did not fancy us return-
> ing to Dublin armed only with condoms, which would have con-
> centrated the mind of the nation on male nether regions; on sex;
> on anything but birth control. Unthinkable. So I bought hundreds
> of packets of aspirin.[17]

McCafferty was quite confident that no one at customs was going to look closely enough at the individual pills to declare them all fakes, so that crisis, at least for the time being, was averted. It also solved a problem for Máirín Johnston, who had taken her partner and one of her children on the train with her. It was close to her son's fourteenth birthday and they had decided that a trip to Belfast would be good fun. She and her family were also interested in the political scene in the North, another incentive for them to make the Contraceptive Train a (less than obvious) family outing. Johnston was also several months pregnant with her fourth child, but McCafferty, in a moment of forgetfulness that morning, had decided that Johnston should be the first woman to go through cus-toms declaring her illegal contraband and refuse to hand it over. She had wanted Johnston to swallow the pill in front of the customs official. "I said, 'Nell, I can't take the pill, I'm pregnant!' She said, 'Well, just put it under your tongue and spit it out later'," Johnston remembers. The fact that they were not actually successful in obtaining the pill made it less of a problem for Johnston to swallow.

Since Johnston was occupied most of the day with her own family, she cannot really recall what the atmosphere was like with the other women, who split up into smaller groups after their trip to the chemist. She makes a good guess at what was going on, though. "I believe they set Belfast ablaze in a different way that day from the bombs that were going off," she says. Of the television footage that exists from the arrival of the train in Dublin, the clip of Máirín Johnston confronting the cus-toms officials is perhaps the best embodiment of the spirit of coura-geousness that each woman must have summoned in her own way to do what she did that day. Several of the women who had gone before Johnston actually had given up their contraceptives, but, as McCafferty had wished, Johnston was the first one to refuse to hand over her purchases. The customs officer asked her if she had contraceptives and she said yes, pulling a tube of spermicidal jelly out of her purse. He said he'd have to take it from her and she said, in her broad Dublin accent, "It's my jelly. You're not getting it." She stuck her aspirin under her tongue, saying, of course, it was the pill. The customs officer told her she was breaking the law, but in the end, he let her through. De Burca's reception committee, including Johnston's younger children, were all on the platform shouting "Let them through!" "It was a great day because they couldn't do anything about it and it proved how stupid the law was," Johnston said. "It proved that if you organised well enough, you could confront anything, and women were a force to be reckoned with, definitely," she says.

Marie McMahon was not quite as calm, cool and collected as Johnston proved herself to be. McMahon looked so young that when she approached the chemists' counter to buy her contraceptives to bring back, he would not sell them to her because he thought she was under the age of eighteen. She was very afraid of being caught on camera and being seen by her mother, at once breaking the law and her mother's heart. "It would be the biggest disgrace of all time for her to see her daughter who was single and young talking about such a thing as contraception, let alone going on a train and bringing them back," McMahon says. "There's actually a few pictures of me, and whatever the camera is focused on, I'm hiding behind it." Her mother totally disapproved of McMahon's involvement in the women's movement, mostly, Marie thinks, because she was afraid no one would want to marry her daughter. She never knew that Marie had been on the train until Marie appeared on RTÉ's 2001 thirtieth anniversary programme commemorating the day. She was not upset when Marie looked right at the camera and said, "Hiya, ma." "We all changed our mothers' views quite a bit," McMahon says. "And some of us changed our father's views, too."

McMahon was not the only one who was nervous that day. McCafferty and Kenny also feared their mothers' reactions, but they were also a little worried about what their editors at the *Times* and the *Press* respectively would say. They had each taken their reporters' activism and participation in pickets and demonstrations in stride, but would they see this media stunt as really having gone too far? Kenny especially was on thin ice with Tim Pat Coogan. There was also the chance that the women would not even reach Dublin with their contraband – that they would be stopped right across the border and their entire plan for the public arrival through customs would be ruined.

Kenny was not so worried that it was preventing her from having a little fun on the train ride back to Dublin. Both McCafferty and Levine remember hearing about her blowing up condoms like balloons and then letting them fly around the aisles, and Levine's help was enlisted for the second time that day to try to subdue Kenny. One of the other organisers asked if Levine would take Kenny in her own carriage and try to calm her down. Besides blowing up the condoms, Kenny was "beside herself with excitement" and greatly offending a passenger with a child who was unassociated with the IWLM. "Her chat was unsuitable in front of the child, even though Mary always said the most outrageous things in polite English," Levine wrote. "I can't remember if the woman left the carriage or not. Certainly, she wrote to the papers the following week saying how disgraceful we had been".[18] Levine knew that worry would calm her down, and started bringing up problems that were on her own mind. What if de Burca's welcome committee had already been arrested at the station for disturbing the peace? What if they were arrested themselves upon their arrival and their whole protest was for naught? It worked and Kenny settled down.

For the aura of exuberance and excitement that the others remember surrounding her that day, Kenny has a different recollection of the journey. She recalls detaching herself from the group in Belfast and spending most of the day alone at the cinema. It was also the first time she remembers experiencing a deep pain in one leg, a condition that worsened over the years until it culminated in her need for a hip replacement. Like the earlier protest at the Haddington Road church, Kenny says her overriding memory of the day is one of embarrassment. Even though she realised intuitively that the Contraceptive Train was the type of effective protest that would eventually open doors for women, at the time she felt there was something deeply vulgar in its nature. Of the IWLM members who were also on the train and in the receiving crowd that day, Kenny is alone in this sentiment. But her recollections of confronting the customs officials at the station are echoed by some of the other women. "There's a big difference in life between the theory and the practice of things," Kenny says. Though the IWLM had talked at length about patriarchal laws and oppression, seeing the actual faces of the customs men at Connolly station was a different experience from what many of the women had expected. "They just looked so wretched and pathetic and embarrassed and they didn't know where to look and I felt so sorry for them and I thought, oh my God, we're this bunch of harridans descending on these poor helpless men," Kenny says. Although none of the other IWLM members refer to the customs men quite as sympathetically, they do remember the officials' embarrassment at being confronted by a crowd of condom, jelly and pill-wielding women determined to break the law, high on adrenaline and the excitement of the statement they were trying to make. Marching into the station from the platform, before the customs officials could stop them, some of the women threw their packets over the barriers or slid them through to the waiting crowd.

The IWLM women held back from the other women who were not associated with the Contraceptive Train, those who had taken the same trip to Belfast that thousands of other women had taken for cheaper clothes and merchandise. The women's liberationists unfurled their black cloth banner with the white stenciled lettering "Irish Women's Liberation Movement", which Máirín Johnston and her partner had painted, and made their way through customs. They declared their contraceptives and handed them over, or declared them and refused to hand them over, or threw them over to the crowd, or popped the aspirin tablets that were supposed to be birth control pills. They could hear the strains of "We Shall Overcome" and the other shouts from the crowd. When it became clear that the customs officials really were at a loss as to what to do with these women, but that arresting them was not an option, the women who had taken the train merged with the crowd that Máirín de Burca had organised. McCafferty had prepared a statement on the train to read to the crowd and the media at the station, from which reporters quoted extensively in their articles about the train that appeared in the papers two days later:

> By default the government upheld the Constitutional rights of
> Irish men and women allowing for freedom of conscience and the
> right to control one's life . . . We further accuse the State of
> criminal irresponsibility in permitting 26,000 women in this
> country to use the only contraceptive pill legally available to
> them, imported as a "cycle regulator", simply because this is a
> technical evasion of the law – despite the fact that such ovulants
> are, in many cases, medically unsuitable and damaging to women
> who might otherwise, in all conscience, choose other methods, at
> present illegal.[19]

McCafferty's statement articulates the point the IWLM was trying so
hard to prove with the Contraceptive Train – the hypocrisy inherent in
the state's refusal to repeal the ban on contraceptives and its simultane-
ous (and now obvious) failure to enforce it. The group had accomplished
its aim in exposing that hypocrisy and proving by its example that
women would be effectively free from then on to import contraceptives
from the North into the Republic without any interference from law enforcement officials. In her memoir, McCafferty wrote of her one regret
from that day – that she passed the statement which she had written on to
someone else to read. Conscious of the charges that the women's liberation movement was made up not of ordinary women but "uppity com-
mies who had infiltrated and taken fiendish control of women's pages in
the media", McCafferty handed the statement over to an unknown
branch member named Colette O'Neill, thus losing her own "place in
history as the apotheosis of Irish womankind".[20] O'Neill read the statement and was photographed at the forefront of the group, and she and
Mary Kenny were the only two women on the train who appeared on *The
Late Late Show* that night to talk about the experience. Some of the
IWLM women wondered if the protest would have been even more successful if any of the group *had* been arrested, and if the crowd had then
left the train station and made their way to the nearest Garda station to
read the statement again and challenge the guards directly. Nothing happened, and the protestors drifted off to their homes to watch *The Late
Late Show*. McCafferty and Kenny talked later that night, after each had
seen her editor and determined that her job was still safe.

Mary Robinson, for all of her determination and legal brilliance, failed in both March and May of 1971 to get the Senate to add her Contraceptive Bill to its order paper.[21] Despite Robinson's efforts, and those of the IWLM and of the feminist groups like Irish Women United who continued the fight for legal contraception, it was not until 1979 that the government finally passed the Family Planning Act. The Act allowed only "*bona fide*" (married) couples access to contraceptive devices other than the pill with a doctor's prescription. Family planning centres in Dublin and in five other cities were selling condoms without prescriptions by this time, a violation of the law which the government ignored until 1985, when the Fine Gael–Labour government finally amended the Family Planning Act to permit the legal sale of condoms by clinics and a small number of pharmacies. It had been fairly easy for the government to turn a blind eye to the clinics' sale of condoms because of their clever way around the law by accepting "donations". As late as 1990, the Irish Family Planning Association (IFPA) was fined £500 in Dublin District Court for selling condoms in the city's Virgin Megastore, and it was not until 1992 that the government extended legislation further to allow supermarkets and other retail shops to sell condoms. The British medical journal *The Lancet* cited the Virgin Megastore incident as "the first time in recent decades that any person or institution of integrity in any part of the world has been fined for practising preventative medicine".[22] Legislative changes in the contraception laws were obviously a long time coming, far behind the momentum of the Contraceptive Train that day in May 1971.

Although Robinson had failed to get the Senate to grant a reading of her Contraceptive Bill that year, officially labelled the "Family Planning" Bill, she succeeded in highlighting the gap that existed between the issues the male politicians were willing to examine and the issues with which the rest of the country was most concerned. In his biography of Robinson, John Horgan asks what relevance the parliament itself had if everybody in the country was talking about contraception in 1971 except the TDs.[23] Along with the exposition of the hypocrisy inherent in the ban on contraceptives, this was another point the IWLM repeatedly presented to the public.

The IWLM also played a central role, through the media, in diminishing the Catholic church's power in that decade despite the difficulties the women's liberation movement encountered in their campaign due to the church's resistance. The IWLM journalists' focus on the issue despite the church's mighty influence at the time eventually yielded tremendous results:

> If the power of the Catholic church in Ireland has begun to dwindle in recent years it is not so much that it can no longer limit other power blocs and alliances, but that its control of moral practice and discourse is being eroded by the development of mass communications. The media have lifted the veil of silence which previously shrouded moral issues . . .

> It is the media that have shattered the myth that it is bad luck to criticise the priest. It is the media that have broken the tradition of not criticising the church and its teachings in public. It is the media that have forced the church into giving a public account of itself . . .[24]

"We separated church and state," Nell McCafferty says simply when asked what the IWLM's legacy is, as if it were a feat that any group of friends meeting in a beloved restaurant once a week could accomplish over coffee. "We started a revolution that overturned the entire country. We set the seeds that destroyed the authority of the Catholic church, though mind you, they mostly destroyed themselves with their sexual scandals. I can't think of a greater success story," she says. She's careful to point out that it was never the IWLM's intention to destroy the church, and that God and faith are still around, as they should be. "I'm glad people have a God they can believe in," she says. "*I* want to believe. Because I want the party to continue."

The party for the IWLM founders was almost over even as they were celebrating the incredible triumph that had been the Contraceptive Train in May 1971. There were still protests to plan and meetings to be held, and not a single one of the founders can remember a "last" meeting. The end, like the beginning, was never as definite as that. A meeting between the founders was held early that summer and then, simply, no more were called. The movement went on, though, and several of the founders were extremely active in visiting the branch groups that had been born the night of the Mansion House meeting, the night that many of the founders identify clearly as the death of their original small group.

McCafferty in particular, one of the architects of the Contraceptive Train and mouthpiece of the movement, was far from finished with her work for women's liberation. As the founder group disintegrated, she was one of the most active in reaching out to branch groups, lecturing, infuriating, and making people laugh, merging journalism and activism into her own particular brand of feminism. The two characteristics her fellow founders cite most often about McCafferty from their days in the movement are her fondness for provoking a good row and her ability to cheer people up with a good laugh. The civil rights activist from Derry with a gift for public speaking can still captivate, enrage, and charm an audience, whether in print or in person, with little visible effort – one of the things that hasn't changed at all since her days in the IWLM.

15

The Derrywoman

"What I brought from the civil rights movement to the women's movement? Rise up. Rise up, and have the facts on your hands, and if your cause is just you cannot go wrong. That, and the revolution is a glorious thing. It's a happy thing to throw off your shackles, wonderful . . ." — Nell McCafferty, on the civil rights movement and the Irish Women's Liberation Movement

"She wasn't particularly radical, but the times were." — Journalist Gene Kerrigan on Nell McCafferty[1]

When Marie McMahon thinks of Nell McCafferty's role in the IWLM, she remembers something besides Nell's way with a crowd, her brilliant writing or her enjoyment of a good argument, all characteristics some of the other founders mention first. "I just don't think there would have been any women's movement without Nell," McMahon says. "Because she was such a powerful force in her own way."

McCafferty snorts derisively when asked why she became a journalist, saying she wanted to go into the profession because she couldn't think of anything else to do. She was trained as a teacher, and had earned her degree from Queen's University in Belfast, but could not find work in her native Derry in the mid-sixties because the Protestant schools knew she was a Catholic, and the Catholics thought she wasn't a proper Catholic. They all thought she was a communist of some kind. "Kissing the bishop's ring and offering one's services" was how people went about getting teaching jobs at the Catholic schools in those days, and McCafferty hadn't even been to see the bishop at all. After college she had spent some time in Israel working on a kibbutz, which seemed to further confuse the Catholics. They could not figure out why she would be working for no wages for Jews if she truly was a good Catholic.

McCafferty had some poetry published while studying at Queen's, and she was interested in writing from an early age. She was unemployed and on the dole in 1968 when *Observer* journalist Mary Holland (later to join *The Irish Times*) arrived in Derry to report on the civil rights movement. McCafferty was a volunteer secretary of the Derry Labour Party, writing small pieces for its magazine, and she knew which sources gave accurate information. Holland was irate when she was given inaccurate information for a piece she was writing about Royal Ulster Constabulary (RUC) officers in Derry being abusive to demonstrators, leading her to greatly exaggerate the number of officers in her article. "She was furious with this because you get one fact wrong and the whole story sinks," McCafferty says. "All the journalists came to me because I always got the facts right. Always. And *then* I give them my interpretation of the facts because I'm objective about the facts and subjective about my interpretation," she says.

McCafferty got to know Holland and the other journalists covering the North better, taking them around Derry and supplying them with solid information. She was enchanted with Holland's talent as a journalist and the power of her writing. Sometime in early 1970 Holland and an *Irish Times* journalist remarked how inconvenient it was for the paper to send several reporters to Derry when they were all coming to McCafferty for information anyway, and suggested that they simply hire her. This made sense to the editors, and McCafferty was to write a few trial pieces for the paper. One of her first pieces tested her ability to write objectively on a subject about which she was very passionate, and admittedly biased – a profile of the Reverend Ian Paisley, whom she calls the "demagogue and anti-Christ in the North" today, and was the Protestant Unionist candidate for parliament then. Paisley was the favourite politician of anti-civil rights Protestants at the time. "I wrote about him as people saw him," she says. "I followed him around and I saw why people followed him, and I saw him as a force in the land, and I recorded that. And I didn't write as a Fenian or a Socialist, and I said, this is Ian Paisley and this is what I see. I'm very good at that," she says – having admitted that she doesn't do modesty. McCafferty has practised various kinds of journalism over the years, but what she enjoys the most is going to the street where something happened and writing about how it feels to be there among the people. She takes the classic example of Germany during the Second World War and says that if she were a reporter in that time and place, she would write objectively about the Nazis, telling what it was like to be among the masses. Then later, she would write a piece about why she thought the Nazis were wrong. "First you've got to tell what people are, stand among them, be of them," she says.

In McCafferty's opinion, her articles could be powerful and illuminating enough to cause ripples among her readership without much of her own commentary or opinion at all – the idea being that good, insightful journalism could change society simply by reflecting it. Even if she tries to be as objective as possible about the *facts*, though, none of McCafferty's stories are devoid of *feeling*. She may have come to journalism accidentally, but once she was in the profession, she was as much of a crusading journalist as any of her colleagues. She made no secret about using journalism to bear witness to the struggles of the oppressed, whether it was the civil rights activists in the North, or Irish women, North and South:

> It is the modest ambition of every journalist to write a front page story – the big one at the top left hand side, with large headlines, that tells the world the main event of the day. The front page story tells what happened, where, when and gives the explanation usually of the person in charge. If you want to know how the rest of us feel about it, you turn to the inside pages.

> I discovered, early on, that I'd never be able to write a front page story. I'd be inclined to argue with the person in charge, and feel obliged to give the other version in brackets. I discovered this particularly on Bloody Sunday in Derry, when I was lying on the street while people around me got shot dead. I saw everything while the other reporter was at the back. He, rightly, wrote the front page story, because somebody had to provide all the deadly details. Had it been up to me to phone the officer, the row would

still be going on and the story would never have been written. My version appeared on the inside pages. I wrote about how the rest of us felt, lying on the ground.[2]

As a child, McCafferty was not interested in dolls or prams and often ended up playing with all-male gangs of children in her street. Her first recollection of being treated unfairly because of her gender was during a childhood game where another gang of boys arrived from a few streets over. They lined up to play, and the leader of the other gang looked at McCafferty, all of about ten years of age, and declared authoritatively that girls weren't allowed to play. "And for one long tremulous moment, my gang nearly disowned me. They didn't, but there was a moment where I thought, Holy God," she says. Her brother defended her, but she clearly remembers the terrible awkwardness of that feeling of exclusion. By the time she was a teenager, McCafferty knew that she was a homosexual. She was certainly old enough to realise that people would think of her as different in a negative way because of her sexuality, a conclusion she reached as a result of social pressures and mores, and the fact that the topic of homosexuality was virtually unmentionable. McCafferty went to the nuns for advice. Instead of preaching to her or judging her, one nun told her that she might have to live with it for the rest of her life.

In college, she wore dresses and heels in an effort to fit in, feeling ridiculous most of the time and more awkward than ever before. It was only when she travelled to France as a young graduate in the mid-sixties that she realised she would always be more comfortable being true to her own sense of style, even if it did shun conventions of femininity and style. She worked in a boarding school in Cannes teaching English conversation skills to French secondary school girls, but her real motivation in moving to Cannes, besides avoiding the real working world for another year, was to see the film stars that spring during the annual film festival. McCafferty has always loved film stars. She only traded her fancy, frilly clothes for jeans near the end of her time there, on the last day of school, and one of her colleagues told her that she now had a totally different kind of allure because she looked so much more at ease. From then on, that struggle to fit into people's perceptions of how a woman should look and act became less urgent for McCafferty. "You don't realise you were gorgeous until you're about sixty as I am now," she says. "Don't forget, I had already trained myself to be alone because I was born gay . . . but there were some things you couldn't do without a man, like go dancing. I loved dancing, and those fuckers couldn't dance. I had to ask them. And then I was liberated from all that . . . feminism got me out of that shite."

Colm Tóibín wrote a piece for *Magill* in 1985 on McCafferty's impact on the country through her roles as both journalist and feminist:

> Nell McCafferty's achievement as a journalist has been inseparable from feminism. As a feminist she was written from the point of view of women who have little stake in the world as it is. The women's movement has set itself the task of creating a new perspective on almost everything in people's lives, not just of achieving concessions from time to time. That new perspective is much easier to present in the relatively direct world of journalism than it is in the often stifling machinery of politics. She has applied that perspective to everything that has come her way. In doing that she has proved that there is always another way of looking at things.[3]

For all of her subsequent professional successes, McCafferty's early days as a Dublin journalist got off to a shaky start. She arrived a day late for her job at *The Irish Times* because she was scheduled to appear in a Derry court due to a civil rights offence for which she had been arrested, along with Bernadette Devlin, the previous week in Omagh, the main town in Devlin's constituency in parliament. The waiting list for government housing in Omagh was horrendously long and Catholics consistently found themselves at the bottom. McCafferty, Devlin and fellow activist Eamonn McCann had gone to a Unionist-dominated City Council session, disrupting the meeting and planting themselves on the floor. McCafferty was fined £20 and left the court directly, suitcase in hand, for Dublin and *The Irish Times,* where she was uncertain what kind of a reaction to expect from news editor Donal Foley. There was no plausible hope that Foley would not have read about the court case since the high-profile Devlin had been involved. When Foley arrived late to the office, he was welcoming and understanding, but he told McCafferty she'd have to give up this kind of thing now that she was a journalist. "I was panicking inside," she wrote. "He had hired me precisely because I came from the Bogside, and now I was being told not to act like a Bogsider anymore".[4] When one of the sub-editors directed her to the women's page desk in the newsroom and told her to read the page to get a better idea of what she would be writing, it did little to quell her fears – what she knew about cooking, fashion and babies, which were still a large part of the page amid the edgier material in 1970, was minimal at best. It was not until she met the women's page staff, including Mary Maher, and went for her first liquid lunch on her first day at the paper, that she started to feel a little more at home.

The Derry Labour Party was the last organised political group in which McCafferty was to claim membership. "I was a stranger in a strange land when I came to Dublin," she says. It was only a few short months between her arrival at *The Irish Times*, though, and the formation of the IWLM. By the time the group was in its infancy and had begun their first meetings at Gaj's, McCafferty's articles on women and women's rights indicated the rapid development of both her skill as a writer and her confidence as a feminist. Her October 1970 piece on what women's liberation meant to her, which appeared along with those on the same topic authored by Maher, Binchy and Mary Cummins, showed that she was coming into her own as a journalist:

> Women's Liberation is seeing the dread on another woman's face when she finds she's going to have another, or a first baby, and she still hasn't got a house, and someone says "God's will", and if you find an exceptional priest he'll tell you "for God's sake" to go on the pill.

> Women's Liberation is being turned away from an all-night café at Kelly's Corner, Rathmines, because I am an unescorted female, and presumably therefore out to make a pound or two. Can't we have tea alone after dark? . . .

> Women's Liberation is saying you can't have children unless men and women come together, and what is born of them is the responsibility of them both, and don't tie me to the kitchen sink, or the empty suburban house all day, every day, in their name . . .

> Women's Liberation is not asking for a better deal. That is a concession. Women's Liberation is saying I am half the human species, and I am now taking my rights, as a human, not a subspecies. Women's Liberation is the participation of women in the liberation of all people.
>
> Women's Liberation is finding it very hard to explain the difference, when you come down to it, except in terms of physical make-up. And men are as different as women, which no-one holds against them. It's the system which divides. Break the system, unite the people.[5]

McCafferty had learned, from her civil rights activism, that the best way to present your argument for change to people who wanted nothing more than for you and your demands to disappear was twofold: put forward the indisputable facts as rationally as possible, and tell the individual stories of people who have been hurt by the injustices you are trying to correct. She also had a seemingly intuitive sense of what needed to be done to get positive publicity, which must have had its roots in her civil rights activism. McCafferty shared that skill with Máirín de Burca and the others who had been heavily involved in political demonstrations and knew how to grab the media's attention.

But while there was much McCafferty learned from the civil rights movement about organisation and publicity, her experience as a leader of the women's liberation movement made her aware of her frustrations with the civil rights leadership and its exclusion, in large part, of women. She had always viewed Bernadette Devlin as the one exception to the rule of all-male civil rights leadership. Even within the Derry Labour Party, there were many women among its members, but none at the forefront of the organisation. "I was conscious of a great deal of silence," McCafferty says. "And even being shy myself, and sometimes feeling excluded." By the time she moved to Dublin and started working for *The Irish Times*, McCafferty was ready to come into her own as a journalist, a feminist and a leader of the women's liberation movement. She insists that while she was aware of other women's oppression in 1970, she didn't feel oppressed herself, and yet she didn't join the IWLM for purely altruistic reasons, either. "I joined it for myself . . . to be recognised as a woman. Away from the all-male platform of the civil rights movement in the North," she says. "Much as I adored the movement and most of the men in it. But I had no voice, and I felt inferior . . . [being in the women's movement] gave me a voice."

Women may have been excluded from participating as leaders in the civil rights movement in the North due to oversight and ignorance rather than any calculated intentions, but the North was a topic that the IWLM deliberately excluded from its discussions in the Republic. The founders realised that they already had more than enough differences to deal with in their discussions of women's issues, and to introduce the most incendiary political topic of the times into the mix would have been unwise. That was fine with McCafferty, who thinks Gaj's group handled the Northern question well by leaving it out of their sessions. "I didn't want any of them to touch the North," she says. "First, they would have been wrong and I would have been right, and I just didn't want them interfering in the North and talking about us being killers and murderers . . . the North has dogged my life. And I think we were right to exclude it." It was no secret that McCafferty and Marie McMahon were staunchly on one side of the argument about the armed struggle, while Máirín de Burca, the unfaltering pacifist, was on the other. The North was an entirely different matter from other topics that weren't discussed at meetings – namely divorce and abortion – which were left out because of what the founders all describe as simple innocence. Although the IWLM mentions divorce very briefly in *Chains or Change*, there were so many other more basic and, at the time, more important issues that needed attention that it would have made no sense to include it as one of the group's main demands. "Didn't occur to us," McCafferty says of both abortion and divorce. "Imagine us not discussing divorce! It's not that we were afraid, it never entered our minds or our vocabulary."

Although the founders discussed sexuality in the consciousness-raising sessions, at varying levels of comfort for each woman, the topic of gay sexuality never arose. It was still too taboo to talk about. Judging from Mary Maher and Maeve Binchy's reactions to writing about a lesbian late in 1970, it was probably more a matter of innocence, as it was with abortion and divorce, than any deliberate decision to avoid the topic. The founders were still trying to put words to their oppression, and

they were mired down in the process of creating the vocabulary necessary to talk about it. Lesbianism would have been particularly challenging and awkward for them to discuss. But McCafferty still finds it difficult to believe that, as the meetings wore on and the consciousness-
raising sessions progressed, the rest of the IWLM women didn't become
aware of her lesbianism.

It is not that she was particularly open or forthcoming in the consciousness-raising discussions about her sexuality; in fact, some of the
founders remember that she could be just as reluctant about discussing
personal matters as any of them, even if she was sometimes quicker to
criticise others' silence. It was the fact that she had a brief but quite public affair with one of the other founders that makes her certain that the
IWLM women must have known she was gay while the group was still
together. "Sure they all knew at the consciousness-raising sessions,"
McCafferty says. "We were practically sitting there holding hands." The
relationship began on New Year's Eve in 1970, and lasted a couple of
months. The other founder was less discreet than McCafferty had expected; she burst into the Shelbourne Hotel on New Year's Day 1971,
kicked open the doors, and announced that she was in love with Nell.
Today, it still puzzles McCafferty that the assembled media did not write
a word about her sexuality, even after her longtime lover and journalist
Nuala O'Faolain's memoir *Are You Somebody?* was published in the
nineties, naming Nell and detailing their relationship. "Maybe it was unspeakable and maybe they were being kind, but they've never used it
against me since," McCafferty says of the media's handling of the 1971
New Year's incident and O'Faolain's revelations. It was only after she
announced in February 2003 that one of the themes of her upcoming
memoir was being born gay that a few tabloids, *Ireland on Sunday* and
the *Sunday World*, wrote what McCafferty characterises as "slightly
sleazy" pieces about her sexuality. At first she was surprised to see a
change in the respectful tone of the media to which she had grown accustomed. "Then I thought, no, this is probably very fair, if you're a public
figure and you've broken your silence they're entitled to say whatever
they want about you," she says.

One other way in which McCafferty's homosexuality affected her
feminism was in the freedom which being "beholden to no man" allowed

her in her arguments. It is not that the other founders' relationships and marriages necessarily restrained them from their activism; but, as Eimer Philbin Bowman and others described, due to their membership in the liberation movement some women experienced tensions in their relationships with husbands or male partners. This could be something as simple as Máirín Johnston's difficulty in finding someone to mind her children so she could attend nighttime meetings when her partner was working the night shift. McCafferty was free of those tensions and strains, which she thinks might be part of the reason she gave no corner to the opposition, which she calls "the boss class, the male class". She thinks she would have been relentless and persistent in her arguments for women's rights anyway, but it was easier for her because she did not have to answer to any man. "Any male transgressed, I would have had him for breakfast. Wouldn't have cost me a thought," she says. "I had no partner, no husband, I had no children. The last great battleground of feminism is the home, that man in those kitchens rattling those pots and pans."

McCafferty became known early on in the life of the IWLM as someone who could be depended on to deliver forceful arguments that were backed with accurate facts. She did it fearlessly, and with confidence. She was charismatic, but as her career as a journalist was in its infancy, she was able to convey the strength of her arguments in print just as well as in person. She possessed both wit and warmth, but is probably unable to commit even charitable acts without at least a measure of sarcasm. Frank Crummey remembers McCafferty slipping him a cheque for a down-and-out woman he was defending in court once with a "Here you are, you little bollocks". McCafferty spent a lot of time in the courts for her long-running "In the Eyes of the Law" column in the seventies, in which she exposed the sad reality that the Irish courtroom was the last place most ordinary citizens could expect to find fairness and justice, least of all women:

> There's no place like a courtroom to dismiss the nonsensical notion entertained by housewives that they are in any degree independent of their husbands . . . frantic efforts were being made to secure independent bail for the 64 Sinn Féin (Gardiner Place) defendants who had been arrested, and held in custody, for picketing the homes of politicians. Several of those who offered them-

selves as Bailsmen were women. They assured District Justice O hUaidhaigh that they were joint owners, with their husbands, of their own homes. "I've never seen so many women owning houses," he commented. "This women's lib. is going to be the ruin of us all. I suppose it's all right if you're married to them."[6]

Most of her "In the Eyes of the Law" articles proved McCafferty's notion that simply observing society, in this case the inner workings of the court system, was enough to expose hypocrisy and injustice without even venturing to comment on it herself. Give them the rope, and most of the time, they would hang themselves.

Long after the IWLM disintegrated, McCafferty remained active in other women's rights groups and as a journalist writing about women's rights. When the IWLM began its decline (McCafferty agrees that the night of the Mansion House meeting was effectively the end of the founder group) she continued to travel to branch groups in an effort to keep the movement's momentum. Even at the time, she realised that it would be difficult to capture and sustain the euphoria that had bolstered the IWLM in its early days. She concedes that one of the IWLM's biggest problems what that it had allowed itself to be used for other socialist groups purposes. She remembers the IWLM marching in the 1971 May Day parade and being relegated to a place at the back of the procession. None of the women was asked to speak. "The May Day parade very clearly showed if you hitch your wagon to any male-dominated or male-organised institutions, you are dead," she says.

However, in her eyes it was mainly the IWLM's inability to structure itself that was its undoing – a thousand women showed up the night of the Mansion House meeting, and the founders did not know what to do with them, simple as that. But would the IWLM founders have been able to continue even if they were experts at organisation and structure? "I don't think any of us would have had the stamina," McCafferty says. "There were twelve of us. Who's got time to do it? Who's got the energy? We may not have been able to structure it, but we were into ego, by God. We were a very close-knit, warm group, even with the tensions, and then suddenly our lovely wee Monday night meetings are all gone and you have strangers in the house and in the room."

McCafferty, Marie McMahon, Fionnuala O'Connor and Mary Anderson were the original IWLM founders who did the bulk of the travelling to branch meetings, working with and speaking to the groups of women, trying to provide some kind of focus for the faltering movement. They discovered that it was mainly two of the founders' aims that some of the branch groups had trouble accepting – one-family/one-house, and contraception for all women, regardless of age or marital status. Shortly after the Mansion House meeting, the founders had haphazardly decided it would be best to keep the branches meeting separately for about six months so they could figure out for themselves what they wanted to do in their own areas of Dublin. A delegate from each branch would attend the Gaj's meeting with the founders on the first Monday of each month. The idea was that this system would lead to a better liaison and feeling of belonging between the branches and the founder group. However, the IWLM founders felt they had no choice but to try to impose some structure on the movement, given its recent tidal wave of expansion, and this made both the branches and the founders themselves uncomfortable. McCafferty felt as though their intimate group was being swallowed by this mass of other women who were joining, and while it was gratifying to see that they had moved so many women to take action, the IWLM founders weren't entirely prepared to work with them. They were simply at a loss as to what to do with everyone.[7]

Although most of the founders were wary of leading the movement and the new branches it now included, they were, by default, the only ones who really had much of a right to apply any kind of structure and rules. Just how much power they should have in controlling the movement became, almost immediately, a matter of contention. For a short while, it seemed that the branches and the founders could work very well together under the system of having a branch delegate attend one meeting a month, with the branches working otherwise mostly on their own. Founders and branch members alike agreed upon the Contraceptive Train under this system, even though there were significant numbers who voted against the majority decision to go ahead with the train. After the train, things deteriorated between some such dissenters and the founders. There were those who felt that the Contraceptive Train had been undignified and had given the movement a bad name, even if they agreed with the campaign to legalise contraception.

On the evening that the Forcible Entry Bill was passed in the Dáil, in the late summer of 1971, the founders created even more tension between themselves and the branch groups. This was the same night that Máirín de Burca and Mary Anderson were arrested in the incident that began their famous case that challenged the Juries Act. The Sutton Branch participated in the protest against the bill outside the Dáil, and had produced a newsletter called *Object*, selling 150 copies at the demonstration. Some of the founders were unhappy with the content of the newsletter, especially a satirical piece titled "Ballad of the Belfast Train", commemorating the Contraceptive Train – they thought it was too bawdy. The newsletter's authors found that hypocritical coming from the same group whose journalist members had written so many daring articles themselves and had devised so many controversial protests, including the Contraceptive Train itself. The incident also highlighted the conflict between the idea of each group acting as it saw fit within the framework of the six aims and the reality of the founder group reserving the right to "hold a watching brief on all activities and to vet them for orthodoxy".[8]

By the autumn of 1971, almost exactly one year after the IWLM's founding, the membership numbers in many of the branch groups created at the Mansion House meeting had fallen drastically, and many of the founders themselves had left the movement. Mary Maher, busy with her two infant daughters and her job at *The Irish Times*, found it too difficult to sustain the same level of activism that she had the year before. Mary Kenny had left Ireland for her job as features editor at London's *Evening Standard* in the mid-summer of 1971, and the *Irish Press* women's page was never the same. Moira Woods's husband was very ill, and she devoted much of her time to his care. Margaret Gaj's husband was also unwell, and she focused on his care, on running her restaurant, and on her other political activities. Máirín de Burca's Sinn Féin membership made many of the women in the branches uncomfortable. They saw de Burca as the most direct link between the women's liberation movement and the nationalist movement, which many did not approve of if only because they felt, as Nuala Fennell had, that the women's movement should concentrate solely on "feminist" issues. De Burca's responsibilities with Sinn Féin and her activism in other political causes were more than enough to fill her schedule. Nuala Fennell had left the movement in the most public manner of any of the founders by sending her resignation letter to the papers that June of 1971. The other founders drifted off in their own ways, to concentrate on careers, families and, in some cases, other political and women's organisations that were yet to be founded.

Nell McCafferty kept going to some meetings of the women's groups, which were becoming increasingly scattered and disjointed. The remaining IWLM branch groups restructured themselves in the absence of the founder group and in the face of their own falling numbers. Active membership had fallen to such small numbers in the branches that it made sense to hold only one meeting fortnightly, in an effort to counter-act the feeling of isolation that many of the branches were experiencing since they were too small to continue on their own as separate entities. The energy that had been so electric in its promise on the night of the Mansion House meeting only five or six months earlier had proved too difficult to harness and now seemed to be draining away almost com-pletely. By December 1971, only a single "Fownes St. Group" remained, named for the location of its eventual fixed meeting place.

McCafferty continued to speak to other women's assemblies in an ef-fort to restore some of the movement's former life and enthusiasm. "There were other women's groups, some of them struggled on, but there was a wilderness then," McCafferty says. "I remember being very lonely about it." In that wilderness, it was hard to know exactly what her own role should be, so McCafferty chose simply to continue spreading the arguments and messages of the movement wherever she could, speaking at as many as five meetings a week and appearing anywhere in front of crowds of any size. "I kept on trundling, I was getting invitations from everywhere and I believed in speaking," she says. Other IWLM founders and women's liberationists also took up the mantle to help spread the message, especially those with a specific field of expertise, like Moira Woods with women's health and contraception. McCafferty had no such specialisation, but felt that the movement's message could do with a bit of humour at times. "I made speeches about bras," she says. "An entire meeting I talked about the bra, just for fun. Because of the talk of equal wages and all that boring shite, and somebody else I knew the week behind me would outline the demands of the movement. I was just there to cheer them up," she says.

McCafferty continued speaking and, like the other IWLM founder journalists, writing about women's issues throughout the seventies. When the next cohesive, radical feminist organisation, Irish Women United (IWU) formed in June 1975, McCafferty was there, along with Marie McMahon. IWU was an umbrella organisation, led by trade union-ist Anne Speed, which attracted women who adhered to many left-wing political organisations, including the Movement for a Socialist Republic, the Communist Party of Ireland, the Socialist Worker's Movement, the Irish Republican Socialist Party and the International Lesbian Caucus.[9] Speed herself was a member of the Revolutionary Marxist Group. IWU used the IWLM's six aims, as well as the Working Women's Charter of the Irish Transport and General Workers' Union, as a basis for its own manifesto. They added free contraception, self-determined sexuality, equal pay based on a national minimum wage, and the establishment of women's centres to the IWLM's demands, demonstrating that they were willing to appear more radical than the IWLM had been. The women who formed IWU were more politicised than most of the IWLM foun-ders had been, but politics was nevertheless a divisive factor within that group, just as it had been within the IWLM. Northern Ireland was less of an unspeakable issue in IWU than in the IWLM, where it had not been discussed openly at all. Many IWU members had believed that the group's founding was based more firmly on the ideals of radical femi-nism than any of the competing political ideologies that the women brought to it. Individual members' politics became such a preoccupation within the group that at one point it was written into the minutes that members must state their political affiliations upon speaking.[10]

Like the IWLM, IWU planned demonstrations and pickets that it knew were certain to catch the media's attention. Members picketed the Archbishop's residence in general protest at the church's policies toward women's rights and staged a sit-in at the offices of the Federated Union of Employers in protest at the organisation's delay in implementing equal pay. They stormed male-only recreational areas and facilities around Dublin, like the Forty Foot bathing place at Sandycove and the Fitzwilliam Lawn Tennis Club, painting their insignia on the tennis court. In the summer of 1976, IWU formed its Contraceptive Action Programme CAP), which became one of its main lobbying programmes. Although the CAP was a key mobilising issue for IWU, by 1976 contraception was less of a burning issue than it had been in the IWLM's days because of the advent of family planning clinics around Dublin and other cities, which as previously discussed were able to bypass the laws against selling contraceptives by making them available for free in exchange for "donations". IWU built on the IWLM's activism but, in many ways, took it further, discussing abortion in some depth but deciding not to campaign for it for fear of alienating too many women. IWU was also an organisation where lesbians were free to express themselves, and their views, openly.[11] When the group disintegrated in 1977, it was largely due to internal divisions and ideological differences between the cliques of radical feminists, socialists and radical lesbians and Republicans among its members. The group had done much to keep women's issues in the public eye and on politicians' agendas.

McCafferty continued to write and speak about women's equality, never shying away from the most controversial issues of the day. It was not until 1980 that one of her columns sparked a serious, prolonged debate in the feminist community that was played out, at first, in the pages of *The Irish Times*. Throughout the seventies and her membership in both the IWLM and IWU, McCafferty had managed to keep her civil rights activism in the North separate from her feminist activism in the South, but that changed with the plight of the women prisoners at Armagh prison in the winter of 1980 and the beginning of the "dirt strike" there. McCafferty's article detailed the background of the events leading up to the prisoners' protest, which involved the smearing of their own excrement, urine and menstrual blood on the walls of their cells and the refusal of showers for over 200 days:

> The position of Britain is, briefly, that those who commit offences against the State are criminals. The position of Republicans is, briefly, that having been charged with scheduled or political offences, in consequence of which they are denied the right to trial by jury and must appear before a special Diplock court, they are by definition political prisoners. In support of their case, Republicans point to the existence of political prisoners within

Northern Ireland jails who were sentenced before March 1st
1976. The British case for criminalisation is arbitrary, resting on
the decision to abolish political status after that date.[12]

In February 1980, legislation was pending in Britain that would deny
retrospective political status to those who were facing conviction for acts
committed before March 1976. As a result, the authorities revoked prisoners' rights to wear civilian clothes, which projected their own self-
image as political prisoners, not criminals, and expressed sympathy with
Republican causes. The women wore their outfits – black berets and
skirts – occasionally in the exercise yard when conducting a political
parade in commemoration or in celebration of some Republican happening on the outside. In early February, the prison governor at Armagh in-
formed the thirty-two women inmates that their cells would be searched
for the berets and skirts and that the garments would be confiscated. The
women resisted, some were injured, and they were confined to their cells
for twenty-four hours without access to toilets or showers; this marked
the beginning of their protest. McCafferty's article four months later argued that it was wrong for feminists, North and South, to ignore the Armagh women's plight:

> It is my belief that Armagh is a feminist issue that demands our
> support. I believe that the 32 women there have been denied one
> of the fundamental rights of women, the right to bodily integrity,
> and I suggest that an objective examination of the events that
> gave rise to the dirt strike will support this contention . . . the
> menstrual blood on the walls of Armagh prison smells to high
> heaven. Shall we turn our noses up?

The week following the publication of McCafferty's article in *The Irish
Times* saw some of her old colleagues writing letters disagreeing with
her belief that Armagh was a feminist issue, among them Máirín de
Burca and Nuala Fennell. Several of the feminists opposed to McCafferty's view argued that Armagh was not a feminist issue because the
prisoners' actions were dictated by male politicians and, in turn, brought
misery to many other Northern women. De Burca's response focused on
what she saw as the tragedy of the movement's male leadership in the
North using women for its own means, often placing them in danger by

encouraging them to carry out violent acts. De Burca's pacifism and abhorrence of what she saw as men's willingness to exploit women's eagerness to participate in the cause come through strongly in her letter. She pointed out that a woman could pull a trigger and stop a bullet just as effectively as any man, and that men had manipulated women with rhetoric that included "a thin version of feminist jargon" combined with "Mother of Ireland stuff" to put them in the right frame of mind:

> . . . Women were just as good at going to prison as men, too, and could be relied upon to parrot the prison protests as efficiently as they had done the terrorism outside. They had not been encouraged to question the basis of this whole physical force merry-go-round so why should they suddenly discover their common sisterhood with other women prisoners? . . . Our male masters had told us that we could only be freed by death and destruction, so we obediently shot and bombed and helped them to shoot and bomb . . .[13]

McCafferty thought that it was only fair that Mary Maher, who was then her editor, turn the page over the following week to those feminists who agreed with her. As McCafferty tells it, Maher refused, and McCafferty felt her refusal amounted to censorship, although she continued to write for Maher for another month or two before resigning. Máirín Johnston is one IWLM founder who today agrees with McCafferty that the Armagh women deserved much more solid support from the feminist community than they received. In any case, the Armagh issue became one of the most divisive for feminists at the beginning of a decade that was to bring many more of the same, including the abortion referendum in 1983.

When McCafferty thinks of the IWLM's legacy, she sees the group's impact on the country as only positive. Contraception, equal pay, the severance of the previously unbreakable bonds between church and state, and the general sense of much higher expectations amongst women are the biggest advancements in the past three decades that she feels the IWLM helped bring about. "We put money into the pockets of both women and men – and men resisted it then – we gave them money, we gave them sex, Jesus, what more can you ask for in this world?" she says. She concedes that sex existed before the IWLM, but she sees the

successful fight for contraception as the beginning of the nation's accep-
tance that women, too, were entitled to enjoy sex, without the constant
fear of pregnancy.

As the Armagh issue demonstrates, McCafferty has had passionate,
albeit measured, disagreements with some of her feminist colleagues
well after the IWLM's disintegration. Despite these incidents, and impressed as she already was with the IWLM founders in 1970, the years
have done little to dull her esteem for them. "I suppose I was slightly
stunned at their intelligence," she says. "Just amazed at the gifts and talents they had, which doesn't make them Einstein, but by God they were
amazing. Ah, it was deeper than that, it was happy. It was a very happy
time . . . you could not wait for Monday nights."

Where They Are (and What They Think) Now

"The women's liberation movement was a success story. I don't care what anybody says, it was a success story. . . . I've been in a lot of organisations that have split from time to time, but this is what I call a nice split. The women's movement didn't stop, you see. It went on. They [the founders] saw where they wanted to be and they went off and did it. All the things they founded are still there." — Máirín de Burca

"I see this group as just a stopping-off point for a whole range of people who were making this journey of their time in their own individual ways. . . . There was this sort of coming together at this moment in time, and in all the years afterwards I was so taken that everybody had sort of splintered off in their own directions and accomplished something important in their own fields . . . you always had a bond with them, even if you mightn't have retained a friendship with them. With any one of them, there was a bond." — Dr Eimer Philbin Bowman

"The founder only passes by once," American journalist Bob Edwards wrote of the legendary Edward R. Murrow, the man who had a profound influence on the birth of broadcast journalism in the US in the 1940s. "Murrow's accomplishments can't be duplicated because he was writing on a blank page".[1] The same could be said of the women, collectively, who founded the Irish Women's Liberation Movement. Each one of them discovered that as individuals they possessed the capability within themselves to create social change. As they came together and worked with each other, they enhanced each other's talents, gave each other confidence, and discovered that the differences in their backgrounds contributed more to their group's successes than to its failures. It is unfair to judge later activists and their accomplishments by the same standards because the IWLM was able to make up its own rules. It was a group that was very much of its own time and place. "I don't think you could invent something like the Irish Women's Liberation Movement," founder Nuala Fennell says. "You couldn't invent it, it was a once-off."

Of the threads that bound the IWLM founders together in spite of their differences, stories are the strongest – theirs and other women's, spoken and written. The patrons at Gaj's, their beloved restaurant and unofficial headquarters, loved telling their own stories and hearing other people's. The mix of people who ate at Gaj's in itself demonstrated how much easier it is for people to relate to, understand and enjoy each other's company if they're willing to listen to each other for a while, and share something of themselves in turn. Margaret Gaj, perhaps, enjoyed that kind of exchange the most, although, as many of her patrons remember, she was less inclined to tell her own stories than to want to hear others'. It was in this environment that the IWLM founders got to know each other through the telling of their own stories in the consciousness-raising sessions and, in even smaller numbers, over tea or a meal after the meetings. In telling tales from their own lives and listening to others', they found that their stories were closer to each others' than they ever would have realised had they not started the most simple, and powerful, of all exercises – conversation. The journalists among them widened that circle of discovery and solidarity among women. It was through their stories on the women's pages of the three newspapers that Irish women nationwide got to know them, their fellow countrywomen, and themselves better.

In her own way, each of the founders is a storyteller, even if she is not a journalist or a writer by trade. At the very least, her story is tied in history to the larger story of the women's movement for equal rights. It is a story worthy of the telling, especially today, when so few young people really understand the desperation of the oppressed and the great personal risks the women faced in fighting that oppression. "May you live in interesting times" reads a Chinese proverb, but some argue that the words are less of a benign adage than a curse. The IWLM women, though some of them have suffered more than others as a result of their roles in the movement, would not have exchanged the excitement and opportunity of their times for the chance to belong to a less tumultuous generation. As Mary Maher says today, she's sure glad she was there.

Late in 2004, thirty-three years after the IWLM introduced itself to the nation on *The Late Late Show*, Nell McCafferty appeared again on the programme to talk about her new memoir and revealed that the government still had files on many of the IWLM founders, which it refused to open. She had written to the government, she told Pat Kenny, under the Freedom of Information Act to see if they would give it to her, and they refused. The reason? "I'm a threat to the security, defence, and safety of this state," she said, speaking into the camera with a sardonic smile. One senses at least a hint of pride in her expression – the activists of the sixties and seventies, and probably many of those who ate at Gaj's regularly, would have been shamed and embarrassed had the government not kept a file on them. As Mary Kenny had felt back then, you probably were not accomplishing anything if you weren't kicking up a little dust. McCafferty continues her story, clearly enjoying herself. Although she does not have access to the file on herself, she has discovered that it is comprised entirely of the reports of a Special Branch officer who followed her for the month of April 1971. It was, perhaps, the IWLM's most momentous month, as it was sandwiched between the group's appearance on *The Late Late Show* and the Contraception Train, as well as the month of the Mansion House meeting.

The story gets better, McCafferty's tone implies, because it was not just her whom the Special Branch was keeping an eye on. Most of the IWLM founders, and some others outside the group who were sympathetic to their cause, including future Irish president Mary Robinson, were also followed that month. So was the scholar and teacher Sister Margaret MacCurtain (known affectionately as Sister Ben). McCafferty says that the Special Branch officer who was ordered to follow Mary Kenny for a month must have thought he had died and gone to heaven.

"If you'd like our nation to be happy, open the file on Mary Kenny just in case some people have forgotten how to enjoy themselves," she says. "And on Sister Ben, because she's a historian. And every school child would read them and say, I never knew history could be such fun. Open those two files and overnight this island becomes a land of saints and scholars," she says. "There's a hole in the heart of the history of this country if we don't understand why and how us women constituted, then and now, a threat to the safety, defence and security of this state."

Mary Maher had interviewed TD and future Taoiseach Garret Fitz-Gerald the winter before the IWLM formed and had closed her article by asking him what he thought was hopeful in Ireland. "Probably that a country that was so unwilling to change is now so open to it," FitzGerald said. "The immediate effect is confusion, even disorder, but on the other hand it's hopeful to be in a society where change is no longer resisted – not by the church, by the schools, by the people . . ."[2] The kind of confusion and disorder as a direct result of change that FitzGerald spoke about in 1970 goes a long way in answering McCafferty's question about how the government could have labelled the IWLM founders as threats to the safety, defence and security of the state. The definition of the word "revolution" is the complete overthrow of an established government or political system. The IWLM founders were not literally trying to overthrow the government. But the confidence and determination with which they presented their demands and, just as important, the attention they began to attract, was sufficient to constitute a very real and powerful threat to those in control of the government at the time. In this context, it is easier to understand how the mostly male government officials could have seen the IWLM founders' actions as compromising the security of *its own power* within the state. The church had certainly identified the IWLM as a clear threat to its power, and was quite right in doing so. The group was among the first to present any serious and public challenges to the church's authority, which paved the way for others to do the same, thus contributing to the severe weakening of the church's influence in Ireland.

Other threads that bound the IWLM founders together included intellectual curiosity and respect for education. Among the original five founders – Gaj, de Burca, Maher, Johnston and Woods, only two – Maher and Woods – had earned university degrees. But despite their lack of diplomas and degrees, Gaj, de Burca, Johnston and the other founders who had left school early were far from uneducated. Through a combination of independent reading, surrounding themselves with like-minded friends and colleagues, often living abroad for some time, and engaging in the political causes that were setting the scene for the great drama that was unfolding in their society before their eyes, those who lacked a formal education educated themselves by other means. Mrs Gaj, for one, has found that she has learned more from her customers and her years in the restaurant business than she could ever have expected to learn inside the walls of any classroom.

Máirín de Burca had been attending political meetings and protesting since the age of fourteen, and she was unfailingly articulate and adept at expressing herself through the printed word. After leaving the IWLM in 1971 and then Sinn Féin in 1977 out of tiredness and a yearning for something different, she built herself a fine career in journalism. It was not an easy transition, though, from the world of politics and activism to her new, although related, career. In her first year after leaving Sinn Féin, she worked as a typist in the Post Office Engineering Union, but the position was hard-won. De Burca was almost as unemployable in Ireland at the time as any suspected communist whose name was on the blacklist in 1950s America. She was registered with several employment agencies, none of which contacted her with any opportunities. Her eventual saviour was an outsider, a woman from Liverpool at one of the agencies who asked de Burca if there was something she ought to know about her past. She was putting forward de Burca's name only to hear, again and again, "Not her. Anyone but her." De Burca gave the woman a brief synopsis of her political involvement and arrest record, and it all started to make sense. Now the woman started to see that finding de Burca a job would be a challenge, and a worthy one. Although she might not have understood the intricacies of Irish politics, she felt it was wrong for de Burca to be labelled as unemployable because of her history when she was clearly capable, and quite often over-qualified, for the jobs for which she was applying. When the job at the union came up, she sent in two names only, de Burca's and another woman's whose tests had proven she could not type or spell. If they did not pick de Burca, it would be a very clear case of discrimination. De Burca did get the job, and re-

members the Liverpool woman's kindness today with gratitude. De
Burca's hardship in finding a job was one of the more frustrating consequences of her activism which made her a target for society's disap-
proval long after her protesting days.

Throughout her year as a typist, de Burca was looking wholeheartedly for a full-time job in journalism. It was not even necessarily that,
like her IWLM journalist friends, she saw the profession as another way
to provoke change – she actually found journalism, after coming from
politics, frustrating in that sense. "In politics you get a problem and follow it to its logical conclusion," she says. "You can't do that with journalism. You write it up and then you're on to the next thing and you
don't know what happened to Joe Bloggs who had a terrible time with
the police . . . in politics, even if you didn't have a satisfactory outcome,
you knew what happened in the end." It was more that de Burca had
known it was time for her to leave politics, and she had more potential
than being a typist was allowing her to utilise. She eventually got a job
with the current affairs magazine *Hibernia* as the seventies drew to a
close, but after only a year on staff it failed due to costs awarded against
it in a libel suit. *The Sunday Tribune* hired heavily from the *Hibernia*
staff, and de Burca was among the *Tribune's* recruits.

As a journalist, de Burca was a jack-of-all-trades. She wrote about
politics, produced book reviews and did general reporting. She enjoyed the
work, but found that because she was dealing with so many different people on a daily basis, and so many different *kinds* of people, there were few
hard and fast rules for journalists to follow. It was an unsettling realisation.
She remembers, for instance, being assigned to go out to the countryside
and interview the parents of a young woman who had been killed in a car
accident two days after the death. De Burca was uneasy about the assignment, thinking it disrespectful to show up on the mourning family's door-
step asking for an interview. She told the photographer that if the family
even hinted they didn't want to give an interview, they would leave immediately. Instead, the parents welcomed de Burca and the photographer in
and it became clear that they wanted to talk about their daughter, especially to someone who wasn't from their hometown. "It meant that you
couldn't even lay down that kind of rule, that you don't go out and talk to
somebody the day after their daughter died," de Burca says.

No longer a full-time journalist, de Burca will be a politically active person in some capacity until the day she dies. If she were young again, she would want to focus on the international dimension of women's rights issues, concentrating on pacifism and the poor treatment of women in many developing countries, and especially those like Afghanistan and Iraq that have recently suffered so much violence and upheaval. She views the internet as something of a magical tool for activists, for getting their messages out, recruiting and organising. It's a far cry from the methods she and her fellow radicals used to get attention in the seventies, which included rigging the public phone boxes so they could call the newspapers from the scene of a demonstration free of charge (you would never call the press beforehand in case the police got wind of it, she notes). De Burca likes to think of the ultimate result of her role as an IWLM founder in terms of the contribution she has made to women's lives – that women can do things today that they could never have done when she helped found the IWLM. She is especially proud of the fact that women's expectations in both their professional and personal lives are so much higher now than they were then. She is happy if that's what she can leave behind her, along with the fact that she and Mary Anderson successfully challenged the Juries Act and gave women a little more dignity by ensuring that they were treated exactly as men were in regard to jury service. "As long as people study law in Ireland my name will be remembered because I changed the law and it's part of the course now . . . I'm not religious, and I don't believe in a life hereafter, I believe when you're dead you're dead. But in some *small* way my name will live on and that's very selfish and egotistical, but I like that," she says.

Máirín Johnston's name will live on, too, not only because of her role in the women's liberation movement, but through her work as an author. The same woman who, even today, finds it outlandish that she ever held a job at the Institute for Advanced Studies, went on to author two adult, non-fiction books and one children's book. *Dublin Belles* is a series of interviews with Dublin women in reflection of their own lives and their city as the twentieth century drew to a close. *Around the Banks of Pimlico* is a historical account of life in the Liberties from the 1850s to the 1950s, into which Johnston weaves her own family's story and her personal experiences growing up there.

Soon after the IWLM's disintegration, Johnston felt a similar loneliness to McCafferty's about the wilderness that had, all of a sudden, opened up in the women's movement. She soon found her niche. Johnston continued her childcare work, bringing her "travelling crèche" to trade union and feminist meetings and conventions, allowing women the freedom to attend meetings about fighting for equal pay and running for office, until she felt she needed to stop in order to focus more fully on raising her own family. She knew the women in the organisations appreciated her help, and the opportunities it allowed them to get directly involved in asserting their rights. She also joined IWU's Contraceptive Action Programme in the mid-seventies, although she was never as heavily involved in the group as she had been in the IWLM. She takes great satisfaction in thinking about what the IWLM founders, who used their particular talents and abilities to their highest potential, accomplished after the group's disintegration.

There are times when she wishes, though, that today's young women had a better sense of the IWLM's accomplishments. "They seem to think things were always as they are," she says. "The women today, as they are today, could never, ever have conceived of living through what we had to live through. The climate of opinion is so totally different." As Johnston ages, she is experiencing the long-term consequences of some of the discriminatory laws against women that the IWLM fought in the early days of the liberation movement. The civil service, local authorities, and health board did not remove the marriage bar, for instance, until 1973, and legislation toward equal pay for women was not enacted until even later in the seventies, largely at the urging of the EEC. Today, the state ignores the consequences of the marriage bar and the lack of equal pay legislation to which the women in Johnston's generation were subject for at least part of their working lives. As a result, women who never worked outside of the home, worked for a number of years and then stayed home to raise children, or were forced out of their jobs by the marriage bar, are ineligible for the state's full, contributory pension payments. Johnston explains that she and many women receive only a non-contributory pension. Besides being a smaller amount, the state pays non-contributory pensions to those whom it classifies as never having contributed anything to the state. Johnston, who has worked in factories, the Institute for Advanced Studies, and in childcare, staying home at times to raise her four children, is justifiably upset that the state feels she has not contributed anything to it. "I didn't choose to stay at home, the law said I had to stay at home," she says. "But then the law turned around and said, you're not entitled to a full pension because you made no contribution," she says. She points out that the hypocrisy inherent in this system is reinforced by Article 41 of the Constitution, which explicitly confines a woman's role to the home:

> 41.2.1 In particular, the State recognises that by her life within the home, woman gives to the state a support without which the common good cannot be achieved.
>
> 41.2.2. The state shall, therefore, endeavour to ensure that mothers shall not be obliged by economic necessity to engage in labour to the neglect of their duties in the home.

Interestingly, the Constitution does acknowledge that women contribute to the state's common good in staying home, but the word "work" is never used. Instead, the phrase "her life within the home" makes it clear that in the state's eyes, a woman's whole existence should be confined to the home. Therefore, even if a woman makes some valuable contribution to the state in staying at home, it is obviously not *as* valuable as a working man's contribution when determining pension payments. Also, the words "woman" and "mother" are interchangeable in the text, thus reinforcing women liberationists' argument during the contraception campaign that the state viewed them as nothing but "baby machines". Over the past several years Johnston has considered, briefly, taking the state to court over the pension issue. "Although I still get very angry at times and I still feel that inside me, and it's not that my mind has gotten old. But the knees are giving, the ankles are giving, the heart is giving, and it's the old body and muscles." She's aware of the battles for equal rights that women have yet to face, but her own days manning the barricades are over. For all the causes with which she was involved throughout her life, Johnston ascribes to the idea that one of the most revolutionary things a person can do on this earth is to raise her children to be peaceful, generous and fair. In that sense, her four grown children are solid representations of her own legacy in the women's liberation movement just as much as her ride on the Contraceptive Train and her appearance on *The Late Late Show* during her days with the IWLM.

Marie McMahon, although one of the youngest among the IWLM founders, felt the strain of years of heavy activism as the seventies ended. If it was possible for McMahon to be even less employable than Máirín de Burca because of her history of political involvement, that was the case as she struggled to find her own niche. The publicity from the bogus charges of prostitution reinforced her near-pariah status in the eyes of potential employers. Her urge to edit much of the material from political organisations that came across her desk in her years as a typesetter, as well as her respect for her journalist colleagues in the IWLM, made McMahon think she might be interested in journalism. She would have liked to try to break into some kind of career in the media, but the fear that she had no realistic chance of being hired prevented her from even applying for many positions. At the same time, it was difficult for her to see some feminists who hadn't "dirtied their bibs", as she had, using the women's liberation movement as a means of advancing their careers.

McMahon drifted for a while, and in the early eighties she gave birth to her son and encountered the struggles and rewards of raising a child as a single mother. She spent nearly a year in France with her baby after selling her share in her typesetting business, returning to Dublin to face the recession and all the difficulties it brought. "I kind of led a pretty destitute existence in the late eighties," McMahon says. But the same resourcefulness that she had drawn upon in her snap creation of the *Chains or Change* cover design led McMahon to take advantage of the government's offer of subsidies to people who were setting up co-ops during the eighties. She began a desktop publishing business, Verbatim, around 1990, working in collaboration with The Attic Press to produce many of that company's books on feminist subjects. By the end of the nineties, though, McMahon wanted to challenge herself and her own abilities further. "I would have considered myself to be a monkey because I had sat at some sort of typing machine or another from the age of twelve till the age of forty, producing other people's stuff," she says. "I've been told I underestimate what I actually did; I did a lot of editing, but I'd never really used my creative ideas, I'd never tried to produce my own creative ideas and I'd never been educated, which was a huge thing." In her mid-fifties, McMahon went to night classes and earned her college degree – in journalism. She is still not sure if she's ready to put her degree to use and apply for a job in the media. At the moment, it's enough that she proved to herself that she was capable of completing the programme. The confidence that she began to build in the IWLM meetings, and that she realised it was possible for women to cultivate within themselves, has culminated in the receipt of her degree – no small accomplishment for a woman who began working at the age of fourteen and thought she had left school, along with the hope of any kind of a fulfilling career, behind.

Two of the Marys – Kenny and Sheerin – also received their degrees as mature students, proving how much the IWLM founders, as a group and as individuals, valued education. Kenny received her degree in French Studies from Birkbeck College, London University in the mid-nineties; Sheerin earned her English Literature degree, with honours, through the Open University at Trinity College and is currently at work on a Master's degree. Sheerin continued to work in public relations following the IWLM's disintegration, dabbling in short-story writing and freelance journalism throughout the seventies before eventually going back to work for the civil service as a press officer for the Government Information Services. She feels that one of Ireland's most insidious problems today is the drink culture. It is not by any means strictly a women's issue, but she feels that it is not entirely necessary to divide the nation's challenges into gender-specific categories anymore. Sheerin thinks it is wrong to dismiss the over-indulgence of alcohol, as many do, as a symptom of Ireland's history as an oppressed nation. For women, the risks of getting very drunk and compromising their judgement is especially harmful, Sheerin says. "I'm very in favour of sexual activity, but youngsters are experimenting with sex when they don't even need to and so often it's because they are drunk and I think this is very detrimental," she says. She would like to see some better state efforts in educating people about the risks associated with heavy drinking, along the lines of the government's recent public relations campaign to curb cigarette smoking. Although she has always viewed herself as one of the less publicly visible founders of the IWLM, Sheerin is no less proud of the group's accomplishments. "Certainly for such a small group in a short time, it made a terrific impact. I think it was a great touchstone."

Nuala Fennell left politics in 1992 to start her own public affairs agency, Political Communications Ltd., the following year. She is the IWLM founder cited most often by the other founders as having directly brought about practical improvements in women's lives after the IWLM's disintegration, in spite of the tense circumstances of her resignation from the group and the hard feelings on both her and the other founders' sides. As Máirín Johnston has noted, the years have softened all of the IWLM founders a bit – "knocked our corners off", as she puts it. Marie McMahon remembers that Fennell, who never made any secret of the fact that she was opposed to breaking the law in the name of activism during the IWLM's days, was wary of her. "She used to call me 'picket-happy Marie'," McMahon smiles now. Years ago, McMahon would have seen Fennell's going into politics as joining the forces of the enemy. Today, she feels that the more women who are in positions of political power, the better for women in general. "Her stance would have been a very courageous one because she came from such a different background politically," McMahon says. "And her stance in the women's liberation movement was purely a sense of her awareness of discrimination against women, and she had no hidden agenda . . . if she decided to go for the big fish and do something in government, well, looking back on it, fair play to her." Fennell has moved from journalism to politics to the private sector since her time in the IWLM, but among her proudest accomplishments are the practical women's organisations she helped found during the seventies, including AIM, the family law reform lobby, and Women's Aid, which provided refuge for battered wives. As the other IWLM founders have come to respect Fennell's achievements, she recognises that she and the IWLM simply represented different strands of the women's movement, and in the end, there is no real cause for enduring bitterness about the past. "At the end of the day, there was empathy between me and the group and what we were doing," Fennell says.

Dr Moira Woods, as one of the founders most immersed in left-wing causes, represented almost the opposite end of the political spectrum as Fennell. But like Fennell, Dr Woods went on to do very practical work for women. Woods's husband, also a doctor, had been ill, and he died shortly after the IWLM's disintegration. Woods was instrumental in the 1978 founding of one of Dublin's first women's clinics, the Well Woman Centre, and she continued to campaign actively for the repeal of the laws banning contraception. The Well Woman Centre has expanded its services significantly since its founding, operating clinics today at three different Dublin locations. She also pioneered the treatment of child sex abuse in Ireland, acting as Director of the Sexual Assault Treatment Unit in the Rotunda Hospital for years.

In early 2002, Moira Woods was found guilty of professional misconduct by the Medical Council's Fitness to Practise Committee relating to her diagnosis of sexual abuse of children in three families in the 1980s. The allegations were all related to Dr Woods's alleged failure to follow proper procedures when determining victims of child sexual abuse. Of fifty-five allegations, relating to five children from three separate families, that the individuals involved had been falsely accused in the 1980s of sex abuse by Dr Woods while she was director of the Sexual Assault Treatment Unit (SATU) in the Rotunda Hospital, the Fitness to Practise Committee found Dr Woods guilty of thirteen allegations.[3] The Committee found that Woods had not followed the protocols recommended by international experts and adopted by the SATU in a number of the cases.[4] The Committee also found that Dr Woods had not taken the appropriate approach to validation, in certain cases failing to gather all the evidence that was available, and in others failing to review cases or findings.[5]

Dr Woods told *The Irish Times*, in a statement on 30 January 2002, that "she was disappointed at the findings, and her work was motivated by the best interests of the children at all times".[6] The Committee did not recommend striking Dr Woods off the register of medical practitioners, but it did stipulate that she would have to undergo retraining and professional development and that she only engage in the same type of work as part of a multi-disciplinary team. Woods's supporters, among them many of the IWLM founders, as well as journalist (now Ombudsman) Emily O'Reilly, have made what they see as a connection between Dr Woods's active campaigning against the 1983 abortion referendum and the allegations brought against her. They believe that Dr Woods's outspokenness and opposition to the anti-abortion campaigners made her a target.

O'Reilly noted that Dr Woods was centre-stage during the 1983 controversy and emerged again as a key figure in the 1992 "X" case as the doctor who treated the fourteen-year-old girl involved, a role which, O'Reilly stated, ". . . led to [Woods's] vilification by elements of the anti-abortion movement, who characterised the controversy as a deliberate attempt to overturn the result of the 1983 referendum".[7] O'Reilly also pointed out that the "X" case became public in 1992, and that the complaints that sparked the lengthy Medical Council investigation into Woods's work at the Rotunda Hospital were made one month later, although the initial complaints related to a case that dated back to 1985.[8] It was shortly after the case was decided that Woods moved permanently from Ireland to Italy, a country she had loved since she was a young girl. Several of the IWLM founders have visited Woods under the sunny Tuscan skies.

Mary Kenny's pride in the IWLM's achievements still stands today, despite the changes in her ideology and her writing. "I regret that I was such a show-off and exhibitionist and that I could be such a pain in the butt in that way. And I certainly regret my excessive drinking. But I don't regret, or criticise, anything within the programme of that movement, which I think on the whole was really very good," she says. Kenny also finds it tedious, though understandable, that the first thing so many people remember about her is her participation in the Contraception Train. She knows her obituary will mention that she was on the train, and she would like to be remembered more for other aspects of her life, both professional and personal. She does find it rewarding to hear from women who remember how cheeky she was and who found a bit of that strength, confidence and irreverence in themselves. In some of her most recent writing, though, Kenny is ambivalent about the movement's achievements:

> I am constantly approached by young researchers – often from America – who ask to interview me because I was involved in founding a feminist movement in Ireland back in the Seventies. Bless their optimistic little hearts, they are full of admiration for what has been achieved for women over these past thirty years or so. But as I stand by the kitchen sink, brillo pad in hand, getting down to the pots and pans, I ponder that the most basic form of female slavery still remains just as it was: the subjection of

household chores. Indeed, a recent survey found that women to-day do more housework than they did thirty years ago, because standards have risen with more appliances. Where exactly did all this liberation come in?[9]

Kenny's musings echoed McCafferty's in her opinion that women will not truly be liberated until it is just as normal for a man to cook the meals, do the housework and mind the children as it is for a woman. The two IWLM founders are correct that, thirty-six years after the beginning of the women's liberation movement, that is simply not the case in the majority of households, although many young couples today would argue that there is a more equal sharing of the chores than they had witnessed in their parents' relationships. Change may come slowly, but, it seems, it is also inevitable.

Mary Kenny was one of the IWLM's most controversial figures in the group's earliest days because of her outrageousness. After the IWLM's disintegration, she provoked heated responses from many of the same people she had fought beside for women's rights because of her newfound conservatism. Although she sometimes speaks of her time with the IWLM as if it was not only another lifetime, but someone else's besides, she has not changed so much as to be unrecognisable. In the same 2004 column in which she derided housework, the woman famed for fun and ego in her younger days claimed that she sees her funeral "as the last chance to throw a really good party, and since I had a rather hurried and secretive wedding, a last opportunity to be the star at one's own obsequies". She further requested that all the ladies wear hats. "Please! Can't one have full dress for the last party?" she wrote. What could possibly be a better tribute to a woman who, at age sixty, still manages to be resplendent even when she's trying to look matronly?

Kenny has also proven in the last several years, in the face of much doubt as to the sincerity of her convictions, that she is willing to endure significant personal sacrifice in order to stand by her beliefs. After working for several years at London's *Daily Express* in a pensionable post, she resigned when Richard Desmond bought the company because he had, as Kenny put it, "made his fortune in quite seamy magazines". Nell McCafferty mentions the incident as an example of the media's willingness to criticise Kenny for her inconsistencies and, conversely, its failure to acknowledge the morality of her decision to resign. "She resigned her pensionable job, and did I hear a word of praise for Mary Kenny doing that? Not one. It was a very brave and wonderful thing she did," McCafferty says. If Kenny were in the room at the moment, McCafferty says, "I'd probably tell her to shut up and keep the glow of yesteryear, unless, Mary, you were going to have a drink." Kenny could be fun, and at equal turns, irritating. Still, in many ways, McCafferty feels that Kenny endured more than her share of unfair sneering over the years.

When Kenny thinks of how the IWLM will be remembered in years to come, she fears that the group's aims and activities will be distorted, specifically by those writers with, as she puts it, a left-wing slant. "If you look at entries in the current *Encyclopedia of Ireland*, a lot of them are written by younger feminists now . . . and they have a very strong doctrinaire of left-wing feminist deconstruction, and that to me is actually a betrayal." Kenny claims that these younger feminist historians have placed a heavy emphasis on abortion as a key mobilising issue in the earliest days of the women's liberation movement, when that simply was not the case. The other IWLM founders' recollections of their meetings and discussions confirm that abortion was not on the group's agenda. Kenny argues that contraception never would have had the prominence it did as one of the group's demands if it had chosen to take on the abortion issue, which was simply never an option. "I'm displeased about the sort of rewriting of history in a way that things are not seen in the context of their time," she says.

A striking photo of Kenny from the late sixties, sitting on a desk in the RTÉ offices, mini-skirted, one leg crossed over the other, features a poster in the background reading "If it's timid, it's not today". That's as accurate a description of Kenny herself in the context of her own time, during the earliest days of women's liberation, as this researcher has encountered.

Most of the other journalists among the IWLM founders, like Kenny, continued to write and report long into the decades following the group's disintegration, although there are a few exceptions. Mary Anderson, *Irish Independent* journalist and Máirín de Burca's courtroom partner in challenging the Juries Act, had emigrated first to Oxford to study Politics at Ruskin College, and then to America by the start of the eighties to join an alternative lifestyles ranch. She has very little contact with any of the other IWLM founders, and has since changed her name to Emerald O'Leary. June Levine remembers Anderson's fervour over women's wrongs. "Her energy matched her anger and often, when she spoke, it seemed as if all female rage was channelling itself through her. She had a love-hate relationship with journalism when she left . . ."[10]

Anderson's editor at the *Independent*, Mary McCutchan, continued to work in journalism and married another journalist, Eamonn Fingleton. McCutchan died in a car crash in London in the mid-seventies, along with her infant twins. McCutchan's smart writing style and easy smile in the photo that occasionally accompanied her stories indicate that she shared the best of the qualities that defined most of the IWLM founders – a sharp wit and good humour.

June Levine freelanced for radio, TV and several national newspapers throughout the seventies, writing a full feature page for *The Sunday Independent* before landing a permanent job as a researcher on the *Late Late Show* with Gay Byrne, which she held for five years. She went back to freelancing after leaving RTÉ, contributing to *Southside* newspapers. Her 1982 memoir *Sisters* details much of the IWLM's work, and she is also the co-author of *Lyn: A Story of Prostitution*, Lyn Madden's memoir. Madden is the former Dublin prostitute who sat at Mrs Gaj's regular lunchtime table, an old friend of both Mrs Gaj and Marie McMahon. Levine also wrote a novel, *A Season of Weddings*, examining the themes of marriage and bisexuality and based on her own experiences travelling and living in India.

Mary Maher and Nell McCafferty both enjoyed long careers in journalism. Maher stayed with *The Irish Times* for more than thirty-five years and was never bored. For a long period, she worked as a sub-editor on the foreign desk, mainly because it was an overnight shift and it allowed her more time during the day to spend with her two daughters, although she found the schedule a strain on her marriage. The women's page in the *Times* was gradually phased out until it was dropped completely in the late seventies, amid the general feeling that it had served its purpose. Since women were now making more of the headlines in their own right, many journalists, male and female, felt that there was no need to have a separate page devoted only to women's issues.

Maher started another women's page in 1980 that ran once a week as a collective of pieces from the female staff journalists. By that time, they were much more up-front about the issues that the first women's pages had been forced to either ignore completely or tiptoe around, including abortion. She led the *Irish Times* chapter of the National Union of Journalists for years and remains active in the organisation. She has said that she would not have been interested in journalism if she had not been allowed to be a campaigning journalist, and that she never had much desire to do straight reporting – she was always more interested in politics and advocacy. Her retirement from *The Irish Times* did nothing to diminish that interest, and Maher is finding the time and opportunities to get more actively involved in politics in different ways. The 2004 American presidential election led Maher to several months of work in Pittsburgh, Pennsylvania for Democratic candidate John Kerry's campaign. She wrote a novel, *The Devil's Card*, and edited a collection of women's writing, *If Only: Short Stories of Love and Divorce*. She has also written several forewords for colleagues' collections of articles, including Mary Holland's posthumous anthology of work, published in late 2004.

One of Maher's parting thoughts about the IWLM is the huge role that she believes humour played in the group's successes. "We really could not have got through the meetings if we didn't laugh a lot," she says. Humour, the pub, and singing – all were tied into the revolutionary movements of the sixties and seventies. Maher has not lost her taste for any of them, least of all a good laugh, and she enjoys music immensely, especially traditional ballads and tunes. Any time she sings these days, she sings like she means it and, one surmises, mostly for the fun.

It was Maher who recently reminded McCafferty what she had said during a 1971 IWLM consciousness-raising session in Gaj's when each woman had to say what she liked about herself. McCafferty had said she could always make herself laugh. For a woman whose defining characteristics included biting sarcasm and dry wit, which at turns involved deep cynicism, McCafferty's laugh was probably among the loudest at those meetings. She ends her memoir optimistically, with her belief that the world has changed slowly, but for the better in her lifetime. "The best is yet to come," she wrote. "While we await that glorious day, the sensible response is to laugh and be a disorderly woman."[11]

After leaving *The Irish Times* for good in the early eighties, McCafferty freelanced for *In Dublin* and *Magill* magazines, among others, and wrote a regular column for the *Irish Press*. She had published her first collection of her newspaper and magazine articles by the mid-eighties, and authored several books of historical non-fiction on subjects like the Civil Rights activist Peggy Deery and, later, the Kerry Babies case. She was given a slot during the eighties on RTÉ's weekly *Women's Programme* as a commentator on the print media, where she created her trademark sign-off – "Goodnight, sisters" – always delivered with a wink that she says was inspired by the reassuring wink *Irish Times* editor Douglas Gageby gave her upon her return to the newsroom the night of the Contraception Train.

McCafferty doesn't do much journalistic writing now, a piece here and there in a freelance capacity, and though she appears to be as lively, and acerbic, as ever, she is tired in the same way as many of the other IWLM founders following many years of activism. "When the ceasefire happened in Northern Ireland in 1994 and I tuned into the top ten music programme, I realised I had not listened to music hardly at all since 1971 apart from Springsteen," McCafferty says. "I gave my entire everything to civil rights, to the North and to the South. And I was wrong . . . and I slightly regret it. I wish I had taken more time off to go to the movies, and I would have been the better woman for it," she says. Now she's scanning the papers trying to figure out what she should be as interested in as the causes of her youth, and finds it "quite worrying" that she isn't able to come up with much.

That aside, when McCafferty talks about how women's problems have changed from the early seventies to today, she's very passionate, and concerned. "Jesus Christ, we're back at the beginning," she says. "Women are now doing two jobs, one at home, and one outside the home . . . we haven't got the balance right." She makes the point that the IWLM, and every women's rights group to follow, were correct to fight so hard for women's equal rights in the workplace, but that better career opportunities have not solved the problem of how women are supposed to raise families while working. Women staying home with their babies is a wonderful thing that should be applauded and encouraged, she says, but they are often punished financially, by the loss of job opportunity, and sometimes even by their partners for making that choice. On the other hand, there are many women rising at 6.00 am so they can drop their kids off at a crèche or school and make it to work by nine, putting themselves and their families on an exhausting treadmill.

McCafferty remembers that one of the first questions Máirín de Burca presciently raised within the IWLM was how to ensure that women would have every opportunity for the top jobs and still be able to devote the necessary time to their families and other areas of their lives. De Burca used the specific example of the position of the editor-in-chief of *The Irish Times*, asking what woman in her right mind would want the job. "We were all thinking she was off the wall – it's loads of money, a big job," McCafferty says. Now she understands de Burca's point better, and the wrenching difficulties women face in their efforts to balance their personal and professional lives. "Who is going to change the world so that women can spend more time with their children?" McCafferty asks. "Are women getting to that stage now? That's for women to decide. The ones with babies. Oh, it's a tough one," she says.

McCafferty's deep love and respect for her mother, who passed away in December 2004 in her mid-nineties, were probably the most consistent thing in her life from childhood to mature adulthood. Shortly before her mother's death, she said, "I know everyone loves their mother, but I *like* my mother. I actually enjoy her, being in her company, talking to her." It's odd for McCafferty to have reached a time in her life where she's without a cause, but she wants to pick up where she left off in her younger days of travel, planning trips to places she's never seen. She doesn't deny herself the small indulgence of celebrating herself and the IWLM founders as they were in 1970. "We were free, lovely, young and full of confidence." She also basks in the praise of some of the letters she occasionally receives, even now, from women applauding her role in the women's movement. She reads a few lines from one recent letter: "'Lucky me, being sixteen in 1970 when you all burst on the scene. You will never know the difference you made to some of our lives. Your group hauled us by the lapels into another world planets away from the one we grew up in, that to us was a new way of thinking.'" McCafferty puts the letter down and smiles. "She's absolutely bloody right."

In February 2006, McCafferty suffered a heart attack and underwent triple bypass surgery, and at the time of this writing was recovering in Dublin. Just before her heart attack, she had been in New Orleans reporting on the aftermath of Hurricane Katrina, prompting the headline of an affectionate article written by her colleague Larissa Nolan the weekend following her surgery in the *Sunday Independent,* "Whirlwind Nell Still Kicking up a Storm Despite Wee Bypass."[12]

There is some disagreement, even today, among the IWLM founders as to exactly who qualifies as a founder member. There is no question that the five women who met at Bewley's – Gaj, de Burca, Maher, Woods and Johnston – were founders, and little debate over whether McCafferty, McMahon, Levine and Kenny were also present at the group's creation, for that first meeting at Mary Maher's house. But there are other women whose roles are less clear. For example, several of the founders mention that the poet Eavan Boland was present at the first meetings at Gaj's, and that she was a vocal and enthusiastic participant in discussions. But she seems to have dropped out of the group quickly, and was not influential in planning or carrying out any of the IWLM's major protests. Fionnuala O'Connor was the ex-schoolteacher who was waiting tables at Gaj's and later became a journalist, but she doesn't consider her own role in the IWLM as significant enough to define her as a founding member of the group. Other founders remember her at the first meetings and as an active member throughout the IWLM's lifespan. There were many other women who dropped in and out of the meetings and worked alongside the IWLM, albeit on its periphery. Mary Robinson was one of those women, and many of the founders remember her legal advice and support as invaluable. Though the IWLM's loose structure caused the group many problems and accelerated its demise, it also allowed for the casual contribution of ideas from several brilliant women who might not have felt as comfortable at that time participating in a more strictly regimented group that required permanent membership. Some of the IWLM's non-members, or droppers-in, were certainly as important to the group's success in their own ways as were the founders themselves.

The IWLM founders are from undeniably varied backgrounds. Class, nationality and age were some of the divisive factors that threatened to separate them even before they gathered for their first meeting. But these dozen or so women found that they were more alike than unalike, and that was a discovery they made together mostly through conversation and the honest sharing of their own personal stories. In the thirty-six years since the group's founding, there have been dramatic improvements in all of the areas of discrimination they fought, both through the law and through the changes in the country's very psyche. The IWLM founders knew in 1970 that the nation's mentality about how women deserved to be treated must be challenged and changed in order to unleash the necessary impetus for real improvements in women's lives through the law. In their newspaper articles, on television and out in the streets on protests, the IWLM was teaching Ireland how *human beings* should relate to each other more respectfully, regardless of gender, as they had taught themselves how to relate to each other within their own group, regardless of their differences. All of the founders take great satisfaction in knowing that today's young women will never have to face the same obstacles that they did; that their own enthusiasm and courage as young women ensured the improvement of the next generation's quality of life. Women face different obstacles now, requiring different solutions from the problems of the past, but at least they may see options and new possibilities where before there were no choices.

It may be true that the founder only passes by once, but the IWLM founders have exhibited what American feminist Jo Freeman calls "the phoenix-like quality" of the women's movement in their collective accomplishments, which are as varied as they are valuable. So many of the IWLM founders continued the work that they started in the IWLM through their contributions in the media, politics and medicine. In the end, what might be the most common characteristic between the founders is their sustained belief that, as Garret FitzGerald told Mary Maher in 1971, a country that was so resistant to change would some day finally prove itself to be so much more open to it. They started one of the most radical, peaceful and profound social movements in history, proving that even a small group of true believers has the power, under the right circumstances, to irreversibly transform a nation.

Notes

Introduction

1. McCafferty, Nell, 1984, *The Best of Nell*, Dublin: Attic Press, p. 10.

2. Luther P. Gerlach and Virginia H, Hine, 1970, *People, Power, Change: Movements of Social Transformation*, Indianapolis: Bobbs-Merrill, p. xvi; quoted in Daherlup, Drude (ed.), 1986, *The New Women's Movement*, London: Sage, p. 6.

3. Cullen, Mary, 1985, *Telling it Our Way: Feminist History*; quoted in Steiner-Scott, Liz (ed.), 1985, *Personally Speaking , , , Women's Thoughts on Women's Issues*, Dublin: Attic Press, p. 264.

Chapter 1: Not Just a Restaurant

1. Sweetman, Rosita, 9 April 1970, "Painless Paying", *Irish Press*, p. 6.

2. Geraghty, Des, 1994, *Luke Kelly: A Memoir*, Dublin: Basement Press, pp. 104–107.

3. Ibid, p. 107.

4. Boland, Rosita, 30 October 2004, "No Charm, No Personality – and now no Bewley's", *Irish Times*, p. 3.

5. Leahy, Alice, 1995, *Not Just a Bed for the Night*, Dublin: Marino, p. 91.

Chapter 2: The Universal Activist

1. "25 Most Influential Irishwomen" (no author), 9 March 1971, *Irish Press*, p. 6.

2. McCafferty, Nell, 4 May 1971, "Women in Court: Confronting the Law", *Irish Times*.

3. "Three Fined for Egg-Throwing – Nixon Visit Recalled" (no author), 18 November 1970, *Irish Press*.

4.   O'Sullivan, Phillip, 11 May 1971, "Why Don't Irishwomen Make Good Jurors?", *Irish Independent*, p. 8.

5.   *Irish Times,* 13 December 1975, editorial (untitled, no author), p. C-1.

Chapter 3: A Journalist Crosses the Pond

1.   Gillespie, Elgy, 2003, *Changing the Times*, Dublin: Lilliput, p. 246.

2.   "The Female Homosexual" (no author), 30 November 1970, *Irish Times*, p. 6.

3.   Kenny, Mary, 24 August 1970, "What is Women's Lib About?", *Irish Press*.

4.   Kenny, Mary, 31 August 1970, "Just One More Time", *Irish Press*.

5.   Maher, Mary, 8 October 1970, "The Most Difficult Civil Rights Struggle", *Irish Times*, p. 6.

6.   Martin, Janet, 15 October 1970, "The Facts About Women's Wrongs", *Irish Independent*, p. 8.

7.   Foley, Donal, 1977, *Three Villages: An Autobiography*, Dublin: Egoist Press, p. 96.

8.   Holland, Mary, 2004, *How Far We Have Traveled*, Dublin: Townhouse, p. ix.

Chapter 5: Two Different Doctors

1.   Kenny, Mary, 8 October 1970, "Heart of a Revolutionary", *Irish Press*, p. 8.

2.   Ibid.

3.   Ibid.

4.   Ibid.

5.   Ibid.

6.   "1,500 March in Dublin Anti-Nixon Protest" (no author), 5 October 1970, *Irish Independent*, p. 20.

7.   Levine, June, 1982, *Sisters: The Personal Story of an Irish Feminist*, Dublin: Ward River Press, p. 154.

8.   Madden, Lyn and Levine, June, 1987, *Lyn: A Story of Prostitution*, Dublin: Attic Press, Acknowledgements.

9.   Kenny, Mary, 8 October 1970, op. cit.

Chapter 6: Chains or Change

1.   *Chains or Change*, 1971, pamphlet published by the Irish Women's Liberation Movement.

2.   Maher, Mary, 9 March 1971, Untitled article, *Irish Times*, p. 6.

3.   Kenny, Mary, 25 September 1969, "Equal Pay – The Facts", *Irish Press*.

4.   Maher, Mary, 12 September 1968, "Equal Pay – Women are Sick of Nothing but Promises", *Irish Times*, p. 6.

5. Martin, Janet, 10 September 1970, "Does Your Daughter Want to Type?" *Irish Independent*, p. 6.

6. McCutchan, Mary, 23 February 1971, "Women Fighting for Their Rights Have a Top Man's Support", *Irish Independent*, p. 6.

7. *Chains or Change*, op cit.

8. Ibid.

9. Richards, Maura, 1998, *Single Issue*, Dublin: Poolbeg, p. 46.

10. *Chains or Change*, op. cit.

11. "The Civil Wrongs of Irishwomen" (no author), 24 March 1971, *Irish Press*.

Chapter 7: Paying the Price

1. *Chains or Change*, op. cit.

2. Maher, Mary, 12 November 1968, "Students in the North", *Irish Times*, p. 12.

3. De Burca, Máirín, 21 September 1978, *Hibernia*, "A Woman's Place," p. 6.

Chapter 8: Hats and Hotpants

1. Kenny, Mary, 2003, *Germany Calling*, Dublin: New Island, p. 3.

2. Kenny, Mary, August 1968, "Get Out", *Irishwoman's Journal*, p. 7.

3. Ibid.

4. O'Muirithille, Risteard, June 1983, "The Wide Boy", *Magill*, p. 63.

5. Levine, June, 5 April 1970, "Meeting Mary's Mammy", *Irish Press*, p. 6.

6. Boylan, Clare, 17 August 1970, "Mary – The Militant Feminist", *Irish Press*, p. 6.

7. Kenny, Mary, 3 August 1970, "Having a Ball in the Hat Shop", *Irish Press*, p. 6.

8. Kenny, Mary, 30 July 1970, "One Girl All Alone on the Town", *Irish Press*, p. 8.

9. Ibid.

10. Kenny, Mary, 2 March 1970, "Bouquet for Us", *Irish Press*, p. 6.

11. Kenny, Mary, 30 March 1970, "Should Journalists Be Active in Politics?" *Irish Press*, p. 6.

12. Levine, June, 1982, *Sisters: The Personal Story of an Irish Feminist*, Dublin: Ward River Press, p. 183.

13. Kenny, Mary, 13 October 1970, Untitled Article, *Irish Press*, p. 8.

14. Kenny, Mary, 31 May 1971, Untitled Interview with Parliamentary Secretary to the Taoiseach, *Irish Press*, p. 6.

15. Levine, June, 1982, op. cit.

16. *Irish Press*, 28 April 1971, "Women's Lib – Its Crisis", p. 7.

17. Kenny, Mary, 1 May 2004, "The Protestor and the Vacuum Cleaner", *Irish Independent*, p. 5.

Chapter 9: Showtime

1. Tóibín, Colm, January 1985, "Gay Byrne – Filling the Hall", *Magill*, p. 21.
2. Ibid.
3. Byrne, Gay, 1972, *To Whom it Concerns: Ten Years of The Late Late Show*, Dublin: Gill & Macmillan, p. 154.
4. Ibid., p. 142.
5. Levine, June, 1982, *Sisters: The Personal Story of an Irish Feminist,* Dublin: Ward River Press, p. 163–4.
6. Ibid, p. 166.
7. Ibid., p. 167.
8. Flanagan, Maeve, 1998, *Dev, Lady Chatterly, and Me: A '60s Suburban Childhood*, Dublin: Marino, p. 61.
9. Ibid, p. 58.
10. Ibid, p. 62.
11. Richards, Maura, 1998, *Single Issue,* Dublin: Poolbeg, p. 45.

Chapter 10: Finding Her Place

1. Levine, June, June 1968, "The Work Ahead", *Irishwoman's Journal,* Vol. 3, no. 8.
2. Johnston, Máirín, 1988, *Dublin Belles,* Dublin: Attic Press, p. 104.
3. Ibid, p. 105.
4. Ibid, p. 104.
5. Ibid, p. 107.
6. Ibid, p. 108.
7. Levine, June, 1982, *Sisters: The Personal Story of an Irish Feminist,* Dublin: Ward River Press, p. 36.
8. Ibid., pp. 40–45.
9. Ibid, p. 58.
10. Ibid., p. 70.
11. Ibid., p. 82.
12. Ibid., p. 85.
13. Ibid, p. 86.
14. Ibid., p. 87.
15. Ibid., p. 90.
16. Ibid., p. 113.

17. Ibid., p. 136.

18. Ibid., p. 44.

19. Ibid., p. 54.

20. McCafferty, Nell, 2004, *Nell*, Dublin: Penguin, p. 281.

21. Levine, June, June 1969, "Editorially Speaking" column, *Irishwomen's Journal*, Vol. 4, No. 8.

22. Connolly, Linda, 2002, *The Irish Women's Movement – From Revolution to Devolution*, New York: Palgrave, p. 112.

23. *Hoodwinked*, television documentary directed by Trish McAdam, Dublin: East Lane Films, broadcast on RTÉ, 1997.

24. Heverin, Aileen, 2000, *The Irish Countrywomen's Association – A History 1910–2000*, Dublin: Wolfhound Press, p. 17.

25. Connolly, Linda, 2002, op. cit, p. 106.

26. Maher, Mary, 27 October 1971, "The Interim Report on Equal Pay by the Commission on the Status of Women is Out Today, So What?" *Irish Times*, p. 6.

27. McCutchan, Mary, 27 October 1971, "Equal Pay for Women by 1977?" *Irish Independent*, p. 7.

Chapter 11: Standing Room Only

1. "Women's Lib Goes Public" (no author), 14 April 1971, *Irish Times*, p. 6.

2. Maher, Mary, 9 March 1971, *Irish Times*, p. 6.

3. Gillespie, Elgy, 15 April 1971, "Women Seek Real Equality", *Irish Times*, p. 1.

4. McCafferty, Nell, 2004, *Nell*, Dublin: Penguin, p. 220.

5. McCafferty, Nell, 2002, "The Child was a Bastard and the Mother a Whore", *The Sunday Tribune*, p. 11.

6. Ibid.

7. Richards, Maura, 1998, *Single Issue*, Dublin: Poolbeg, p. 45.

8. Kenny, Mary, 3 May 1971, "The Suffering Sex", *Irish Press*, p. 6.

9. Ibid.

10. Brennan, Pat, April 1979, "Women in Revolt", *Magill*, p. 38.

11. Ibid.

12. Ibid.

Chapter 12: Odd One Out

1. Fennell, Nuala, 1971, "Letter of Resignation from the Irish Women's Liberation Movement"; quoted in Bourke, Angela, (ed.) *Field Day Anthology of Women's Writing, Volume Five: Irish Women's Writing and Traditions*, Cork: Cork University Press, 2002, p. 201.

2. Ibid.

3. Quoted in Levine, June, 1982, *Sisters: The Personal Story of an Irish Feminist,* Dublin: Ward River Press, p. 233.

4. Ibid.

5. McCafferty, Nell, 2004, *Nell,* Dublin: Penguin, p. 299.

6. Fennell, Nuala and Arnold, Mavis, 1987, *Irish Women – Agenda for Practical Action: A Fair Deal for Women, December 1982–1987, Four Years of Achievement*, Department of Women's Affairs and Family Law Reform, Dublin: The Stationery Office.

7. Levine, June, 1982, *Sisters: The Personal Story of an Irish Feminist,* Dublin: Ward River Press, p. 243.

8. De Burca, Máirín, March 1983, "No, Minister", *Magill*, p. 20.

9. Ibid.

10. Brennan, Pat, 1983, Interview with Nuala Fennell, from *Women's Political Association Journal*, quoted in Bourke, Angela (ed.), *Field Day Anthology of Women's Writing, Volume Five: Irish Women's Writing and Traditions*, Cork: Cork University Press, 2002, pp. 242–43.

11. McCafferty, Nell, 22 September 1983, "Caoineadh Mhná na hÉireann", *In Dublin*; quoted in *The Best of Nell*, 1984, Dublin: Attic Press, pp. 58–62.

12. Levine, June, 1982, *Sisters: The Personal Story of an Irish Feminist*, Dublin: Ward River Press, p. 246.

Chapter 13: Learning Feminism Backwards

1. Sweetman, Rosita, 6 January 1971, "Midnight in Marlborough House", *Irish Press*, p. 8.

2. Kenny, Mary, 4 January 1971, "Newspaper Frustration", *Irish Press*, p. 8.

3. Quoted in Sweetman, Rosita, 1979, *On Our Backs: Sexual Attitudes in a Changing Ireland,* London: Pan, p. 156.

Chapter 14: All Aboard

1. *Hoodwinked,* television documentary directed by Trish McAdam, Dublin: East Lane Films, broadcast on RTÉ, 1997.

2. "Contraception: The Two Basic Problems" (no author), 15 December 1970, *Irish Times*, p. 6.

3. Horgan, John, 1997, *Mary Robinson: An Independent Voice*, Dublin: O'Brien Press, pp. 33–34.

4. "Contraception: The Two Basic Problems", op. cit.

5. Martin, Janet, 27 October 1970, "Growing Opposition to Birth Control Laws", *Irish Independent*, p. 6.

6. Kenny, Mary, 3 November 1970, *Irish Press*, p. 6.

7. Martin, Janet, 27 October 1970, op. cit.

8. Poll, 22 December 1970, *Irish Times,* p. 6.

9. *Hoodwinked*, television documentary directed by Trish McAdam, Dublin: East Lane Films, broadcast on RTÉ, 1997.

10. "Brainwashing" (no author), 4 May 1971, *Irish Independent*, p. 6.

11. Kenny, Mary, 22 March 1971, "The Contraceptive Laws: The Fact, Not the Fiction", *Irish Press*, p. 6.

12. Ibid.

13. "Women Protest in Pro-Cathedral" (no author), *Irish Times,* 29 March 1971.

14. Fennell, Nuala, 7 April 1970, "Day Tripper to Belfast", *Irish Press*, p. 6.

15. Levine, June, 1982, *Sisters: The Personal Story of an Irish Feminist*, p. 175.

16. McCafferty, Nell, 2004, *Nell*, Dublin: Penguin, p. 223.

17. Ibid, p. 223.

18. Levine, June, 1982, op. cit, p. 179.

19. Coghlan, Denis, 24 May 1971, "Dublin Customs Officials Knew What Hit Them!" *Irish Times*, p. 13.

20. McCafferty, Nell, 2004, op. cit, p. 226.

21. Horgan, John, 1997, op. cit, p. 211.

22. *The Lancet,* 26 May 1990, "Ireland: Murphy's Law", p. 1268.

23. Horgan, John, 1997, op. cit, p. 38.

24. Inglis, Tom, *Moral Monopoly: The Catholic Church in Modern Irish Society*; quoted in O'Toole, Michael, 1992, *More Kicks Than Pence: A Life in Irish Journalism, Dublin: Poolbeg Press.*

Chapter 15: The Derrywoman

1. Kerrigan, Gene, December 1984, "The Essential Nell", *Magill*, p. 21.

2. McCafferty, Nell, 1984, *The Best of Nell*, Dublin: Attic Press, p. 14.

3. Tóibín, Colm, January 1985, "Keeping the Faith", *Magill*, p. 22.

4. McCafferty, Nell, 2004, *Nell*, Dublin: Penguin, p. 191.

5. McCafferty, Nell, 8 October 1970, "Born of Small Memories", *Irish Times*, p. 6.

6. McCafferty, Nell, 5 December 1972, "Housewives' Independence Notions Disappear in the Courtroom", *Irish Times*.

7. Flynn, Mary, 1980, "Memoir of the Irish Women's Liberation Movement", in Bourke, Angela (ed.), *Field Day Anthology of Women's Writing, Volume Five: Irish Women's Writing and Traditions*, Cork: Cork University Press, 2002, p. 203–205.

8. Ibid.

9.   Fennell, Nuala and Arnold, Mavis, 1987, *Irish Women – Agenda for Prac-
     tical Action: A Fair Deal for Women, December 1982–1987, Four Years of
     Achievement,* Department of Women's Affairs and Family Law Reform,
     Dublin: The Stationery Office, p. 11.

10. Ibid., p. 13.

11. Connolly, Linda, 2002, *The Irish Women's Movement: From Revolution to
     Devolution,* New York: Palgrave, p. 139.

12. McCafferty, Nell, 17 June 1980, "It is my Belief that Armagh is a Feminist
     Issue", *Irish Times*; in *The Best of Nell,* Dublin: Attic Press, 1984, pp. 130–
     34.

13. Levine, June, 1982, *Sisters: The Personal Story of an Irish Feminist,* Dub-
     lin: Ward River Press, p. 201.

Chapter 16: Where They Are (and What They Think) Now

1.   Edwards, Bob, 2004, *Edward R. Murrow and the Birth of Broadcast Jour-
     nalism*, Hoboken: John Wiley & Sons, p. 153.

2.   Maher, Mary, 5 February 1970, "Garret FitzGerald", *Irish Times*, p. 10.

3.   Coulter, Carol, 30 January 2002, "Medical Council Finds Dr Woods Guilty
     of Professional Misconduct", *Irish Times*.

4.   Coulter, Carol, 26 January 2002, "Woods Found Guilty of Professional
     Misconduct in Abuse Cases", *Irish Times*.

5.   Ibid.

6.   Coulter, Carol, 30 January 2002, op. cit.

7.   O'Reilly, Emily, 3 February 2003, "Woods: Zealous Campaigner who has
     Lived with Controversy", *Sunday Business Post*.

8.   Ibid.

9.   Kenny, Mary, 30 October 2004, "No Housework in Heaven", *Irish Inde-
     pendent*, p. 5.

10. Levine, June, 1982, *Sisters: The Personal Story of an Irish Feminist*, Dub-
     lin: Ward River Press, p. 138.

11. McCafferty, Nell, *Nell,* Dublin: Penguin, 2004, p. 422.

12. Nolan, Larissa, 5 March 2006, Whirlwind Nell Still Kicking up a Storm
     Despite Wee Bypass", *Sunday Independent*.

Index

abortion, 74–5, 156–8, 198, 223–4, 226, 228
Action, Information, Motivation (AIM), 115, 153–5
Anderson, Mary, 27, 28, 54, 106, 112, 162, 202, 217, 226
Andrews, David, 100
Are You Somebody?,, 199
Arnold, Mavis, 96
Around the Banks of Pimlico, 217
apartheid, 15

Bardwell, Leland, 173
Best of Nell, The, 3
Bewley's Café, 1, 3, 17–18, 46, 52, 84, 131
Binchy, Maeve, 37–9, 41–2, 94, 116, 176, 186, 198
Boland, Eavan, 3, 28, 63, 65, 231
Bowes pub, 40
Bowman, Eimer Philbin, 63–8, 81, 109–10, 211
Bowman, John, 81
Boylan, Clare, 96
Brennan, Pat, 144, 156
Browne, Dr Noel, 14
Byrne, Gay, 5, 108–12, 227

Campbell, Patrick, 17
capitalism, 59
Catholic Church, 168, 174, 187, 188

Chains or Change, 5, 69–78, 79–80, 85, 89, 96, 99, 106, 110, 112, 126, 140, 154, 159, 162, 198
Cherish, 141
Chicago Tribune, 33
civil rights movement (US), 29–30
class issues, 3, 10, 51–3
Collins, Pan, 107
Commission on the Status of Women (CSW), 128–9
Communist Party, 15, 16, 50, 62, 100, 205
Connolly, Linda, 3, 127
Conroy, Róisín, 87, 133, 140
consciousness-raising, 4–5, 53–6, 57, 60, 68, 79, 89, 122–4, 148, 228
contraception, 1, 19, 36, 37, 55, 65, 71, 76, 81, 120, 121, 127, 139, 167–80, 183, 187
Contraception Bill (1971), 6, 144, 175, 187
Contraception Train, 150, 163, 167–89, 202, 213, 220, 224, 229
Contraceptive Action Programme (CAP), 206, 218
Coogan, Tim Pat, 94, 95, 184
Costello, Joe, 12
Country Girls, 178
Cribben, Meena, 172
Criminal Law Act (1935), 168
Crowe, Caitriona, 167

Crummey, Frank, 9, 10, 13, 19, 20,
    62, 89, 164, 200
Cullen, Mary 6, 107–8
Cummins, Mary, 41, 196

D'Alton, Pauline, 97
Daily Express, 225
Day by Day, 86
de Burca, Máirín, 16, 17, 21–32, 41,
    45, 47, 49, 51, 52, 54, 55, 59, 60,
    66, 71, 77, 85, 88, 95, 98, 99, 100,
    106, 112, 118, 130, 142, 144, 149,
    151–2, 155–6, 163, 179, 180,
    183–5, 197–8, 203, 207–8,
    214–17, 220, 226, 230
Deery, Peggy, 229
Delacroix, Eugene, 69
Democratic Youth Movement, 49
Denehy, Dennis, 24
Desmond, Richard, 225
de Valera, Eamon, 24, 134
Devil's Card, The, 228
Devlin, Bernadette, 195
divorce, 74–5, 198
Doolan, Lelia, 107
Dublin Belles, 118, 217
Dublin Housing Action Committee,
    15, 23, 27, 77, 83

Edwards, Bob, 211
equal pay, 31, 36, 37, 51, 65, 71–3,
    85, 96, 129, 130, 135, 136, 139,
    143
Equal Pay Act, 136
Evening Standard (UK), 93, 122,
    203

Family Home Protection Act
    (1976), 154
Family Planning Act (1979), 187
Fathers Come First, 163
Female Eunuch, The, 26
Feminine Mystique, The, 26, 34, 66,
    119, 135
Fennell, Nuala, 4, 54, 63, 147–58,
    159, 177, 203, 212, 222
Fertility Guidance Clinic, 170, 171

Fingleton, Eamonn, 227
Firestone, Shulamith, 162
FitzGerald, Garret, 20, 111–13, 130,
    158, 214, 232
Flanagan, Maeve, 113–15
Flynn, Mary, 141, 144–6
Fogarty, Michael and Phillis, 73
Foley, Donal, 16, 35, 36, 40, 43, 195
Forcible Entry and Occupation Bill,
    27, 112, 116, 152, 203
Freedom of Information Act, 213
Freeman, Jo, 232
Friedan, Betty, 26, 34, 66, 119, 135

Gageby, Douglas, 94, 228
Gaj, Margaret, 10–20, 21, 45, 60,
    61, 86, 99, 140, 212, 215
Gaj's Restaurant, 9–20, 32, 41, 55,
    66–8, 82, 85, 89, 104, 107, 124,
    125
Geraghty, Des, 15, 16, 35, 81
Gillespie, Elgy, 35, 139
Greer, Germaine, 26, 162
Griffith Barracks campaign, 15

Heaphy, Helen, 140–1
Hibernia, 88
Holland, Mary, 44, 192
homosexuality, 37–8, 197–9
Hoodwinked, 167, 173
Horgan, John, 87
Hurricane Katrina, 231
Hussey, Gemma, 87, 157

*If Only: Short Stories of Love and
    Divorce*, 228
Institute for Advanced Studies, 50,
    217
International Lesbian Caucus, 205
International Planned Parenthood
    Association, 171
Irish Anti-Apartheid Movement, 23
Irish Countrywomen's Association,
    128, 172
Irish Family Planning Association
    (IFPA), 169, 171, 187

Irish Housewives' Association, 97, 127–8

Irish Independent, 2, 27, 28, 36, 42, 43, 59, 73, 100, 102

Irish Movement for Peace and Justice, 177

Irish Press, 2, 36, 40, 42, 43, 57, 72, 82, 93, 96, 101, 122, 134, 147, 165

Irish Republican Socialist Party, 205

Irish Society for the Prevention of Cruelty to Children (ISPCC), 13

Irish Times, 2, 12, 16, 28, 32, 33, 34, 38, 41, 42, 43, 72, 84, 100, 120, 139, 173, 192

Irish Voice on Vietnam, 23, 35, 62

Irish Workers' Party, 15

Irish Women United, 187, 205

Irishwoman's Journal, 92, 120, 122, 126, 135

Jacob's Biscuit factory, 47

Johnston, Máirín, 16, 17, 31, 46, 47–56, 57, 74, 77, 79, 80, 81, 96, 102, 104, 106, 107, 118, 122, 123, 138, 142, 151–2, 169, 176–7, 182–3, 185, 200, 208, 215, 217–19, 222, 231

Johnston, Roy, 49

Jong, Erica, 1

Juries Act, 29, 112, 217, 226

Keery, Neville, 97

Kelly, Ivan, 138

Kelly, Luke, 15

Kenny, Mary, 6, 36, 40–1, 54, 57, 58, 69–70, 72, 78, 89, 91–104, 107, 111, 113, 114, 122, 143–4 147–51, 159, 161–2, 171–2, 175–7, 179–80, 183–6, 203, 213–14, 221, 224–6, 231

Kenny, Pat, 86, 213

Kerry, John, 228

Labour Party, 15, 16, 62, 178

"Lady Liberty Leading the People", 69

Late, Late Show, The, 5, 6, 65, 104, 105–16, 126, 130–1, 137, 145, 160, 164, 167, 175, 186, 213, 220, 227

Leahy, Alice, 116

Levine, June, 60, 73, 80, 95, 98, 99, 106, 117–27, 155, 164, 180–1, 184, 227, 231

Longford, Lady Christine, 9, 14

Lyn: A Story of Prostitution, 227

MacCurtain, Sister Margaret, 213

Madden, Lyn, 14, 61, 86, 227

Magill, 94, 155, 195, 229

Maher, Mary, 16, 17, 32, 33–45, 47, 53, 54, 62, 72, 80, 81, 95, 98, 106, 112, 122, 129–30, 135, 138, 142, 145, 148–9, 156, 180, 196, 198, 203, 208, 213, 214, 227–8, 231–2

Mansion House meeting, 133, 136–45, 149, 167, 178, 189, 201, 213

Markievicz, Constance, 59

marriage bar, 3, 64, 71–3, 80

Martin, Janet, 42, 73, 171, 172

May Day march, 143, 201

McCafferty, Nell, 3, 24, 25, 38, 41, 54, 81, 88, 95, 102, 106–8, 113, 125, 138–40, 150–3, 156–8, 178–86, 188–9, 191–209, 213–14, 218, 225–31

McCann, Eamonn, 195

McCutchan, Mary, 36, 54, 73, 100, 129, 174, 227

McDevitt, Deirdre, 153

McEnroy, Monica, 172

McMahon, Marie, 9, 24–6, 52, 55, 61, 70, 79–89, 96, 102, 106, 118, 137, 140, 152, 162, 183, 191, 198, 202, 205, 220–2, 227, 231

McQuaid, Archbishop John Charles, 168–70, 172, 174, 176

Millet, Kate, 135, 162

Moorhouse, Jack, 48

Movement for a Socialist Republic, 205

Murrow, Edward R., 211

Nafisi, Azar, 19
Nixon, Richard, 24, 59
Nolan, Larissa, 231

O'Brien, Edna, 178
O'Connell, Dr John, 87
O'Connor, Fionnuala, 84, 87, 88, 144, 202, 231
O'Faolain, Nuala, 199
O'Leary, Michael, 87
O'Muirithille, Risteard, 94, 95
O'Neill, Colette, 186
On Our Backs, 163
On Our Knees, 163
O'Reilly, Emily, 223
Orpen, Hilary, 138
O'Sullivan, Sean, 120

Packard, Vance, 37
Paisley, Rev Ian, 192
Pearl Bar, 40
People's Democracy, 83–4, 178
Political Communications Ltd, 222
Post Office Engineering Union, 215
Prisoners' Rights Organisation, 12
Provisional IRA, 23, 25

Quinn, Bernadette, 153
Quinn, Ruairi, 87

Randall, Dr Paddy, 62
Reading Lolita in Tehran, 19
republicanism, 21, 83, 206, 207
Revolutionary Marxist Group, 205
Richards, Maura (nee O'Dea), 75–6, 115, 141
Robinson, Mary, 6, 28, 107, 129, 138, 144, 162, 171, 175, 176, 187, 231
Roche, Margaret, 115
RTE, 16, 100, 104, 111, 160

Season of Weddings, A, 227
Seven Days, 160
Sexual Assault Treatment Unit, 223
Sexual Politics, 135
Sexual Wilderness, The, 37
Shannon-Shiel, Deirdre, 12

Sheerin, Mary, 17, 43, 61, 63, 106, 113, 133–6, 148, 221
Single Issue, 75
single mothers, *see* unmarried mothers
Sinn Féin, 15, 22–4, 27, 31, 62, 100, 203, 215
Social Welfare Act (1974), 154
Socialist Worker's Movement, 205
Speed, Anne, 205
Suffragettes, 56
Sweetman, Rosita, 9, 54, 82, 95, 125, 159–65

Tallman, Cyril, 178
Three Villages, 43
Tóibín, Colm, 105, 109, 195
Turkel, Studs, 6
Tweedy, Hilda, 128

Ulysses, 118
UN International Convention on Civil and Political Rights, 28
Universal Declaration of Human Rights, 169
unmarried mothers, 74–6, 96, 121

Vietnam War, 15, 23–5, 31, 35, 85

Well Woman Centre, 60, 66, 223
West, Richard, 101
Widows Association, 128
Women Graduates' Association, 128
Women in Top Jobs, 73
Women's Aid, 153, 155
Women's Educational Resource and Research Centre, 127
Women's Political Association (WPA), 51
Women's Programme, 228
Woods, Dr Moira, 16, 17, 52, 57–62, 102, 138, 142, 176, 203–4, 214, 222–4, 132
working class, 48, 51–3

"X" case, 224